Intellectual Leadership, Higher Education and Precarious Times

Perspectives on Leadership in Higher Education

Series Editors: Tanya Fitzgerald, Helen M Gunter and Jon Nixon

Perspectives on Leadership in Higher Education provides a forum for distinctive, and sometimes divergent, ideas on what intellectual leadership means within the context of higher education as it develops within the twenty-first century. Authors from across a number of nation states critically explore these issues with reference to academic and research informed practice and development, institutional management and governance, the remapping of knowledge as well as sector-wide policy development.

Advisory Board:
Sarah Aiston (Teesside University, UK), Michael Apple (University of Wisconsin-Madison, USA), Ronald Barnett (University of London, UK), Hamish Coates (Tsingshua University, China), Ann Corbett (London School of Economics, UK), Rosemary Deem (Royal Holloway, University of London, UK), Kevin Dougherty (Teachers College, Columbia University, USA), Claus Emmeche (University of Copenhagen, Denmark), Ase Gornitzka (University of Oslo, Norway), Chris Husbands (Sheffield Hallam University, UK), Will Hutton (Academy of Social Sciences, UK), Fred Inglis (University of Warwick, UK), Niilo Kaaupi (University of Strasbourg, France), Eric Lybec (University of Manchester, UK), Bruce Macfarlane (Education University of Hong Kong), Jani Ursin (University of Jyväskylä, Finland), Yuki Takahashi (Tsuda University, Japan), Ly Tran (Deakin University, Australia) and Leesa Wheelahan (University of Toronto, Canada)

Also available in the series:
Cosmopolitan Perspectives on Academic Leadership in Higher Education, edited by Feng Su and Margaret Wood
Mass Intellectuality and Democratic Leadership in Higher Education, edited by Richard Hall and Joss Winn
Leadership in Higher Education from a Transrelational Perspective, Christopher M. Branson, Maureen Marra, Margaret Franken and Dawn Penney
Leadership for Sustainability in Higher Education Janet Haddock-Fraser, Peter Rands and Stephen Scoffham
Scholarly Leadership in Higher Education, Wayne J. Urban
Exploring Consensual Leadership in Higher Education, edited by Lynne Gornall, Brychan Thomas and Lucy Sweetman
Disrupting Leadership in Entrepreneurial Universities, Jillian Blackmore

Intellectual Leadership, Higher Education and Precarious Times

Edited by
Tanya Fitzgerald, Helen M Gunter and Jon Nixon

BLOOMSBURY ACADEMIC
LONDON • NEW YORK • OXFORD • NEW DELHI • SYDNEY

BLOOMSBURY ACADEMIC

Bloomsbury Publishing Plc, 50 Bedford Square, London, WC1B 3DP, UK
Bloomsbury Publishing Inc, 1359 Broadway, New York, NY 10018, USA
Bloomsbury Publishing Ireland, 29 Earlsfort Terrace, Dublin 2, D02 AY28, Ireland

BLOOMSBURY, BLOOMSBURY ACADEMIC and the Diana logo are
trademarks of Bloomsbury Publishing Plc

First published in Great Britain 2024
This paperback edition published in 2026

Copyright © Tanya Fitzgerald, Helen M Gunter and Jon Nixon, 2024

Tanya Fitzgerald, Helen M Gunter and Jon Nixon have asserted their right under the Copyright,
Designs and Patents Act, 1988, to be identified as Editors of this work.

Cover image © Jobalou / iStock

All rights reserved. No part of this publication may be: i) reproduced or transmitted in any form,
electronic or mechanical, including photocopying, recording or by means of any information storage
or retrieval system without prior permission in writing from the publishers; or ii) used or reproduced
in any way for the training, development or operation of artificial intelligence (AI) technologies,
including generative AI technologies. The rights holders expressly reserve this publication from the
text and data mining exception as per Article 4(3) of the Digital Single Market Directive (EU) 2019/790.

Bloomsbury Publishing Plc does not have any control over, or responsibility for,
any third-party websites referred to or in this book. All internet addresses
given in this book were correct at the time of going to press. The author and
publisher regret any inconvenience caused if addresses have changed or sites
have ceased to exist, but can accept no responsibility for any such changes.

A catalogue record for this book is available from the British Library.

Library of Congress Cataloging-in-Publication Data
Names: Fitzgerald, Tanya, 1960- editor. | Gunter, Helen, editor. | Nixon, Jon, editor.
Title: Intellectual leadership, higher education and precarious times /
edited by Tanya Fitzgerald, Helen M Gunter and Jon Nixon.
Description: First edition. | New York : Bloomsbury Academic, 2024. |
Series: Perspectives on leadership in higher education | Includes
bibliographical references and index. |
Summary: "This book draws on interdisciplinary social science and philosophical
frameworks to offer new dimensions to debate about intellectual leadership and
higher education. The chapters are focused on provoking readers to think critically about
intellectual leadership in precarious times. The contributors frame critical questions
about the unevenness, ambivalences, and disruptions that now mark everyday life and
interactions. In the precarious present and, what has changed and why? What might
now be the new social reality within which we work?"– Provided by publisher.
Identifiers: LCCN 2023051003 (print) | LCCN 2023051004 (ebook) |
ISBN 9781350291805 (hb) | ISBN 9781350291843 (pb) |
ISBN 9781350291829 (ebook) | ISBN 9781350291812 (ePDF)
Subjects: LCSH: Education, Higher–Research. | Intellectuals–Research. |
Teaching, Freedom of. | Academic freedom. | Educational leadership.
Classification: LCC LB2326.3 .I584 2024 (print) | LCC LB2326.3 (ebook) |
DDC 378.0072–dc23/eng/20240110
LC record available at https://lccn.loc.gov/2023051003
LC ebook record available at https://lccn.loc.gov/2023051004

ISBN:	HB:	978-1-3502-9180-5
	PB:	978-1-3502-9184-3
	ePDF:	978-1-3502-9181-2
	eBook:	978-1-3502-9182-9

Series: Perspectives on Leadership in Higher Education

Typeset by Integra Software Services Pvt. Ltd.

For product safety related questions contact productsafety@bloomsbury.com.

To find out more about our authors and books visit www.bloomsbury.com
and sign up for our newsletters.

Dedicated to
Jon Nixon
1950–2023
Scholar, mentor and friend

Contents

List of Contributors		viii
1	Intellectual Leadership, Higher Education and Precarious Times *Tanya Fitzgerald, Helen M Gunter and Jon Nixon, Editors*	1
2	When Intellectual Leadership Dies: Critical Voice vs Self-Censorship in Precarious Universities *Anatoly Oleksiyenko*	21
3	Governance of the Marketized University in Precarious Times *Steven Jones*	41
4	The Geopolitics of International Higher Education, Transnational Intellectual Collaboration and Leadership *Ly Thi Tran, Jill Blackmore and Diep Thi Bich Nguyen*	61
5	On the Abolition of Intellectual Leadership *Richard Hall*	81
6	Irish Academia: Nirvana for Gender Equality and Female Leadership? *Pat O'Connor*	101
7	Thinking Plurality: Academic Leadership, Precarious Institutions and Collegial Bodies as Member States in an Epistemic Union *Sharon Rider*	121
8	Enabling Intellectual Leadership in Precarious Times: The Contribution of the Professional Doctorate *Elizabeth Parr, Janet Lord, Stephen M Rayner and Rachel Stenhouse*	139
9	Crises and the Emergence of 'Estates' within Australian Universities *James Waghorne*	159
10	The Need for Critical Intellectual Leadership in US Community Colleges during Precarious Times *David L. Levinson and Katherine R. Rowell*	179
11	Thinking Critically about Intellectual Leadership in Precarious Times *Tanya Fitzgerald, Helen M Gunter and Jon Nixon, Editors*	197
Index		207

List of Contributors

Jill Blackmore, AM, PhD, is Alfred Deakin Professor in Education, Faculty of Arts and Education, Deakin University, Australia, a Fellow of the Australian Academy of Social Sciences and President of the Australian Association of University Professors. She researches from a feminist perspective education policy and governance; international and intercultural education; leadership and organizational change; spatial redesign and innovative pedagogies; and teachers' and academics' work, health and well-being. Recent projects are on school autonomy reform and the geopolitics of transnational education and student mobility. Her latest publication is *Disrupting Leadership in the Entrepreneurial University: Disengagement and Diversity* (2022, Bloomsbury).

Tanya Fitzgerald is Professor of Higher Education, a Senior Fellow of the Higher Education Academy, Fellow of the Royal Historical Society and Dean of the Graduate School of Education at the University of Western Australia, Australia. Scholarly publications include 11 books, 100+ book chapters and journal articles, and she has served as editor for both academic journals and book series. Current projects include a history of scholarly women and academic diplomacy, and an analysis of the biographies and career trajectories of vice-chancellors of the top 100 universities.

Helen M Gunter is Professor Emerita in The Manchester Institute of Education, University of Manchester, UK. She is a Fellow of the Academy of Social Sciences and recipient of the BELMAS Distinguished Service Award 2016. Her research focuses on the political sociology of knowledge production in the field of education policy. Her most recent book is *A Political Sociology of Education Policy* (2023, Policy Press).

Richard Hall is Professor of Education and Technology at De Montfort University, UK. A UK National Teaching Fellow, Richard writes about the political economy of higher education. He is the author of *The Hopeless University: Intellectual Work at The End of The End of History* (Mayfly Books, 2021) and *The Alienated Academic: The Struggle for Autonomy Inside the University* (Palgrave Macmillan,

2018). Richard is an independent visitor for a looked-after child, a governor of the Leicester Primary Pupil Referral Unit and a trade union negotiator. He writes about life in higher education at http://richard-hall.org.

Steven Jones is currently Head of Manchester Institute of Education, which is part of the University of Manchester, UK. He is Professor of Higher Education, and conducts research into policy and practice. His academic background is in Linguistics, and he brings the tools of critical discourse analysis to his examination of the university sector. Steven has co-authored public reports for the *Sutton Trust*, the *Joseph Rowntree Foundation* and *Advance HE* that explore how socially disadvantaged young people conceptualize, engage with and perform at university. He is particularly interested in how students' cultural and social capital affects their experiences, from application to employment. His latest book, *Universities under Fire: Hostile Discourses and Integrity Deficits in Higher Education* (Palgrave Macmillan, 2022), explores the ways in which the contemporary university is talked about and talks about itself. Always keen to disseminate his work to as wide a range of audiences as possible, Steven has presented research findings to *HM Treasury*, *Universities UK* and the *Association of School and College Leaders*, as well as giving evidence to the *All-Party Parliamentary University Group* in the House of Commons, participating in roundtables for the *Social Mobility Commission* and addressing the *Sunday Times Festival of Education*. He created the *H.E. Watch* blog, writes op-ed pieces for the *Guardian* and was listed as one of JISC's top fifty social media influencers in HE.

David L. Levinson, PhD, is President Emeritus, Connecticut State Colleges and Universities (CSCU), USA. Having served CSCU and its antecedent for over seventeen years, Dr Levinson was President of Norwalk Community College, Vice President of Community Colleges, Presidential Fellow and Interim President of Connecticut State Community College. He is the general editor of *Education and Sociology: An Encyclopedia* (RoutledgeFalmer) and author of *Community Colleges: A Reference Handbook* (ABC-CLIO). His publications have appeared in *The American Sociologist*, *Community College Journal of Research and Practice* and the *American Prospect*. He has taught at Bergen Community College, Massachusetts Bay Community College, Norwalk Community College, Sacred Heart University, Teachers College, Columbia University and the University of Massachusetts at Amherst. Dr Levinson received the Connecticut Higher Education Excellence Award from the New England Board of Higher Education and a Distinguished Teaching Award from the University of Massachusetts at Amherst.

Janet Lord has worked as a social sciences teacher and a lecturer in HE for many years, specializing in education studies, teacher education and social sciences. She has a professional doctorate in education from the University of Manchester, UK. Janet has experience in school governance and educational consultancy. Her research and writing concern pedagogy, student experience, assessment, the nature of critical spaces in HE and in initial teacher education. Janet is currently a senior lecturer in Education Studies at Manchester Metropolitan University, UK.

Diep Thi Bich Nguyen is a Research Fellow at School of Education, Deakin University, Australia. She obtained a master's degree on Lifelong Learning from Institute of Education, University College London in 2010, and a PhD degree on academic capacity building for internationalization from Deakin University in 2021. Her research areas include staff capacity building, geopolitics in international education, international student support, student mobility, English-medium instruction and graduate employability.

Jon Nixon was a Visiting Professor at Middlesex University, UK. His main research and scholarly interests were in the field of intellectual history particularly as it relates to educational and political thought. Among his most recently authored books are *Erich Auerbach and the Secular World: Literary Criticism, Historiography, Post-Colonial Theory and Beyond* (Routledge, 2022), *Rosa Luxemburg and the Struggle for Democratic Renewal* (Pluto Press, 2018) and *Hannah Arendt and the Politics of Friendship* (Bloomsbury, 2015). He has also written widely in the field of higher education policy and practice, and was working on a study of mid-twentieth- and early-twenty-first-century literary fiction entitled *Narratives of Memory and Loss*.

Pat O'Connor is Professor Emeritus of Sociology and Social Policy, University of Limerick (UL), Ireland, and Visiting full Professor, Geary Institute, University College Dublin, Ireland. Her core research interest is gender inequality: focusing particularly on the gendering of leadership, power and institutional resistance in higher education and more broadly on the gendering of organizations, excellence and careers. She became the first female professor of sociology in Ireland (1997); the first female full professor in any discipline in UL (1997) and the first female faculty dean (2000) there. She has held visiting professorships at London, Aveiro, Linkoping, Deakin and Melbourne and is on the Advisory Boards of a number of EU-funded research projects. Her 120 publications include 8 books, over 80 peer-reviewed journal articles and 30 book chapters.

Anatoly Oleksiyenko is Professor of International Higher Education at the Education University of Hong Kong (EdUHK). His research focuses on dilemmas of agency and leadership in the developing contexts and transforming systems of higher education. He is a world-leading critic of post-Soviet academia, especially regarding the problems of knowledge production and geopolitics. His research papers have been published in the globally influential journals such as *Higher Education, Studies in Higher Education, Minerva, Higher Education Policy* and *Higher Education Quarterly*. Oleksiyenko's paper 'On the Shoulders of Giants? Global science, resource asymmetries, and repositioning of research universities in China and Russia' (Comparative Education Review) received CIES-HESIG's Best Article Award in 2016, and his book *Global Mobility and Higher Learning* (Routledge) won the Best Book Award from CIES' SIG International Students and Study Abroad in 2019. Professor Oleksiyenko holds a PhD in Higher Education from OISE-University of Toronto.

Elizabeth Parr is a Senior Professional Tutor in Initial Teacher Education at Liverpool Hope University, UK. Prior to this, she led the School Direct programme and the Masters of Education with QTS. Elizabeth also has experience as a primary school teacher and governor in schools across the northwest of England. She successfully completed her Doctorate of Education with her research focusing on professional perceptions of community-oriented primary schools. Elizabeth's research interests include school-community relationships, the development of children's writing over time and Primary English.

Stephen M Rayner is Senior Lecturer and Deputy Head of the Manchester Institute of Education, UK. He has worked in and with schools in England for more than thirty years as a teacher, senior leader, governor and education advisor. Stephen's research interests include policy, school leadership, school collaboration and teacher education. His doctoral thesis was a study of the Academies programme in England as a dynamic process of systemic change.

Sharon Rider is Professor of Theoretical Philosophy at Uppsala University, Sweden. Her work focuses on the cultural conditions for autonomy, responsibility and knowledge, and how these might be conceptualized in ways that neither reject nor rely on conventional notions of rational agency. Her books on education include *World Class Universities: A Contested Concept* (Springer 2020, with MA Peters, M Hyvönen & T Besley), *Post-truth, Fake News: Viral Modernity and Higher Education* (Springer 2018, with Peters, Hyvönen & Besley) and *Transformations in Research, Higher Education and the Academic Market: The Breakdown of Scientific Thought* (Springer 2013, with Y Hasselberg & A Waluszewski).

Katherine R. Rowell has taught sociology at Sinclair Community College in Dayton, Ohio, USA, since 1996. She is the founding director of the Sinclair Community College Center for Teaching and Learning (2008–13). She currently serves as the advisor to the Honors Program at Sinclair Community College. Dr Rowell has won numerous awards for teaching excellence: American Sociological Association Teaching Excellence Award (2012), Outstanding Community College Professor of the Year by the Council for Advancement of Scholarship and Education and the Carnegie Foundation in 2005, 'Who's Who among America's Teachers' (1996, 1997, 2002, and 2004) and the 2005 North Central Sociological Professor of the Year. Dr Rowell earned bachelor's and master's degrees from Wright State University in Dayton, Ohio, and a PhD from Ohio State University. She is a recent recipient (2022) of the American Society of Learned Communities Community College fellowship to support her research on children and eviction.

Rachel Stenhouse has worked in education for over fifteen years, teaching in both primary and secondary schools before taking on her current role as a Senior Lecturer in Education at Manchester Metropolitan University, UK, specializing in primary mathematics. She has also been a governor of a primary school for more than five years. Since completing her Doctorate of Education, her main research areas have been mathematics education and social justice. She has also done work on identity, including doctoral student identity, early career research identity and trainee teacher identity.

Ly Thi Tran is a Professor in the School of Education, Deakin University, Australia. Her research focuses on international students across the ELICOS, school, VET and HE sectors, international student graduate employability, the education-migration nexus, geopolitics of student mobilities and staff professional learning in international education.

James Waghorne is official historian of the University of Melbourne, Australia, based in the Centre for the Study of Higher Education. His history of the Melbourne University Student Union (*By Students, For Students*) was published in 2022, and his history (written with Gwilym Croucher) of the Australian Vice-Chancellors' Committee, *Australian Universities*, was published in 2020. He is co-editor of the University of Melbourne's forthcoming Indigenous History, and is Chief Investigator on the 'Expert Nation' and 'Universities and Post-war Recovery' ARC projects, tracing the careers of university graduates who served in the First and Second World Wars.

1

Intellectual Leadership, Higher Education and Precarious Times

Tanya Fitzgerald, Helen M Gunter and Jon Nixon, Editors

Introduction

The research data and analysis reported in this book speak to the precarious times in which we live. The continued rise of right-wing movements and authoritarian governments exposing the fragility of democracy, emerging and real ecological disasters, the legitimation of opinions over facts, vast social and economic inequalities, the corruption of public life, populist anti-intellectualism and the absence of concern for the public good have all wreaked havoc on our institutions and way of life. There is more at work here. There is a deep contempt for truth, civility and democracy. Geiselberger (2017) characterizes this as 'the great regression', whereby citizens are turning away from democratic ideals, values, practices and cultures based on debate, facts, trust and the rule of law. What has emerged too is 'nostalgic nationalism' (Rachman, 2022) based on a rhetoric of an imagined past. What is becoming normalized is the unspeakable, if not the unthinkable; what is needed is the restoration of the values and practices for deliberative democracy, a re-energization of civil society, and a recognition that education is central to this envisioning and civic renaissance.

Our intention is to put on record the attacks on our democratic ideals, values, practices and cultures, and to consider how researchers in higher education engage in the public realm regarding the revitalization of democracy, and how we might continue to promote and exchange ideas, engaging in civic debates underpinned by imagination, opportunities, justice and productive change. What ought we leave behind, to restore to do anew? How might we collectively move forward with public imagination regarding the conditions that make a radical participatory democracy possible? This book is a collective and critical call for researchers, teachers, students in higher education and the wider publics to come together to challenge the underlying condition of precarity and to affirm the possibility of alternative futures.

Our prime intention is to offer new dimensions to the public and professional debates about intellectual leadership and higher education. We locate our concerns within the broad spectrum of institutions that provide continuing post-school education within academic, professional and work-place settings. In this book we are primarily concerned with university and college settings but acknowledge the full range of institutional contexts within which higher education is – and will be – conducted. We frame precarity within a range of research conceptualizations to highlight how expectations of the normal or every day have been set aside (Berlant, 2011). Thus, we question whether alternatives which may have emerged are a new normal, an unthinkable reality. We do this by presenting new thinking about intellectual leadership and higher education within these chapters.

We locate the research reported in this book according to two main standpoints. Our first is that intellectual leadership is traditionally located in the professorial remit and activities within hierarchy and disciplinary excellence (Macfarlane, 2012). While we appreciate the distinctive contribution of the professor, we want to democratize the location and exercise of power by examining inclusive, communal and shared approaches to the development and activist impact of expertise by those at different stages of a 'career', often in partnership with students. More recently, attention has been paid to leadership in higher education that engages with the public mission and purpose of the university/college as a civic and public institution. Connell's (2019) work is a reminder of the role and purposes of higher education and carries a sustained debate about why radical change is now required to overhaul the way in which universities and colleges have become corporate bodies with a commercial focus. Connell argues for universities and colleges to reinvigorate their social contract. This book heeds this call, and we carry this forward in our focus on the economic, social and global contexts of higher education and argue that the past 30+ years of attention to commercialization, marketization and managerialism has ultimately, and potentially, placed universities and colleges at risk. Thus, the way in which the pandemic *impacted* universities (e.g. through income loss) is the issue that draws our attention in this book.

Our second standpoint is that intellectual leadership has been increasingly examined through the changes that have taken place to the sector regarding purposes and identity that continue to impact on research and teaching, where

Collini (2012) asks: what are universities for? For example, there is research that examines governance (Tierney, 2004), the policy environment (Tight, Mok, Huisman & Morphew, 2009), globalization (Roberts & Peters, 2008), internationalizing learning, teaching and curriculum (Peach, 2012), issues of access (Fitzgerald, White & Gunter, 2012), accountability mechanisms (Smyth, 2017), research and researchers (Kenway & Fahey, 2009), academic work (Enders & de Weert, 2009) and the challenges of new managerialism (Deem, Hillyard & Reed, 2007). We engage with such change through thinking about precarity, where Butler (2004) adopts this term as an acknowledgement of dependency, needs, exposure and vulnerabilities, and Berlant (2011) suggests that precarity invokes a 'slow death' due in part to a predictable pattern, replication and reproduction of ordinary life that does not easily permit another alternative to emerge.

We understand that higher education means very different things in different cultural, socio-economic and political contexts. The availability of state-funded schooling, the financial support for students continuing into post-school education and the commitment of the state to publicly funded higher education are crucial elements in what we consider in the development of an equitable system of higher education. But, how – and this is the issue we face – are we to confront these challenges in a time of multiple and escalating precarities? And, in addition how do we embrace the risks necessary for productive change and learning as constructive precarity, while challenging forms of destructive precarity that undermine relationality through fabricated competition.

Precarious times

From the mid-seventeenth century, the word *precarious* has been used in legal parlance to denote the dependence (primarily of ownership) on the favour of others: on entreaty, supplication or prayer. Precarity denotes obligation and dependency, which carry a very different moral and political weight within different societies and polities that are structured within historical periods. Feudal society was based on hierarchical notions of obligation and dependency. Post-feudal capitalism incorporated obligation and dependency into more meritocratically but deeply unequal societies heavily reliant on enslaved labour and the international slave trade that relied upon that labour. Late capitalism, as demonstrated in post-Second World War Western society, has – in its drive towards modernity – recently struggled towards a more democratic, civic and participatory notion of mutual obligation (Axel Honneth (1995) has described this struggle as 'the struggle for recognition'). But, with the rise in the second and third decades of the twenty-first century of economic protectionism (nation against nation), escalating socio-economic inequality (the haves against the have-nots) and cultural and religious antagonisms (the fragmentation of cultural and religious groupings), the position of those on the losing sides of these bitterly contested dichotomies and divides has become increasingly precarious. We are now undoubtedly in precarious times.

Within the field of sociology, the term *precarity* has its origins in Bourdieu's research in Algeria (see Alberti, Bessa, Hardy, Trappmann & Umney, 2018; Bourdieu, Darbel, Rivet & Seibel (1963); Millar (2017) presents a different citation dated 1952). As Bourdieu later showed in his immensely ambitious collaborative project into social suffering in late-twentieth-century French society, 'the "real" suffering of material poverty (*la grande misère*)' is intersected by the positional suffering of diverse individuals and families living on the margins: 'all kinds of ordinary suffering (*la petite misère*)' (Bourdieu et al., 1999, p. 4). Precarity, he and his team of researchers suggested, permeated every aspect of life through the accumulation of 'ordinary suffering'. The notion of precarity has been variously used in reference to 'a labour condition, a class identity, an ontological experience of human existence, [and] a generalized state of the world today' (Millar, 2017, p. 2). As Millar (2017) notes, for Bourdieu precarity is about working conditions, for Standing (2011) it is about a social class, and for Butler (2004) it is about a general condition of life. While these approaches demonstrate both simultaneous and distinctive interpretations, it is the case that all three share forms of precarity that evoke vulnerabilities, insecurities and instabilities that are material, social and psychological. Precarity is an affective condition that is historically located and now pervades society in ways that deeply impact on the security of jobs, housing and well-being. The issue is not just in relation to economic security but also related to near and far global events from acts of terror (see Butler, 2004; Ettlinger, 2007) through to the impact of climate change (see Weston, 2012).

Precarity is, as Berlant (2011) argues, a structurally induced slow death. As she further elucidates, 'precarity provides the dominant structure and experience of the present moment' that affects 'everyone whose bodies and lives are saturated by capitalist forces and rhythms' (p. 192). Such forms of sentient mortality are evident in the interplay of the impact of capital accumulation, competitive consumer markets, managerialist technologies and the ascendance of the corporate organization, on the provision of and access to higher education.

These realities have been investigated as a globalized trend (e.g. Slaughter & Leslie, 1997) with national system investigations (e.g. Courtois & O'Keefe, 2015; Means, 2017), where the only certainty is precarity. The problem is not just gross inequalities in income earnings but – as Thomas Piketty (2014) showed – the gross inequalities in wealth leading to widening gaps of cross-generational wealth accumulation. Notably, while researchers, teachers and students need to embrace change as integral to knowledge production, it is the experience of permanent uncertainty that generates public and private risk in the production of performance data and individualized responsibility.

As Slaughter and Rhoades argued more than two decades ago (and the argument still holds):

> Public colleges and universities emphasize that they support corporate competitiveness through their major role in the global, knowledge-based economy. They stress their role in training advanced students for professional positions close to the technoscience core of knowledge economies, in fostering research that creates high-tech products and processes for corporations, and in preparing undergraduate and community college students to be malleable workers who will fit into (and be retrained for) new information-based jobs and workplaces. In the process, the fundamental social roles of public higher education, including providing increased upward mobility for underserved populations, have been displaced by the economic role of serving corporations' global competitiveness.
>
> (2000, p. 73)

This dismantling of the public provision of and access to higher education means that precarity is implicated in how the citizen is constituted relationally within civil society and certainly with the state. Precarity produces a *precariat* that can be identified through patterns in the workforce (e.g. young and creative industries, Neilson & Rossiter, 2008), where a focus is on those who experience precarity as a feeling that may infuse their entire worldview (Alberti, Bessa, Hardy, Trappmann & Umney, 2018). Higher education has thereby become a site for the production of leading-edge research where funding is dependent on evidence of impact on the economy and teaching outcomes must demonstrate employability. As such all workers in higher education are subjected to feeling unsafe, where research shows a gulf between high-salaried elite roles and an underclass of part-time disposable workers (see Adsit, Doe, Allison, Maggio & Masito, 2015; Ivancheva, Lynch & Keating, 2019). In effect a significant proportion of the workforce has joined the 'working poor' (Ivancheva, 2015), who endure challenging workloads and conditions of service that generate the experience of being trapped in a low-paid, low aspirational job that impacts not only on career opportunities but on the possibility of building a life with a partner and family.

What is being experienced is a process of *precarization*, or the reality of 'the loss of grip over a future that once seemed under control, as more and more areas of life are subordinated to the needs of the economy' (Alberti, Bessa, Hardy, Trappmann & Umney, 2018, p. 449). Consequently, precarization enables understandings about what it means to lose out in work, in personal life and in wider society, but there is some ambivalence regarding this negativity within the debates: not least the case is made about the positivity of having the potential to refuse to conform and so begin anew (see Millar, 2017). What is important to grasp is that this process of precarization cannot be neatly compartmentalized. It is experienced as – and impacts upon – a person's whole way of life and the complexities of social and economic relationships on which they depend. Also, because it is a process, it is cumulative and corrosive. It impacts generationally on persons, families, communities and societies.

Dimensions of precarity

Higher education is at risk for a number of reasons: first, knowledge production has become corporatized within and external to higher education, not least through private think tanks and laboratories combined with financialized research and development (Holmwood & Servós, 2019; Means, 2017); second, the impact of knowledge production on the economy, governance and wider civil society has been commodified through public sector closures and redundancies, and the growth in private consultancy and advisors (Gunter & Mills, 2017); and third, the growth in populist momentum from charismatic leaders combined with 'what works' delivery solutions in everyday practices has marginalized evidence, condoned lying and enabled attacks on academics by government ministers (Gunter, 2018). The Covid-19 pandemic has intensified these trends (Watermeyer et al., 2021), where lockdowns generated the spectre of potential of bankruptcy (Baker, 2020), raised questions about quality in relation to on-line teaching and learning (Mitchell, 2021) and exacerbated mental health issues for staff and students (Bashir, Bashir, Rana, Lambert & Vernallis, 2021; Godber & Atkins, 2021). In addition, the rapid growth in the use of Artificial Intelligence (AI) has demonstrated both productive and destructive impacts on teaching, assessment and research, whereby human intelligence may be eclipsed, and researchers have identified important moral and ethical issues regarding discrimination (see Abdous, 2023; Popenici & Kerr, 2017). In the context of this book, AI might well be considered a form of precarity as it has the potential to disrupt teaching, learning and research.

We recognize that precarity is subject to ongoing debate and conceptual testing (e.g. Alberti, Bessa, Hardy, Trappmann & Umney, 2018; Masquelier, 2019; Neilson & Rossiter, 2008), particularly in higher education (e.g. Burton & Bowman, 2022), and research shows that the experience of higher education can be understood and explained through *contextual precarization*. We therefore distinguish between the complexities of *personal, organizational, existential* and *geopolitical* forms of precarity as a means of understanding and explaining the contexts in which intellectual leadership in higher education is located, while acknowledging that forms of precarity are always complicatedly intertwined.

1. *Personal*: Precarity means that the individual is 'judged personally responsible for their situation' (Näsström & Kalm, 2015, p. 556) and so can be viewed with suspicion and contempt if they 'cannot hack it', or find themselves the subject of attack on social media leading to increased personal security following threats (BBC, 2020a), to 'no-platforming' at conferences (BBC, 2020b) and forced resignations (Adams, 2021). Working lives in higher education are gendered, raced and classed (Arday, 2022; Arday & Mirza, 2018; Cole & Gunter, 2010; Jones, 2022; Warnock, 2016). Data show the impact of precarity on equity: for example, Ivancheva et al. (2019, p. 449) state: 'The price of a successful academic career seems particularly high for women. In Europe, women are increasingly dropping out of academic career paths even when qualified to pursue them.' They go on to argue that precarity is 'antithetical to care in deep and profound ways' (p. 499) and so there are concerns about mental health (Shaw & Ward, 2014), with cases of suicide linked to income targets (Parr, 2014). Representation and recognition are central to the notion of precarity and are deeply embedded in narratives of experiences of working within higher education (see Robson, 2022). Such experiences are structured through social injustices, where Mirza (2018, p. 11) builds on Collins' account of what it means to be an 'outsider-within' (1998, p. 5) as someone who is formally protected from discrimination through organizational equity policies, but who actually works within institutionalized racism regarding whose knowledge counts (see Crenshaw & Roskos-Ewoldsen, 1999).

As Bhopal (2018) argues, public policymaking in general and certainly in education 'works to further perpetuate a society in which whiteness is privileged and prioritised' (p. 5).

2. *Organizational:* Precarity means that the individual is an employee of a 'bottom-line-driven university' (Adsit, Doe, Allison, Maggio & Masito, 2015, p. 21) where brand, business models and consumer choice are what matters. As Jones (2022) shows, academic labour is exploited in a range of ways through zero hours contracts, where 'some universities make use of practices that would make gig economy employers blush' (p. 51). He provides examples to illustrate how and why overwork is endemic, where such work does not necessarily enable a career to be built and the basics for doing the job have to be bid for – from funding for research, through to attendance at conferences. Insecurity is implicit in organizational policy and precarity works in ways that are uneven across the organization, where some staff and courses can be more at risk as what is valued varies (Adsit, Doe, Allison, Maggio & Masito, 2015). Examples from the United States include:

> In 2009 the women's studies program was closed at the University of Guelph; in 2010 the University at Albany suspended five departments in the humanities: the departments of French, Italian, classics, Russian, and theater art; in 2013 the University of Windsor closed its Centre for Studies in Social Justice; in 2014 the University of South Carolina Upstate closed its Center for Women's and Gender Studies. Such programs become considered a financial drain on the institution and opposed to the 'money-making' disciplines, which are externally funded by grants and contracts. Closed departments are seen as inessential to the university because they are not monetarily profitable in the so-called marketplace of ideas that constitutes higher education.
>
> (Adsit, Doe, Allison, Maggio & Masito, 2015, p. 21)

Notably areas of work that expose and problematize corporate models, such as critical management and organizational studies, have been identified for targeted closure (Burrell, 2018).

3. *Existential:* Precarity that is personal and organizational means that higher education can be deemed irrelevant, with cases of mergers and closure (see Higher Ed Dive Team, 2022). The ongoing struggle to avoid closure is evident:

Across the globe, higher education institutions (HEIs) have been radically reshaping teaching and learning in unprecedented ways, and with rare exceptions, education has moved into the online space at breakneck speed. Work practices have altered significantly, placing new pressures on staff and students. Funding for HE has become more precarious than ever, particularly in countries which have been heavily reliant on fees from international students to fund its core business. Questions about universities' and governments' duty of care for the well-being of students encountering economic and emotional hardships and physical isolation have become more urgent. At the same time, the social, psychological, economic and health impacts of the pandemic raise new questions about the future of HE, its purpose and sustainability.

(Green, Anderson, Tait & Tran, 2020, p. 1309)

Higher education has been causally linked to economic growth and hence must operate within and for the economy, and as such not only is the corporate organization at risk of failure but also, to prevent failure, the organization has to redesign purposes and practices in order to survive. Delivery matters more than debate. Consequently, as Gunn and Mintrom (2022) show, 'basic, pure, or blue skies research' (p. 34) is under threat, not least because it is not commercially viable and hence has to be funded by the taxpayer, so the state makes interventions into the purposes of research in ways that are 'coercive', 'mimetic' and 'normative' (p. 52). In other words, as Gunn and Mintrom (2022) state, universities are directed to rise up the global rankings, to at least match internationally successful organizations, and conform to globalized standardized practices whereby a networked and travelling elite of leaders and performers construct and respond to the fear of failure. Indeed, Jones (2022) notes the impact of the Covid-19 pandemic on universities in England: 'With many institutions in financial difficulties and some fearing insolvency, it was imperative that no one displeased an easily threatened government' (p. xi).

4. *Geopoltical:* The world has become increasingly precarious in the period during which this book has been produced. The invasion of Ukraine by Russia on 24 February 2022, the divisions within Europe and the West in response to that invasion, the rise of far-right nationalist parties, the shifting balance of economic power and influence between the superpowers, and the drift towards what Gideon Rachman (2022)

has termed 'the age of the strongman': together, these have created a situation in which personal, organizational and existential risks to persons and institutions have been intensified (e.g. see reforms to HE in the US state of Florida regarding 'woke' and 'freedom of speech', The Economist, 2023; and the dismissal of academics in Turkey; Grove, 2022). The possibility of a liberal order in which intellectual leadership plays a crucial role can now no longer be taken for granted, not even in those parts of the world which embraced social democracy as part of their prized post-Second World War political heritage. Acknowledging the geopolitical dimension of precarity is to recognize that personal, organizational and existential risks play out very differently within different national and regional contexts.

Intellectual leadership

Intellectual leaders – regardless of their institutional positioning – distinguish between truth and untruth, verifiable belief and wishful thinking, fact and fantasy. 'Our concern', as the philosopher Bernard Williams (2002, p. 133), 'is with the virtues of truth'. Those virtues cannot be discovered readymade within a single 'method'. As the philosopher Hans-Georg Gadamer (2001, p. 42) insisted, truth resides in our commitment to 'the questionableness of something and what this requires of us'. Methods matter, but they cannot provide us with a ladder of perfection that inevitably leads us to 'the truth'. The quest for truth is always a messy and muddled affair characterized by false starts, blind alleys, occasional insights, provisional resolutions and leaps of 'the hermeneutical imagination'. Above all, it requires the capacity to listen and to keep the argument going beyond the point of seemingly irreconcilable disagreement. Intellectual leadership is primarily concerned with ensuring that truthfulness matters in social interactions and in wider cultural and political discourse. It is concerned with calling ourselves and others to account through reasoned debate.

The philosopher Richard J. Bernstein (2018) warns of the risk that the routine recourse to untruth has on democratic politics: 'What happened so blatantly in totalitarian societies is being practiced today by leading politicians. In short, there is the constant danger that powerful persuasive techniques are being used to deny factual truth, to transform fact into just another opinion, and to create a world of "alternative facts"' (p. 74).

Democracy, within such a context, becomes – as the political thinker Sheldon S. Wolin puts it – 'managed', 'incorporated', 'fugitive'. Ultimately, it runs the risk of becoming a form of what he termed 'inverted totalitarianism': populism coupled with authoritarianism operating as a totalizing ideology (Wolin, 2010, 2016). The prime responsibility of the intellectual leader under these or any other circumstances is to insist that truth matters – and to challenge any attempt, covert or otherwise, to blur the distinction between truth and untruth.

This involves, to return to Williams's philosophical inquiry into truth and truthfulness, 'the virtue of Accuracy': 'the virtue that encourages people to spend more effort than they might have done in trying to find the truth, and not just to accept any belief-shaped thing that comes into their head' (Williams, 2002, pp. 87–8). This virtue, Williams goes on to argue, is closely related to another of 'the virtues of truth'; namely, 'the virtue of Sincerity'. For, as he puts it, '[i]f we are to rely on what others tell us, they had better be not just sincere but correct; moreover (in the other direction so to speak) if we take care to be right, we need to be honest with ourselves' (Williams, 2002, p. 94). Trust between individuals and communities relies crucially on what Williams calls these 'virtues of truth': virtues that include *accuracy* in sifting the relative merits of 'belief-shaped things', *sincerity* in reporting what we understand to be well-founded beliefs, and *honesty* in calling ourselves to account.

In framing intellectual leadership in these terms, we are relocating our analysis away from the corporate forms of 'luxury leadership' (Gunter, Courtney, Hall & McGinity, 2018) that causally link power with hierarchical structures, roles and behaviours. We recognize that such corporatized intellectual leadership is integral to what Jessop (2018) entitles 'academic capitalism', whereby professors in organizational roles (e.g. President, Dean, Director of a Research Centre) and professionals in administrative organizational roles (e.g. Estates of Campus Management, Finance, HR, Student Services) engage in transformational forms of vision and mission, whereby intellectual leadership is implicated in precarization that is used to build the brand and as a research product it is subject to performance and quality audits. Our position is deeply grounded in the intellectual histories of the field of educational leadership (Gunter, 2016), where we draw on a range of plural resources in order to deliberately highlight the *moral*, *ethical* and *political* dimensions (see Foster, 1986; Greenfield & Ribbins, 1993; Smyth, 1989) to the location and exercise of intellectual leadership.

Following Macfarlane (2011) we recognize the importance of and challenges to the role of the professor in intellectual leadership, where professing is vital to their cosmopolitan role within and beyond the organization. But we go further than this where we recognize that professing is not the especial property of professors, and that the process of professing is educative and communal: 'Leadership is and must be socially critical, it does not reside *in* an individual but in the relationship between individuals, and it is oriented toward social vision and change, not simply, or only, organisational goals' (Foster, 1989, p. 46, emphasis in original). Such relationality is based on a mutually understood moral framework, how *we* envisage *our* ethical ends and purposes and how in addressing those twin concerns *we* relate as informed and critical citizens to the broader polity. Institutions of higher education have traditionally been among the institutions of civil society that have helped sustain the notion of intellectual leadership that this book seeks to evidence and unpack. They have acted – sometimes as a bulwark, sometimes as a critic, sometimes as an interpreter – between state and society. They are central to the survival of a vibrant and vocal civil society.

Such institutions have experienced massive changes in the past three decades. Across England, the United States, Australia and New Zealand, intellectual leadership regarding research and public service has been variously 'managed', 'corporatized' and 'commodified', while HEIs have been positioned to contribute to the knowledge economy and gain a level of competitive advantage in the global marketplace (see Jones, 2022). The cumulative redesign of the state combined with anti-political ideologies are providing the warrant for the dismantling and privatization of public services such as health, welfare and education, where economic and law enforcement policies are being focused on security:

> The promise of public universities to open up social reproduction and to democratise the conditions of knowledge production are put into reverse by marketisation, at the same time as the neutrality of the market is declared. The same neutrality is also attributed to audit measures securing efficiency in the production and distribution of knowledge. The university is no longer aligned with democracy as one of the major institutions of the public sphere, but a knowledge corporation operating in a market, competing for students and producing knowledge products for discrete users.
> (Holmwood & Servós, 2019, p. 318)

At best, institutions of higher education affirm the necessity of public reason and critique within a society that values freedom and democracy, thereby upholding what Stewart Ranson calls 'common literacies of the public sphere' (Ranson, 2018, pp. 42–5). It does so through the practices of inquiry, questioning, dialogue, research and scholarship, and through the organizational structures of cosmopolitan outreach, public service and public participation: practices and structures that rely upon the conditions of public accountability and transparency, mutuality and respect – and trust.

Structure of the book

The chapters are focused on provoking readers to think critically about intellectual leadership in higher education in precarious times. Each contributor has been invited to engage as an intellectual activist and so take up their own perspective on precarity, and to examine the impacts on intellectual leadership. What does it mean to do intellectual work, be an intellectual leader and do intellectual leading? What are the implications for intellectual work and leadership in higher education in precarious times? Thus, the chapters are focused on the idea and realities of precarity, and as such each author examines what this means within a particular HE setting. The reader can begin with the next chapter and follow through in a linear way from strategic examinations of the impact of precarity through to more local, nuanced and individual readings of intellectual leadership in precarious times. Or the reader can dive into the text at any stage and use the contents and index to examine an issue that is pertinent to their interests. As presented, these chapters can be read as offering both a critical analysis of distinctive higher education systems and constructive narratives that point to the possibilities that precarity offers to rethink the value and purposes of higher education and intellectual leadership. We call on our readers to be both intellectually active for themselves and to examine what it means for staff and students to engage in thinking, debate, and argument within higher education at a time of precarity. Therefore, we would encourage narratives to be thought about, spoken and written in ways that challenge the self, and if in a secure context we would want to see readers engage in debates in research papers, social media and blogs.

Our focus on democratizing intellectual leadership means that we address the complexities of knowledge production and how it is implicated in social, political, economic and cultural injustices. Consequently, our authors are not concerned with behaviours for intellectual leadership (e.g. Uslu & Arslan, 2018) or the effective management of intellectual leadership (e.g. Dealtry, 2001). Instead, we begin on the basis that what is presented as known and what is regarded as worth knowing is structured by elite projects. That is, there is a precarity of knowledge and knowledge production if shaped and defined by elites.

Notably, Connell (2007) identifies how there is a need to engage in 'Looking South' because of the dominance of 'Northern theory', where the latter 'embeds the viewpoints, perspectives and problems of metropolitan society, while presenting itself as universal knowledge' (pp. vii–viii). The recognition of different forms of epistemological elitism is evident in a range of work that addresses discriminatory knowledge production regarding class (e.g. Warnock, 2016), gender (e.g. Harding, 1991) and race (e.g. Sullivan & Tuana, 2012), where, for example, Johnson and Joseph-Salisbury (2018, p. 144) engage with Yancy (2008) in order to present an '*episteme of Blackness*' (emphasis in original) and how this is 'a way of knowing that is developed experientially, collectively and intergenerationally'.

We therefore present nine chapters where our authors examine data and analysis that report on research through narratives of working lives, and how they both live what Holland and Lave (2001) identify as 'history in person' but also present narratives of and about intellectual leadership that are at the interface of lived histories and organizational structures. We begin with two chapters from Oleksiyenko and Jones that provide a strategic examination of what it means to do intellectual leadership in precarious times, before we go on to present four chapters – Tran et al., Hall, O'Connor and Rider – that examine these matters in more detail regarding forms of destructive precarity. The final three chapters – Parr et al., Waghorne, Levinson and Rowell – not only recognize the unproductive aspects of precarity but also engage with evidence and analysis about activism as a form of constructive precarity, and how it is integral to intellectual work.

While acknowledging and identifying the destructive impact of precarity on the *personal, organizational, existential* and *geopolitical* dimensions of higher education, the following chapters also highlight the constructive responses being developed across the sector to the challenges being faced at all levels. In particular we as editors wish to highlight the importance of new developments and insights introduced by upcoming generations of academics who are responding with imagination and intelligence to the rapidly changing context within which they are forging a new vision of what higher education might – and should – look like in the third and ensuing decades of the twenty-first century: a vision that challenges existing practices, organizational structures and systems of governance, and that insists on the need to affirm higher education as a *public* good. Such a re-envisioning requires – as Antonio Gramsci reminds us – optimism of the will.

References

Abdous, M. (21 March 2023). How AI is shaping the future of higher ed. *Inside Higher Education*. https://www.insidehighered.com/views/2023/03/22/how-ai-shaping-future-higher-ed-opinion

Adams, R. (28 October 2021). Sussex professor resigns after transgender rights row. *The Guardian*. https://www.theguardian.com/world/2021/oct/28/sussex-professor-kathleen-stock-resigns-after-transgender-rights-row

Adsit, J., Doe, S., Allison, M., Maggio, P., & Masito, M. (2015). Affective activism: Answering institutional productions of precarity in the corporate university. *Feminist Formations*, 27(3), 21–48. https://doi.org/10.1353/ff.2016.0008

Alberti, G., Bessa, I., Hardy, K., Trappmann, V., & Umney, C. (2018). In, against and beyond precarity: Work in insecure times. *Work, Employment and Society*, 32(3), 447–57. https://doi.org/10.1177/0950017018762088

Arday, J. (2022). 'More to prove and more to lose': Race, racism and precarious employment in higher education. *British Journal of Sociology of Education*, 43(4), 513–33. https://doi.org/10.1080/01425692.2022.2074375

Arday, J., & Mirza, H. S. (Eds) (2018). *Dismantling race in higher education*. Palgrave Macmillan.

Baker, S. (6 July 2020). Covid-19 crisis could bankrupt a dozen UK universities, IFS warns. *Times Higher Education*. https://www.timeshighereducation.com/news/covid-19-crisis-could-bankrupt-dozen-uk-universities-ifs-warns

Bashir, A., Bashir, S., Rana, K., Lambert, P., & Vernallis, A. (2021). Post-Covid-19 adaptations: The shifts towards online learning, hybrid course delivery and the implications for biosciences courses in the higher education setting. *Frontiers in Education*, 6. https://www.frontiersin.org/articles/10.3389/feduc.2021.711619/full

BBC (25 January 2020a). Oxford professor given protection following threats from trans activists. *BBC News*. https://www.bbc.com/news/education-51248684

BBC (4 March 2020b). Oxford University professor condemns exclusion from event. *BBC News*. https://www.bbc.com/news/uk-england-oxfordshire-51737206

Berlant, L. (2011). *Cruel optimism*. Duke University Press.

Bernstein, R. J. (2018). *Why read Hannah Arendt now?* Polity Press.

Bhopal, K. (2018). *White privilege, the myth of a post-racial society*. Policy Press.

Bourdieu, P., Darbel, A., Rivet, J.-P., & Seibel, C. (1963). *Travail et travailleurs en Algerie*. Mouton & Co.

Bourdieu, P., et al. (1999). *The weight of the world: Social suffering in contemporary society* (P. P. Ferguson, S. Emanuel, J. Johnson, & S. T. Waryn, Trans.). Polity Press.

Burrell, G. (25 March 2018). The attack on Organization Studies in UK universities – an open letter by Gibson Burrell. *Yiannis Gabriel*. http://www.yiannisgabriel.com/2018/03/the-attack-on-organization-studies-in.html

Burton, S., & Bowman, B. (2022). The academic precariat: Understanding life and labour in the neoliberal academy. *British Journal of Sociology of Education*, 43(4), 497–512. https://doi.org/10.1080/01425692.2022.2076387

Butler, J. (2004). *Precarious life: The power of mourning and violence*. Verso.

Cole, B., & Gunter, H. M. (Eds) (2010). *Changing lives: Women, inclusion and the PhD*. Trentham Books.

Collini, S. (2012). *What are universities for?* Allen Lane.

Collins, P. H. (1998). *Fighting words: Black women and the search for justice*. University of Minneapolis Press.

Connell, R. (2007). *Southern theory*. Polity Press.

Connell, R. W. (2019). *The good university: What universities do and why it is time for radical change*. Monash University Publishing.

Courtois, A., & O'Keefe, T. (2015). Precarity in the ivory cage: Neoliberalism and casualisation of work in the Irish higher education sector. *Journal for Critical Education Policy Studies*, 13(1), 43–66.

Crenshaw, C., & Roskos-Ewoldsen, D. R. (1999). Rhetoric, racist ideology, and intellectual leadership. *Rhetoric & Public Affairs*, 2(2), 275–302. https://doi.org/10.1353/RAP.2010.0053

Dealtry, R. (2001). Managing intellectual leadership in corporate value. *Journal of Workplace Learning*, 13(3), 119–24. https://doi.org/10.1108/13665620110388424

Deem, R., Hillyard, S., & Reed, M. (2007). *Knowledge, higher education and the New Managerialism: The changing management of UK universities*. Oxford University Press.

Enders, J., & de Weert, E. (Eds) (2009). *The changing face of academic life*. Palgrave Macmillan.

Ettlinger, N. (2007). Precarity unbound. *Alternatives*, 32(3), 319–40. https://doi.org/10.1177/030437540703200303

Fitzgerald, T., White, J., & Gunter, H. M. (2012). *Hard labour? Academic work and the changing landscape of higher education*. Emerald.

Foster, W. (1986). *Paradigms and promises*. Prometheus Books.

Foster, W. (1989). Towards a critical practice of leadership. In J. Smyth (Ed.), *Critical perspectives on educational leadership* (pp. 39–62). Falmer Press.

Gadamer, H.-G. (2001). *Gadamer in conversation: Reflections and commentary* (R. E. Palmer, Ed. & Trans.). Yale University Press.

Geiselberger, H. (Ed.) (2017). *The great regression*. Polity Press.

Godber, K. A., & Atkins, D. R. (2021). Covid-19 impacts on teaching and learning: A collaborative autoethnography by two higher education lecturers. *Frontiers in Education*, 6. https://www.frontiersin.org/articles/10.3389/feduc.2021.647524/full

Green, W., Anderson, V., Tait, K., & Tran, L. T. (2020). Precarity, fear and hope: Reflecting and imagining in higher education during a global pandemic. *Higher Education Research & Development*, 39(7), 1309–2. https://doi.org/10.1080/07294360.2020.1826029

Greenfield, T. B., & Ribbins, P. (Eds) (1993). *Greenfield on educational administration*. Routledge.

Grove, J. (2022). Deans fired at Turkish University. *Inside Higher Education*. https://www.insidehighered.com/news/2022/02/04/firing-deans-raises-academic-freedom-concerns-turkey

Gunn, A., & Mintrom, M. (2022). *Public policy and universities*. Cambridge University Press.

Gunter, H. M. (2016). *An intellectual history of school leadership practice and research*. Bloomsbury Press.

Gunter, H. M. (2018). *The politics of public education: Reform ideas and issues*. Policy Press.

Gunter, H. M., & Mills, C. (2017). *Consultants and Consultancy: The case of education*. Springer.

Gunter, H. M., Courtney, S. J., Hall, D., & McGinity, R. (2018). School principals in neoliberal times: A case of luxury leadership? In A. J. Means & K. J. Saltman (Eds), *Handbook of global education reform* (pp. 113–30). Wiley-Blackwell.

Harding, S. (1991). *Whose science? Whose knowledge? Thinking from women's lives?* Cornell University Press.

Higher Ed Dive Team (2022). A look at trends in college consolidation since 2016. *Higher Ed Dive*. https://www.highereddive.com/news/how-many-colleges-and-universities-have-closed-since-2016/539379/

Holland, D., & Lave, J. (2001). History in person, an introduction. In D. Holland & J. Lave (Eds), *History in person* (pp. 3–3). School of American Research Press.

Holmwood, J., & Servós, C. M. (2019). Challenges to public universities: Digitalisation, commodification and precarity. *Social Epistemology*, 33(4), 309–20. https://doi.org/10.1080/02691728.2019.1638986

Honneth, A. (1995). *The struggle for recognition: The moral grammar of social conflicts* (J. Anderson, Trans.). Polity Press (Original work published in Germany in 1992).

Ivancheva, M. P. (2015). The age of precarity and the new challenges to the academic profession. *Studia Universitatis Babes-Bolyai Mathematica*, 60(1), 39–47.

Ivancheva, M., Lynch, K., & Keating, K. (2019). Precarity, gender and care in the neoliberal academy. *Gender, Work and Organisation*, 26(4), 448–62. https://doi.org/10.1111/gwao.12350

Jessop, B. (2018). On academic capitalism. *Critical Policy Studies*, 12(1), 104–9. https://doi.org/10.1080/19460171.2017.1403342

Johnson, A., & Joseph-Salisbury, R. (2018). 'Are you supposed to be in here?' Racial microaggressions and knowledge production in higher education. In J. Arday & H. S. Mirza (Eds), *Dismantling race in higher education* (pp. 143–60). Palgrave Macmillan.

Jones, S. (2022). *Universities under fire*. Palgrave Macmillan.

Kenway, J., & Fahey, J. (Eds) (2009). *Globalising the research imagination*. Routledge.

Macfarlane, B. (2011). Professors as intellectual leaders: Formation, identity and role. *Studies in Higher Education*, 36(1), 57–73. https://doi.org/10.1080/03075070903443734

Macfarlane, B. (2012). *Intellectual leadership in higher education: Renewing the role of the professor*. Routledge.

Masquelier, C. (2019). Bourdieu, Foucault and the politics of precarity. *Distinktion: Journal of Social Theory*, 20(2), 135–55. https://doi.org/10.1080/1600910X.2018.1549999

Means, A. J. (2017). Education for a post-work future: Automation, precarity, and stagnation. *Knowledge Cultures*, 5(1), 21–40. https://doi.org/10.22381/KC5120173

Millar, K. M. (2017). Toward a critical politics of precarity. *Sociology Compass*, 11(6), 1–11. https://doi.org/10.1111/soc4.12483

Mirza, H. (2018). Racism in higher education: 'What then, can be done?' In J. Arday & H. S. Mirza (Eds), *Dismantling race in higher education* (pp. 3–23). Palgrave Macmillan.

Mitchell, N. (18 September 2021). OECD warns UK universities over high fees for 'online' learning. *University World News*. https://www.universityworldnews.com/post.php?story=2021091807211996

Näsström, S., & Kalm, S. (2015). A democratic critique of precarity. *Global Discourse*, 5(4), 556–73. https://doi.org/10.1080/23269995.2014.992119

Neilson, B., & Rossiter, N. (2008). Precarity as a political concept, or, Fordism as exception. *Theory and Society*, 25(7–8), 51–72. https://doi.org/10.1177/0263276408097796

Parr, C. (3 December 2014). Imperial College professor Stefan Grimm 'was given grant income target'. *Times Higher Education*. https://www.timeshighereducation.com/news/imperial-college-professor-stefan-grimm-was-given-grant-income-target/2017369.article

Peach, S. (2012). *Understanding curriculum in higher education*. Lambert Academic Publishing.

Piketty, T. (2014). *Capital in the twenty-first century* (A. Goldhammer, Trans.). Belknap Press/Harvard University.

Popenici, S. A. D. & Kerr, S. (2017). Exploring the impact of artificial intelligence on teaching and learning in higher education. *Research and Practice in Technology Enhanced Learning*, 12(22), 1–3. https://doi.org/10.1186/s41039-017-0062-8

Rachman, G. (2022). *The age of the strongman: How the cult of the leader threatens democracy around the world*. Bodley Head.

Ranson, S. (2018). *Education and democratic participation: The making of learning communities*. Routledge.

Roberts, P., & Peters, M. (2008). *Neoliberalism, higher education and research*. Sense Publishers.

Robson, J. (2022). Stigma and spoiled identities: Rescripting career norms for precariously employed academic staff. *British Journal of Sociology of Education*, 44(1), 183–98. https://doi.org/10.1080/01425692.2022.2137464

Shaw, C., & Ward, L. (6 March 2014). Dark thoughts: Why mental illness is on the rise in academia. *The Guardian*. https://www.theguardian.com/higher-education-network/2014/mar/06/mental-health-academics-growing-problem-pressure-university

Slaughter, S., & Leslie, L. L. (1997). *Academic capitalism: Politics, policies, and the entrepreneurial university*. Johns Hopkins University Press.

Slaughter, S., & Rhoades, G. (2000). The neo-liberal university. *New Labor Forum* (Spring/Summer), 73–9.

Smyth, J. (Ed.) (1989). *Critical perspectives on educational leadership*. Falmer Press.

Smyth, J. (2017). *The toxic university: Zombie leadership, academic rockstars and neoliberal ideology*. Palgrave Macmillan.

Standing, G. (2011). *The precariat: The new dangerous class*. Bloomsbury Academic.

Sullivan, S., & Tuana, N. (Eds) (2012). *Race and epistemologies of ignorance*. SUNY Press.

The Economist (26 January 2023). Ron DeSantis wants to limit free speech in the name of free speech. *The Economist*. https://www.economist.com/united-states/2023/01/26/ron-desantis-wants-to-limit-free-speech-in-the-name-of-free-speech

Tierney, W. (Ed.) (2004). *Competing conceptions of academic governance: Negotiating the perfect storm*. Johns Hopkins University Press.

Tight, M., Mok, K. H., Huisman, J., & Morphew, C. (2009). *The Routledge international handbook of higher education*. Routledge.

Uslu, B., & Arslan, H. (2018). Faculty's academic intellectual leadership: The intermediary relations within universities' organizational components. *International Journal of Leadership in Education*, 21(4), 399–411. http://dx.doi.org/10.1080/13603124.2016.1278044

Warnock, D. M. (2016). Paradise Lost? Patterns and precarity in working-class academic narratives. *Journal of Working-Class Studies*, 1(1), 28–44. https://doi.org/10.13001/jwcs.v1i1.6013

Watermeyer, R., Shankar, K., Crick, T., Knight, C., McGaughey, R., Hardman, J., Suri, V. R., Chung, R., & Phelan, D. (2021). 'Pandemia': A reckoning of UK universities corporate response to COVID-19 and its academic fallout. *British Journal of Sociology of Education*, 42(5–6), 651–66. https://doi.org/10.1080/01425692.2021.1937058

Weston, K. (2012). Political ecologies of the precarious. *Anthropological Quarterly*, 85(2), 429–55. https://doi.org/10.1353/anq.2012.0017

Williams, B. (2002). *Truth and truthfulness: An essay in genealogy*. Princeton University Press.

Wolin, S. S. (2010). *Democracy incorporated: Managed democracy and the specter of inverted totalitarianism*. Princeton University Press.

Wolin, S. S. (2016). *Fugitive democracy and other essays* (N. Xenos, Ed.). Princeton University Press.

Yancy, G. (2008). *Black bodies, white gaze: The continuing significance of race*. Rowman & Littlefield.

2

When Intellectual Leadership Dies: Critical Voice vs Self-Censorship in Precarious Universities

Anatoly Oleksiyenko

Introduction

Intellectual leadership is on its deathbed in precarious colleges and universities affected by corporate cultures that 'trump human dignity, healthy relationships and civic engagement' (Oleksiyenko and Tierney, 2018). Unable to reconcile moral and intellectual dilemmas resulting from excessive managerialism and performative surveillance, many professors abide by corporate logic, instead of boldly standing up against fraudulence and lack of integrity in the academe (Vican, Friedman and Andreasen, 2020). One particular factor contributing to the death of intellectualism in such contexts is a failure of professors to take on leadership in order to refine moral orientations and obligations institutionally and socially (Macfarlane, 2013). Escapes from these responsibilities have created bureaucratic 'iron cages' that punish profitless thinking and spearhead precarity and vulnerability (Oleksiyenko, 2018). Intellectual leadership in higher education is often presented as a championship of factory-like productivity and narcissistic positioning, rather than resistance to corporate maltreatment. As precarious universities increasingly generate dehumanizing agendas and ethically challenging institutional behaviours that affect the lives and futures of new generations of scholars and students, questions about the nature and aims of intellectual leadership loom larger.

In my previous studies, I have examined the challenges of becoming a leader in academic contexts and institutions that restrain intellectual freedom and resilience (Oleksiyenko, 2021a; Oleksiyenko and Ruan, 2019). In this chapter, I contemplate the dilemmas facing intellectuals when they fail to respond to ethical challenges emerging through conflicts between their academic and public engagements in the age of post-truth (Oleksiyenko, 2018; Oleksiyenko and Jackson, 2021; Oleksiyenko and Tierney, 2018). In the following sections, I explore the premises of becoming and being an intellectual in a traditional academic environment (Macfarlane and Cheng, 2008; Merton, 1988), and then consider how precarity perverts the nascence of an intellectual when non-intellectual designs of knowledge production are installed and leadership failures are overlooked (Oleksiyenko, 2018). I illustrate pathological developments in higher education by drawing on the example of precarity in the post-Soviet university context. This allows me to delve deeper into moral issues, which are often marginalized or avoided in the global discourse of higher education, as well as provide insights into cultural variations of precarity in contexts where fear of self-evaluation prevails and leadership failures remain under-examined. My post-Soviet experiences and studies (as a former Soviet and Ukrainian citizen, and a researcher of Russia and Ukraine) provide me with abundant insights into the complexity of such failures.

As I write this chapter, Russia wages a brutal war against Ukraine (bombing and murdering civilians, obliterating schools, universities, museums, churches, theatres and hospitals in Ukraine) (Mounk, 2022; Oleksiyenko, 2022a). Meanwhile, the leaders of 200 Russian universities have expressed support for their government's aggression against a neighbouring country (O'Malley, 2022). Although 7,750 Russian scientists signed a letter opposing the 'senseless war', that letter was removed from the web 'after the Russian parliament made it a criminal offense worth as much as 15 years in prison to call the invasion of Ukraine anything but a "special military operation"' (Overbye, 2022). The suppression of academic voices in Russia has been a clear indication of a major failure of Russian higher education to secure freedom of speech and autonomy of academics, notwithstanding thirty years of post-Soviet reforms (Oleksiyenko, 2021c). As I examine the precarity of these academics during the rule of a nefarious regime in Russia, and consider the motivations for their amoral support of the war in Ukraine, I reflect on a wider range of governance challenges within the contexts of higher education affected by corrupt corporatization and overconfident managerialism in general (Oleksiyenko and Tierney, 2018), and in post-Soviet settings in particular (Oleksiyenko, 2018). This approach allows me to re-examine the notion of uncritical academic engagement with governmental agendas, as well as to rethink the causes of self-inflicted fiascos resulting from compliance with corporate rules (Oleksiyenko, 2021b).

In the following section, I outline the premises of intellectual leadership in academia and explain how they become a caricature in a neoliberal university preoccupied with corporate power. I then bring in a case study from the post-Soviet discourse of corporatization to underscore the challenges of precarious contexts, where universities are turned into armies, as was previously described by Kuraev (2016), and leadership is overwhelmed with malignant institutional growths that kill critical thinking, deform intellectuality and generate depravity. To problematize my investigation, I depict the death of intellectual leadership in the Russian context of a fictionalized post-Soviet university. In the concluding part of this chapter, I elaborate on the primacy of critical thinking, inquiry and integrity as a base for nurturing intellectual leadership.

Becoming an intellectual and a leader in a precarious university

Macfarlane (2013) argues that intellectual leadership can sound like an oxymoron. Indeed, leadership is an alien concept for an intellectual who decides to put aside science in favour of managerial control and prioritize corporate hobnobbing over scholarship. Given that leadership implies organizational politics and power struggles (Manning, 2017), why would an intellectual want to take time away from research, writing and teaching to be embroiled in bureaucracy and organizational tussles? Recognizing the perverse nature of academic leadership in the neoliberal contexts of higher education, where the intellectual gives way to the industrial, Macfarlane (2013) remains hopeful that professors are able to use critical thinking and make good choices considerate of ethical dilemmas in their academic citizenry and public outreach. Macfarlane (2011) also recognizes the difficulties of maintaining a steady moral compass by leaders who are in equal measure responsible for buttressing institutional income and the professional careers of university employees; spearheading significant scientific theories and experiments; and transforming knowledge to enable social and institutional innovations and impacts. At a time when the university increasingly borrows from business designs, quasi-academic leaderists end up exploiting the precarity of their junior staff while claiming to improve institutional performance (Oleksiyenko, 2018). Ultimately, many academics seek to escape the corporate control and labour for their own benefit, rather than for institutional and societal development and prosperity.

Concerns about personal privileges have always been significant in the academe (Kwiek, 2015, 2019; Merton, 1988). For scientists, these are the concerns of prestige-driven intellectual influencers focused on the significance of ideas and the followership of disciples and colleagues. In the neoliberal era, in which the academic proletariat, or precariat, is told to labour hard for institutional fame and the economy – or be laid off and lose income – the concerns regarding impact acquire a different connotation. While status and positions of power and privilege remain unevenly distributed among different scholars working collaboratively on the same problems, as had been the case in the past (Kuhn, 1970; Merton, 1988), the asymmetries in power positions have become goods in neoliberal times – those in a position of cumulative privilege seek to purchase disadvantaged labour to further accumulate more power and benefits (Juntrasook, 2014; Oleksiyenko, Zha, Chirikov and Li, 2018, p. 2020).

The precariat is exposed to intensive bullying by jealous and revengeful 'leaderists' of corporate academia when the former's contributions are measured by similar indicators of revenue generation, prestigious publications and citations to the latter's (Kwiek, 2018; Macfarlane, 2017; Oleksiyenko, 2018). In view of corporate power games, it is not always easy to understand what makes an intellectual leader in the long run, given that precarity is increasingly used by the powerful to manipulate the design of corporate teams and the distribution of benefits. Precarious intellectuals are often at a crossroads – deciding whether to abide by the corporate power gaming, or to abandon an industrially imitative academic career for the real industry. As these intellectuals are engaged in disparate temporal and spatial manifestations of power-making in their universities, communities and networks, they encage themselves into rigid conditionalities set by deceptive renumerations, entitlements and affiliations on campuses and beyond.

The trajectories of an intellectual in the making have different degrees of precarity within disparate contextual domains. Opportunities for growing as an intellectual, and even more so for building an intellectual position and influence, may vary significantly in places that prioritize service (rather than research or teaching) – or what could be termed 'servitude' that contributes to corporate, rather than intellectual powers (Oleksiyenko, 2021b, 2021c). In elite and prestigious research universities focused on developing global science, discourse and networks, a new scholar is most likely to be urged to work hard on influential publications and international communication that would define her career and impact (Norton, 2009; Zuckerman, 1977). This labour is hard because research involves, among other things, numerous proposals to be drafted, revised, validated, approved and revised again. However, in research-intensive communities, creativity and innovation are rewarded and are shaped by a continuous flow of advice and collegial interactions at seminars, symposia and conferences, where idea-makers can improve and enrich their theoretical frameworks, data development strategies and analytical insights. Critical thinking emerges as a foundational norm in developing good science and learning within these collegial networks (Bailin, 2002).

Alas, research – especially internationally peer-reviewed inquiry – is not always a prerogative of universities. In the Soviet (authoritarian/totalitarian) model of the university, genuine non-performativist research was deliberately removed from the university mission menu, and professors were responsible only for recycling the propaganda imposed by the military-industrial complex and ideological bureaus (Kuraev, 2016; Oleksiyenko, 2018, 2021b). Free inquiry and criticism were discouraged and punished – not only in academia, but in the society at large. The Soviet-era university was supposed to serve five-year plan targets aimed at achieving 'an equitable communist society': a dream which paradoxically became bleaker as a growing number of Stakhanovites laboured harder. The university also had to persuade new generations of students, i.e. citizens and workers, that they were living in the superior format of societal and economic organization. Most students were, however, forbidden to travel abroad and investigate whether they indeed had the best societal construct. Meanwhile, professors were regarded as achieving outstanding results if their students learned to abide by dictatorial rule, censor themselves and their peers, avoid dissent-generating questions and narratives, and promulgate their exceptional lifestyle should they happen to meet anyone from abroad. Leadership was primarily defined as exceptional belief and will. While some parallels of such leadership can be found in the neoliberal constructs of academia in the West (Brandist, 2016; Oleksiyenko, 2016; Smolentseva, 2017), it should be noted that there is space for dissent, while disagreeing with 'the only and the right course' of organizational existence in the Soviet space of higher education could land one in the Gulag (Oleksiyenko, 2021b).

Interestingly, however, contemporary researchers observe parallels between the (neo)-Soviet and neoliberal forms of administration in higher education insofar as both benchmark machine-like productivity and accountability, and impose rigid ideology and officious leadership (Brandist, 2016; Oleksiyenko, 2018). When neo-Soviets and neoliberals champion the corporate design of the university, precarity becomes a global scourge. It legitimizes and empowers academic 'leaderists' to exploit labour and crave 'soldierism' (Oleksiyenko, 2018). As in the Soviet knowledge factory, these leaderists churn out empty-headed degree-holders, rather than shape their graduates to be curious, resilient and courageous thinkers and designers of new processes and products (Janosik, Carpenter and Creamer, 2006). The precarious university urges the dissemination or recycling of managerial schemes that promise effective implementation at a lower cost to the public, which is increasingly lacking sophistication in choosing and consuming products generated by degree mills. Structuring their programmes for mass consumption in accordance with industrial or ideological templates, universities often appear as either fakes or cages, in which there is no space or time for intellectual inquiry, and where academics act as either salespersons or minions. In such environments, leadership is increasingly understood as a form of hierarchical compliance and surveillance imposed by corporate results-based management (Fitzgerald, White and Gunter, 2012). This type of leadership is not stimulated by ambitions for intellectual prominence and performance aimed at paradigm-shifts in international communities of critically minded scholarship and peer-review. While corporate universities may have their own prominent strategists and politicians, they primarily act as manipulators of commercial designs that reinforce the legitimacy and power of the already powerful and privileged.

The corporate make-up of the university stimulates powerful, but ill-informed decision making which prioritizes narrow-minded interests over greater societal needs (Green, Hammer and Star, 2009). The corporate university does not tolerate faculty members who raise their voice in defence of freedom, equity and social justice (Slater, 2008). In the corporate frameworks of knowledge development, young scholars are positioned as responsibility-centre budget warriors in charge of industrial or governmental revenue-generation (Oleksiyenko, 2018). The growing presence of corporate language and ethos in university boardrooms and departments muffles the voices of dissent (Fitzgerald, White and Gunter, 2012; Leišytė, 2022). Under the corporate mandates, becoming a professor implies complying with performativity and productivity objectives requiring multi-tasking, hierarchical obedience, self-censorship and competitiveness – all for the sake of calculative agendas and reports (Oleksiyenko, 2022b). Having well-trimmed accounts makes the corporate intellectuals look more geared up for combative engagements in competitive higher education. Meanwhile, very few intellectuals have the courage to criticize the corporate university and its patronage of authoritarianism and nationalism (Nixon, 2021).

The mirror of truth

As precarity increases for intellectuals defying the ideas and practices of the corporate university, questions emerge about the ethics of the modern discourse, as well as about the future of the university. Legacies of the Soviet university, the institutional model which enjoyed inscrutable belief and belligerent competitiveness, can be quite instructive in that regard. In his study on the Soviet legacy of the 'perversion of knowledge', Birstein (2001) provides an excellent account of key problems faced by scientists whose allegiance to the government and ideology was tightly steered and controlled by the corporate elites. While Kuraev (2016) noted that the Soviet model trained professionals in accordance with militarist management and uniformist thinking, Birstein (2001) points out that resistance and defiance did transpire, alas through emigration or defection. The key message emerging from the Soviet period accounts is that when scholars are cultivated to misapply their critical thinking and voice, engage with post-truth politics and promote propaganda, the university ceases to be an intellectual space (also see Oleksiyenko, 2021b).

To illustrate the political complexity and precarity faced by the corporate professoriate, the next section of this chapter will transport the reader to the Russian context of academia and intellectual existence. Gessen (1997) delineates this context as a space of recurrent deadening, where intellectuals fail time and again to communicate the truth, and thus contribute to repeated collapse of their society and state. I would argue that these intellectuals are pressed periodically to face 'the mirror of truth', especially after the collapse, but fail to see a true reflection that might help them to recognize the causes and signs of the deadening, given that the mirror is often cracked, allowing memories to disappear or become twisted, as in the recurring image of the cracked mirror of history evoked in James Joyce's (1922/1960) Ulysses. In the absence of critically minded institutions, which would cultivate freedom of inquiry, speech and reflection, and inform professors' teaching and learning processes, these intellectuals fail to develop a practice that would allow them to grow morally, and thus intellectually. The story below draws on data generated by my previous studies in Russia, conducted between 2012 and 2021 (e.g. see Oleksiyenko, 2016, 2021b, 2021c). I delve into nuances related to the role of hierarchy, compliance, corporate abuse and tongue-tied intellectuals in the context of transformations at post-Soviet universities. In the days when Russia turns into a pariah state and approaches a self-inflicted collapse of historical proportions, it is particularly important to understand the mix of narcissism and superpower ambitions embedded in the corporate idea of the Russian academe and its imperial professoriate.

I have put in front of the mirror of truth a fictional image of Professor Snitchin: the product of proud Soviet intelligentsia obsessed with corporate allegiance to anti-Western sentiments and totalitarian perspectives of the twentieth century, yet pressured to undertake radical change and adopt a more global outlook by his twenty-first-century students. Embedding the transformational perspectives into ethnographic and phenomenological studies of Russian intellectuals (e.g. Brower, 1967; Lipset and Dobson, 1972), the section below illustrates how paths taken and not taken turn intellectuals into corporate soldiers and moral failures. The narrative denotes a range of perspectives on tendencies and practices in the so-called 'Russian world' (Shlapentokh, 2019; Tolstoy and McCaffray, 2015), as presented in the critical literature, which has been shunned by Russian officialdom and its subservient scholars.

The dead intellectual in the glare of the bygone world

Professor Snitchin awaited his doctoral students. They should enter his office any time now. He straightened his tie, double-checked the position of his vintage wire phone and made sure the portraits of his predecessors were all well-aligned on the wall behind him. Professor Snitchin was very proud of the image of his mentor, Professor Stukachov, a Great Patriotic War veteran decked out in military medals. Stukachov's jowly face glared grimly out of the ornate frame, keeping students chained to their chairs with the power of his gaze, while Snitchin delivered one of his endless rants. The meeting would start soon and Snitchin was prepared. He had put together a list of bullet-points to make his statements straight and clear. Albeit, these scribbles were not really necessary, as he always knew what the key message should be: 'remain patriotic!'; 'challenge western writers and arguments!'; 'question any logic justifying the advantages of the West!'; and 'deride your opponent when he draws on western discourse!'; when cornered, deflect by asking 'what about … '. The exclamation marks reinvigorated Snitchin – they brought back memories of his slogan-strewn youth, when Professor Stukachov instilled in him an intense admiration and love of Russia, the world superpower, and the indisputable source of eternal wisdom and peace-making on a chaotic planet.

Professor Snitchin started his academic career at the security department of his university. As an inquisitive student, he proved to be an excellent informant for the personnel department and developed a number of files on university activists. He was asked to stay at the university upon graduation and work with Stukachov on a Candidate of Science degree in the Department of Marxist-Leninist Philosophy and Scientific Communism. A hybrid of propagandist, philosopher and schmoozer, Snitchin continued to do parallel research for the security department. This department needed specialists who could collect data prudently and be smart enough to penetrate individual life-stories and develop evidence on suspicious characters in the student body. Once he embarked on a teaching career, Snitchin was able to trigger provocative conversations in the classrooms and beyond. Claiming to be a member of the avantgarde-intelligentsia (as befitting a Scientific Communism specialist), he also dared to deal in pirated 'forbidden literature' and ask unusual questions, thus attracting young activists, who questioned communism and patriotic scholarship. As his dossier on 'weak and unreliable minds' grew, making the security office's evidential database look impressive in the eyes of the authorities, Snitchin gained a reputation and won trust, which positioned him well for promotion in the university. Besides, he was invited to join the Communist Party and later chaperoned various political campaigns, finally succeeding in being enthroned as leader of the university's party bureau. Professor Stukachov, who recommended him for this position, looked at his student appreciatively. Snitchin was an up-and-coming disciple.

Just as his career was progressing superbly, and new perks and titles were accumulating – making his influence in the university and beyond seemingly unassailable – Snitchin's career entered a zone of turbulence in 1986, when the General Secretary of the Soviet Communist Party, Mikhail Gorbachev, announced the infamous policies of Perestroika and Glasnost. New publications on the Gulag, the KGB, and crimes against intellectuals appeared and were excitedly circulated by Snitchin's impressionable students. Should he have joined the public outcry or muffled it instead before his own activities were disclosed and he became an object for public anger and purges? It was difficult to decide. He chose to do what he did before. He encouraged students to speak. That would show that he was an open-minded intellectual, delegating leadership to his younger colleagues and allowing critical debate. Meanwhile, Snitchin continued to collect files for his private dossier, which might be needed by the government when Glasnost was gone. His hopes and expectations suddenly crashed to smithereens when the putsch failed in the Kremlin and the Soviet Union collapsed.

Ready for the worst, Professor Snitchin was hugely relieved when his university rector told the staff to continue their work. Unlike in other post-communist countries – Poland and East Germany – the Russian government decided not to lay off the former Soviet lecturers. With an economic crisis ensuing and entrepreneurial faculty members leaving the university for the private sector, Snitchin decided to re-orient his lectures towards the market economy, work on sponsored translations from English, and thus make extra income on top of his miserable university salary. He was fortunate to join a World Bank project, which was sponsoring courses for university professors like him to study macro- and micro-economics. He completed a certificate programme and participated in several study visits organized by Western universities. His book translations also allowed him to skilfully plagiarize Western texts, while attributing his authorship to the stolen ideas. As his name and reputation grew inside the emerging marketing studies in Russia, he was invited by various American foundations to join grants committees working in Moscow to evaluate proposals and allocate travel and study grants. Notwithstanding being chastised several times for favouring his university buddies, he retained these positions. At the same time, he entered into a number of feuds with competitors from other universities, who suspected him of corruption and plagiarism. When the American charities withdrew their technical assistance a decade later (after Harvard's disgraceful failure in Russia, see McClintick, 2006), Snitchin started to do more commercial consulting at joint enterprises and made a good income on trade projects. His life was going swimmingly a decade after the Soviet collapse, as the Russian government was presided over by a robust team of Federal Security Bureau (formerly KGB) officers. When this power clique consolidated its control over the nouveau-riche and required people with a profound understanding of both local and Western business rules, Snitchin provided support to the government, advising on how to enhance Russian positions in the global markets.

As Russian oligarchs began to accumulate more money and looked for smarter uses of universities' soft powers abroad, Snitchin became a mediator – linking influential Western and Russian scholars, politicians and businessmen. Having saddled the 'triple helix' rhetoric, he began to build multi-stakeholder networks merging interests in government, industry and the university. He schmoozed in various parlours and connected people from his previous projects, allocating money for foreign research projects, paying for visiting professorships, encouraging donations and giving speeches at various events at major Western universities. Desperate for cash, many American and European counterparts were happy to host Snitchin and his Russian friends, as well as to sign various partnership and investment agreements. The professorial image of Snitchin served these purposes well: he could easily switch from talking about investment and trade to deliberations on the greatness of Dostoevsky and Tolstoy, sprinkling in pleasing references to the critical successes of Russian ballet dancers. He could easily arrange the best seats at overbooked opening nights for a renowned foreign scholar or businessperson. In salon tête-à-têtes, he would never hesitate to emphasize the enigmatic nature of the 'Russian soul' and would easily defy or diffuse any emerging conversations that touched on traditions of Russian corruption, political repressions, poverty and crime. As a result of his successful international career, Snitchin was able to advance his fortunes with personal investments, lavishly supported by his old security office buddies, and bought a villa and a yacht in Italy – something that very few of his university colleagues could ever afford.

In 2014, this windfall ceased. Russia annexed Crimea and invaded Eastern Ukraine, thus generating a storm of Western sanctions and international resentment against the Kremlin. Snitchin was recalled from abroad and had to resume his university position at home. When the Russian government increased the anti-Western rhetoric, Snitchin decided to show how a true intellectual can manifest his patriotic image and position. The portrait of his mentor, Professor Stukachov, in dress military uniform, was mounted over his office armchair, next to President Putin. He removed all the luxurious items in his office and trimmed it with nationalist tricolours and ribbons of St George. He stuffed his bookshelves with publications about the Great Patriotic War, as well as with the old copies from his studies of scientific communism. He also began to write more on the unique Russian culture and character, and made presentations emphasizing the powerful and ancient history of the Russian people. Amplifying Russia's President Putin, and fascist ideologues Ivan Ilyin and Aleksandr Dugin, he began to proclaim the pseudo-historical myths about Russian and Ukrainian people being the same, and about Ukrainian identity and history being faked or imagined. Loyally following the Twitter accounts of Russia's President and the Ministry of Foreign Affairs, he began to circulate these myths on social media, and appeared on *Russia Today* (the country's English-speaking channel broadcasting Russian propaganda abroad) to explain why the Russian invasion of Ukraine was fully justified. He also began to write letters to his foreign friends and op-eds in national and international newspapers to claim how wrong the West had always been, and how it misunderstood the Russian culture and history, while threatening Russian security by expanding NATO. At the same time, Snitchin heaped praise on his foreign friends, who remained Russophile and wrote emails to support him, while nostalgically musing about the lavish parties and generous dinners he threw for them in London or New York.

In February 2022, when Russia started a full-blown unprovoked war in Ukraine, bombing schools, hospitals and universities (including Snitchin's hometown of Kharkiv), and killing hundreds of civilians, among them children, as seeming punishment for rebellious Ukrainians' defiance of the Kremlin's good intention to 'liberate them', Snitchin organized several campaigns to collect signatures in support of the war. He wrote letters to his former colleagues in Kharkiv, chastising them for the lack of support given to the 'Russian liberators and de-nazifiers'. 'How could this betrayal happen in a Russian-speaking city?', he asked in disbelief. When a Russian missile hit Kharkiv University and destroyed the economic faculty, one of his former friends finally responded with, 'go, fuck yourself, you Russian slut!' in perfect, if crude, Russian. Snitchin was too intelligent to quarrel. Redirecting his energies to shoring up the image of Russia's greatness amidst growing 'Russophobia', Snitchin spearheaded several university lectures on Russian 'historical justice and special mission in the world', and spoke widely on the American hypocrisy in relation to NATO's interventions in Yugoslavia and Iraq. As Western economic sanctions began to escalate and foreign businesses withdrew from the Russian market *en masse*, Snitchin placated the Russian public. The sanctions would only benefit the Russian producers in the long run, Snitchin argued, as the oligarchs would have no other option but to invest locally. He became a strong voice in support of President Putin's war-mongering policies and joined the United Russia Party (the dominant pro-presidential force in the Duma) when many others decided to leave it. Snitchin proudly flew patriotic colours to inspire his students to embrace ultranationalism.

Back in his office, Snitchin was steaming, as his students were fifteen minutes late. They did not come on time – this had never happened before. Several times, he checked his email box, cell phone and Apple watch. No messages popped up. When he heard a timid knock on his door, Snitchin furrowed his bushy brows to make himself match the portrait of his mentor more closely. The door was pushed ajar, and five of his students stepped inside in identical white t-shirts with the slogan 'Stop the War!' in screaming red letters. The professor and his students stared at each other; there was silence for a very long and awkward minute. Snitchin peered at the t-shirts again – no, the calligraphy was florid and hard to decipher; it was probably 'stop the maw!' The government banned the use of the word 'war' a day before – there is no war, only a 'special operation'. Taking a deep breath, Snitchin stood up, unclasped the upper button of his shirt and loosed his tie. In his curious gunslinger's gait, he walked over to the standing mirror in the corner of his room – an old friend with whom he enjoyed many a chat, the reflection of his proud and beautiful self-looking back at him, always ready to say something very heroic and memorable. Checking the looking glass always gave him immense pleasure – it never failed to inflate his ego. A quick reassuring glance, and he was ready to face his students.

Falling through the cracks

As it stands, the story of Professor Snitchin has an unhappy ending, given that his image continues to project undefeated arrogance. Yet, there is the hopeful possibility that, one day, the students in Snitchin's office will look at the reflection of their professor and see a deflated ego of a precarious old man, a failed intellectual who uses the cracks in his office mirror to hide unconfessed mistakes of the previous era. The historical precedent of what Nazi Germany's scholars experienced offers hope of a reckoning and re-evaluation (Remy, 2002). In the context of Russia's genocidal war in Ukraine (Ibrahim, 2022; Parker, 2022), the deflation of the egos of the Russian intelligentsia can only happen when there is true punishment for Russia's war crimes in an international criminal court and the court of public opinion. As argued by Radchenko (2022), 'Russia's defeat in this unjust, criminal war against Ukraine may help shift the domestic narrative in Russia towards accepting the country for what it really is, rather than what it has vainly pretended to be'. It is not certain that Snitchin will ever see himself as his students might see him in the mirror of truth. Presenting himself as a loyal intellectual with the safety net of a 'surrogate academic freedom' that allows him to advocate for what he sees as important for his President and the government's corporate agenda, Professor Snitchin is nonetheless likely to face retribution, provided the world rigorously pursues Nuremberg-like trials, which it failed to do after the collapse of the Soviet Union, allowing for Stalinist crimes to go unpunished and thus making it possible for Russians to maintain a false image, stunting any possibility of reform (Haven, 2010; National Museum of Holodomor Genocide, 2022).

Alas, in the age of post-truth, the mirror of truth is clouded in many places – not just Russia. Privileged professors in the West use their powerful voices to 'westsplain' and deny Ukraine's agency to define its right to defence and existence, while legitimizing the right of the Russian terrorist state to invade, annex and obliterate an independent nation (Smolenski & Dutkiewicz, 2022). Kukharskyy et al. (2022) explain clearly why such voices can appear embarrassingly naïve when they rush to broadcast fallacies, rather than verify facts on Ukraine. Protected by tenure and accumulated reputation capital, the powerful 'public intellectuals', living in a wealthy country with a strong military, converse with the imperial powers over the heads of the Ukrainians to address the powerful imperial states, while prioritizing their personal safety and security, and disregarding previous commitments (e.g. the Budapest Memorandum, as explicated by the United Nations (2014) and Pifer (2019)). These so-called intellectuals dare to preach how it might be better to just put up with the mass killing, mass rapes and elimination of Ukrainian identity and culture, accepting servitude to the Russian imperialists. In basic terms, the message of the powerful in defence of the powerful is reprehensible – but completely understandable in view of the hierarchical and hegemonic claims that not only justify, but also promote the 'realities' of competition and precarity in the neoliberal world. These realities correspond well with claims of the realpolitik pundits justifying the inevitability of the super-powerful to dominate and dictate what the disadvantaged should be doing in the world. Within the 'realist' discourse of the 'power über alles', Professor Snitchin cannot but feel that he is on the right side of history while supporting his abusive President's logic: 'not only a return to the traditional fascist battleground, but also a return to traditional fascist language and practice. Other people are there to be colonized. Russia is innocent because of its ancient past. The existence of Ukraine is an international conspiracy. War is the answer' (Snyder, 2022). Why would the neoliberal powerbrokers see anything wrong about Professor Snitchin defending the powers of the Russian president, given that the realpolitik of brutality and precarity marches unchallenged in governments, business and academia locally and globally?

Indeed, within this framework of thinking, the powerful and the wealthy arrogantly lavish attention on the images they enjoy most – i.e. of the glorious and the powerful. The precarious and vulnerable matter the least and are unattractive. As Timothy Snyder points out, 'many Europeans and Americans found it easier to follow Russia's propaganda phantoms than to defend a legal order. Europeans and Americans wasted time asking whether an invasion had taken place, whether Ukraine was a country, and whether it had somehow deserved to be invaded' (2018, p. 10). Lacking any knowledge on Ukrainian history and culture, and having little concern about the invasion of the Donbas in 2014, some Western scholars did not hesitate to spread Kremlin propaganda about 'Ukrainian Nazis'. The righteous leftists shifted the blame for Russia's aggression onto NATO's expression of support for Ukraine, rather than onto Russia itself, while ignoring the Ukrainian preferences and choices in breaking away from Russia (Mintz,

2022). As missile attacks rained on civilians and laid waste Ukrainian cities, some Western scholars engaged in comparativist 'whataboutism', for example, juxtaposing how refugees from Syria and Ukraine were treated, entertaining racist comparisons, while seeking to justify their inaction, or simply riding the old horse of 'blame the evil West' instead of countering the Russian imperialism that was the direct cause of bombings in the two countries. Meanwhile, the rise of fascism in Russia was largely ignored by these critics (Snyder, 2018). One may well ask: How is it possible that educated people in free and privileged societies used their influential voices to deny agency to the sovereign but vulnerable nation of Ukraine in determining its identity, language, history and culture?

Professor Snichin's story sits well in the fear-stricken corporate context in which, months into the genocidal war, Russian universities have failed to produce a single powerful critical voice befitting the stature of Academician Andrei Sakharov and the Helsinki Group intellectuals of the Cold War era (Kaasik, 2021). One could certainly contemplate what kind of precarity made most university professors in Russia too petrified to respond to the perverse declarations made by their university rectors advocating for the war in Ukraine. Clearly, when truth is persistently twisted by professors that resemble Snichin, Russian intellectuals cannot attain sufficient agency and freedom to argue with their authorities, and instead prefer to fake respect for their mentors' ideas and instructions. The Snichin-like leadership can hardly educate new generations of intellectuals and impart them with aptitude in critical reflection and thinking. Unsurprisingly, massive cracks in the mirrors of Russian universities appear to distort rather than reveal truth. Falling through the cracks, young intellectuals are not in a position to learn how to make appropriate judgements on issues investigated, questions raised and conclusions made. Subject to unrepentant Snichin-style leadership, Russian students are unfortunately prone to remain stuck in these cracks, rather than to seek the truth, as long as their mentors discourage or disallow critical thinking.

Concluding remarks

Although much hope was placed on a democratic revival in the tragic Eurasian context, where an untold number of dissidents perished in the Soviet totalitarian machine, the failure to develop an academic profession that could pursue the truth and prevent the deadening of intellectual institutions is one cause of Russia sliding back into feudalism and butchery. Russian war crimes witnessed in Syria and happening now in Ukraine are a recurring reminder to intellectuals of the West as well as of the East to seek the mirror of truth and question their own orientations and purposes in engaging with the corporate elites and oppressive governments.

The following are key questions to guide the discourse of intellectual leadership in the years to come: How can we make sure that wanton deviations of corporate powers do not happen in the process of agenda setting at universities? What signals indicate a threat of such aberrations emerging and undermining the integrity of epistemic processes in our departments, programmes and communities? Should scholars be supportive of any corporate intentions? What does support of the corporate agendas really mean in contexts constructed and controlled by a government pursuing anti-human agendas? How can academics control and resist the corporate powers of the university when anti-human deviations arise and precarity grows? How do we cultivate the courage to ask difficult questions in support of truth-seeking and communicating truth to the powerful?

To ensure that these questions are asked time and again, intellectual leaders should prioritize as their primary professional responsibilities the development and legitimization of universities in which scholars and administrators actively support academic freedom, defend truth-telling and shape agendas for the defence and enhancement of human rights, democratic governance, social justice and equity. True academia should always be self-critical, but also serve as a leading societal critic, and thus actively confront and defy the trends of corporate abuse, fascist rhetoric or imperialist interventions. Intellectuals should keep placing their societies in front of the mirror of truth, while also making sure that their own deadening does not happen as a result of over-inflated egos and corporate abuse.

Acknowledgements

I would like to thank Jon Nixon for his discerning comments and recommendations (in particular for bringing to my attention James Joyce's Ulysses at a time when I was seeking to expand on the metaphor of twisted mirror images in my conceptual approach). His insights and encouragement were invaluable throughout the writing process. I am also grateful to Adrianna Stech, who provided collegial criticism and support in the way only she can during my chapter revisions and reflections on the Ukrainian tragedy. I also thank the Hong Kong Research Grants Council for providing me with funding and encouraging me to spend more time on 'Re-imagining intellectual leadership in post-Soviet higher education'.

References

Bailin, S. (2002). Critical thinking and science education. *Science & Education*, 11(4), 361–75. https://doi.org/10.1023/A:1016042608621

Birstein, V. J. (2001). *The perversion of knowledge: The true story of Soviet science*. Basic Books.

Brandist, C. (5 May 2016). The risks of Soviet-style managerialism in UK universities. *Times Higher Education*, 5. https://www.timeshighereducation.com/comment/the-risks-of-soviet-style-managerialism-in-united-kingdom-universities

Brower, D. R. (1967). The problem of the Russian Intelligentsia. *Slavic Review*, 26(4), 638–47. https://doi.org/10.2307/2492614

Fitzgerald, T., White, J., & Gunter, H. (2012). *Hard labour? Academic work and the changing landscape of higher education*. Emerald Group Publishing.

Gessen, M. (1997). *Dead again: The Russian intelligentsia after communism*. Verso.

Green, W., Hammer, S., & Star, C. (2009). Facing up to the challenge: Why is it so hard to develop graduate attributes? *Higher Education Research & Development*, 28(1), 17–29. https://doi.org/10.1080/07294360802444339

Haven, C. (23 September 2010). Stalin killed millions. A Stanford historian answers the question, was it genocide? *Stanford News*. https://news.stanford.edu/2010/09/23/naimark-stalin-genocide-092310/

Ibrahim, A. (27 May 2022). Russia's war in Ukraine could become genocide. *Foreign Policy Magazine*. https://foreignpolicy.com/2022/05/27/russia-war-ukraine-genocide/

Janosik, S. M., Carpenter, S., & Creamer, D. G. (2006). Beyond professional preparation programs: The role of professional associations in ensuring a high-quality workforce. *College Student Affairs Journal*, 25(2), 228–37.

Joyce, J. (1960). *Ulysses*. The Bodley Head (First published by Shakespeare and Company, Paris, 1922).

Juntrasook, A. (2014). 'You do not have to be the boss to be a leader': Contested meanings of leadership in higher education. *Higher Education Research & Development*, 33(1), 19–31. https://doi.org/10.1080/07294360.2013.864610

Kaasik, P. (24 September 2021). Dissident movement in the Soviet Union. *Communist Crimes* (Portal of The International Museum for the Victims of Communism in Patarei Prison in Tallinn, Estonia). https://communistcrimes.org/en/dissident-movement-soviet-union

Kuhn, T. S. (1970). *The structure of scientific revolutions*. University of Chicago Press.

Kukharskyy, B., Fedyk, A., Gorodnichenko, Y., & Sologub, I. (23 May 2022). Open letter to Noam Chomsky (and other like-minded intellectuals) on the Russia-Ukraine War. *E-Flux Notes*. https://www.e-flux.com/notes/470005/open-letter-to-noam-chomsky-and-other-like-minded-intellectuals-on-the-russia-ukraine-war

Kuraev, A. (2016). Soviet higher education: An alternative construct to the Western university paradigm. *Higher Education*, 71(2), 181–93. https://doi.org/10.1007/s10734-015-9895-5

Kwiek, M. (2015). Inequality in academic knowledge production: The role of research top performers across Europe. In E. Reale & E. Primeri (Eds), *The transformation of university institutional and organizational boundaries* (pp. 203–30). Brill Sense.

Kwiek, M. (2018). International research collaboration and international research orientation: Comparative findings about European academics. *Journal of Studies in International Education*, 22(2), 136–60. https://doi.org/10.1177/1028315317747084

Kwiek, M. (2019). Social stratification in Higher Education: What it means at the micro-level of the individual academic scientist. *Higher Education Quarterly*, 73(4), 419–44. https://doi.org/10.1111/hequ.12221

Leišytė, L. (2022). Performance management under surveillance capitalism in higher education. In C. Sarrico, M. Rosa, & T. Carvalho (Eds), *Research handbook on academic careers and managing academics* (pp. 218–31). Edward Elgar Publishing.

Lipset, S. M., & Dobson, R. B. (1972). The intellectual as critic and rebel: With special reference to the United States and the Soviet Union. *Daedalus*, 101(3), 137–98.

Macfarlane, B. (2011). Professors as intellectual leaders: Formation, identity and role. *Studies in Higher Education*, 36(1), 57–73. https://doi.org/10.1080/03075070903443734

Macfarlane, B. (2013). *Intellectual leadership in higher education: Renewing the role of the university professor*. Routledge.

Macfarlane, B. (2017). The paradox of collaboration: A moral continuum. *Higher Education Research & Development*, 36(3), 472–85. https://doi.org/10.1080/07294360.2017.1288707

Macfarlane, B., & Cheng, M. (2008). Communism, universalism and disinterestedness: Re-examining contemporary support among academics for Merton's scientific norms. *Journal of Academic Ethics*, 6(1), 67–78. http://dx.doi.org/10.1007/s10805-008-9055-y

Manning, K. (2017). *Organizational theory in higher education*. Routledge.

McClintick, D. (2006). How Harvard lost Russia. *Institutional Investor*. https://www.institutionalinvestor.com/article/b150npp3q49x7w/how-harvard-lost-russia

Merton, R. K. (1988). The Matthew effect in science, II: Cumulative advantage and the symbolism of intellectual property. *Isis*, 79(4), 606–23.

Mintz, S. (23 March 2022). Does the Ukraine conflict pit the West against the rest? *Inside Higher Education*. https://www.insidehighered.com/blogs/higher-ed-gamma/does-ukraine-conflict-pit-west-against-rest

Mounk, Y. (25 February 2022). The end of an illusion. *Persuasion*. https://www.persuasion.community/p/mounk-the-end-of-an-illusion

National Museum of Holodomor Genocide (16 March 2022). From Stalin to Putin: Unpunished genocide provokes new crimes. *NMHG*. https://holodomormuseum.org.ua/en/news-museji/from-stalin-to-putin-unpunished-genocide-provokes-new-crimes/

Nixon, J. (2021). Education as promise: Learning from Hannah Arendt. In S. S. E. Bengtsen, S. Robinson, & W. Shumar (Eds), *The university becoming* (pp. 51–65). Springer.

Norton, L. (2009). *Action research in teaching and learning: A practical guide to conducting pedagogical research in universities*. Routledge.

Oleksiyenko, A. (2016). Higher education reforms and center-periphery dilemmas: Ukrainian universities between neo-Soviet and neo-liberal contestations. In J. Zajda & V. Rust (Eds), *Globalisation and higher education reforms* (pp. 133–48). Springer.

Oleksiyenko, A. (2018). Zones of alienation in global higher education: Corporate abuse and leadership failures. *Tertiary Education and Management*, 24(3), 193–205. http://dx.doi.org/10.1080/13583883.2018.1439095

Oleksiyenko, A. V. (2021a). Academic freedom and intellectual dissent in post-soviet Ukraine. *Higher Education Quarterly*, 76(3), 580–94. https://doi.org/10.1111/hequ.12362

Oleksiyenko, A. V. (2021b). Is academic freedom feasible in the post-Soviet space of higher education? *Educational Philosophy and Theory*, 53(11), 1116–26. https://doi.org/10.1080/00131857.2020.1773799

Oleksiyenko, A. V. (2021c). World-class universities and the Soviet legacies of administration: Integrity dilemmas in Russian higher education. *Higher Education Quarterly*, 76(2), 385–98. https://doi.org/10.1111/hequ.12306

Oleksiyenko, A. V. (2022a). Ukrainian academics in the times of war. *Academic Praxis*, 2, 19–26.

Oleksiyenko, A. V. (2022b). On politics in comparative and international higher education. *Revista Española de Educación Comparada*, 40 (enero–junio 2022), 50–68. http://dx.doi.org/10.5944/reec.40.2022.31203

Oleksiyenko, A. V., & Jackson, L. (2021). Freedom of speech, freedom to teach, freedom to learn: The crisis of higher education in the post-truth era. *Educational Philosophy and Theory*, 53(11), 1057–62. https://doi.org/10.1080/00131857.2020.1773800

Oleksiyenko, A., & Ruan, N. (2019). Intellectual leadership and academic communities: Issues for discussion and research. *Higher Education Quarterly*, online first. https://doi.org/10.1111/hequ.12199

Oleksiyenko, A., & Tierney, W. G. (2018). Higher education and human vulnerability: Global failures of corporate design. *Tertiary Education and Management*, 24(3), 187–92. https://doi.org/10.1080/13583883.2018.1439094

Oleksiyenko, A., Zha, Q., Chirikov, I., & Li, J. (2018). *Higher education and international status anxiety: The soviet legacy in China and Russia*. CERC/Springer.

O'Malley, B. (6 March 2022). Russian Union of Rectors backs Putin's action in Ukraine. *The University World News*. https://www.universityworldnews.com/post.php?story=20220306120204111

Overbye, D. (14 March 2022). Russian scientists face isolation following invasion of Ukraine. *New York Times*. https://www.nytimes.com/2022/03/12/science/physics-cern-russia.html

Page, D. (2020). The academic as consumed and consumer. *Journal of Education Policy*, 35(5), 585–601. https://doi.org/10.1080/02680939.2019.1598585

Parker, C. (27 May 2022). Russia has incited genocide in Ukraine, independent experts conclude. *The Washington Post*. https://www.washingtonpost.com/world/2022/05/27/genocide-ukraine-russia-analysis/

Pifer, S. (5 December 2019). Why care about Ukraine and the Budapest Memorandum? *The Brookings Institute*. https://www.brookings.edu/blog/order-from-chaos/2019/12/05/why-care-about-ukraine-and-the-budapest-memorandum/

Radchenko, S. (15 May 2022). Why Russia needs to be humiliated in Ukraine. *The Spectator*. https://www.spectator.co.uk/article/why-russia-needs-to-be-humiliated-in-ukraine

Remy, S. P. (2002). *The Heidelberg myth: The nazification and denazification of a German university*. Harvard University Press.

Shlapentokh, D. (2019). The time of troubles in Alexander Dugin's narrative. *European Review*, 27(1), 143–57. http://dx.doi.org/10.1017/S1062798718000650

Slater, J. J. (2008). The loss of the intellectual: Alienation of the academic voice. In J. J. Slater, D. M. Callejo Pérez, & S. M. Fain (Eds), *The war against the professions* (pp. 3–19). Brill Sense.

Smolenski, J., & Dutkiewicz, J. (4 March 2022). The American pundits who can't resist 'Westsplaining' Ukraine. *The New Republic*. https://newrepublic.com/article/165603/carlson-russia-ukraine-imperialism-nato

Smolentseva, A. (2017). Where Soviet and neoliberal discourses meet: The transformation of the purposes of higher education in Soviet and post-Soviet Russia. *Higher Education*, 74(6), 1091–108. https://dx.doi.org/10.1007%-2Fs10734-017-0111-7

Snyder, T. (2018). *The road to unfreedom: Russia, Europe, America*. Tim Duggan Books.

Snyder, T. (19 May 2022). We should say it. Russia is fascist. *The New York Times*. https://www.nytimes.com/2022/05/19/opinion/russia-fascism-ukraine-putin.html

Tolstoy, A., & McCaffray, E. (2015). Mind games: Alexander Dugin and Russia's war of ideas. *World Affairs*, 177(6), 25–30.

The United Nations (2014). *Memorandum on security assurances in connection with Ukraine's accession to the treaty on the non-proliferation of nuclear weapons*. Budapest, 5 December 1994. https://treaties.un.org/doc/Publication/UNTS/Volume%203007/Part/volume-3007-I-52241.pdf

Vican, S., Friedman, A., & Andreasen, R. (2020). Metrics, money, and managerialism: Faculty experiences of competing logics in higher education. *The Journal of Higher Education*, 91(1), 139–64. https://doi.org/10.1080/00221546.2019.1615332

Zuckerman, H. (1977). *Scientific elite: Nobel laureates in the United States*. Transaction Publishers.

3

Governance of the Marketized University in Precarious Times

Steven Jones

Introduction

In this volume and elsewhere, the *management* of universities receives close critical scrutiny: scholars have judiciously documented changes in how institutions are run, mapping the rise of managerialism and metrics (Deem, Hillyard and Reed, 2007), testifying to the corrosive effects of surveillance regimes and contractual insecurity on staff (Ball, 2012; Hall, 2018; Morrish, 2020), and attempting to hold accountable the senior managers that reward themselves disproportionately to their success in defending the public value of the sector (Giroux, 2014; Smyth, 2017). Less common in the literature have been critiques of university *governance* (though see Rowlands, 2017; Jones and Hillman, 2019; Scott, 2021; Shattock and Horvath, 2019). This chapter redresses the balance by building on and updating previous work, and by examining university governance through a more critical lens. I show how governing bodies in England have been refashioned in the mould of company boardrooms, in part through market-based policy and in part through allied discourses that discipline the sector into acquiescence. Precarity is thus effectively maintained, both materially and discursively, by administrative classes that hitherto served as a bulwark for the university and its work. In such an environment, the danger is that governors become collaborators in a wider political project to privatize higher forms of knowledge (Gunter, 2018).

In this chapter, I use *governance* to capture board-led or council-led oversight of higher education institutions. Following Shattock (2006), I do not include forms of administration that extend to senates, academic boards or departmental meetings. Local governance practices vary according to institutional history, classification and legal status (Shattock, 2012), but most universities have a group of individuals who monitor fiduciary performance, seek to bring accountability and *challenge* to the senior leadership team, and act as custodians of the institution's status. This higher-level strategic navigation contrasts with *management*, which I use to describe those individuals – in senior academic, clerical or 'third space' professional roles (Whitchurch, 2012) – charged with overseeing day-to-day operational matters. Following McCaig (2018), I regard *marketization* as the process through which the principles of private enterprise and commerce come to pervade a sector. With market-based policy comes a fundamental reconceptualization of education: learning becomes commodified; outcome becomes more important than process; and what can be immediately measured at the individual and institutional level becomes valued more highly than any resultant gains at the societal level. In marketized systems, students and applicants are superficially empowered as consumers (Tomlinson, 2017), and academics subjected to dubious *quality* measurement across multiple fronts (Gunn, 2018). As policy insisted on modernization, reform and alignment with often ill-fitting commercial principles (Smyth, 2017), a parallel discursive onslaught ridiculed universities for being *woke*, for *no-platforming* speakers and for politicizing students (Jones, 2022). In such ways, precarity was levied on critical academic research and teaching, especially that assumed to trouble dominant political ideologies. Putting in place university governors sympathetic to the broader political project, or at least unlikely to question it, was essential to the smooth implementation of a market-based system.

I frame my analysis in terms of *intellectual leadership* even though, as Macfarlane (2013, p. 12) and others have acknowledged, it is an ambiguous term. Like Macfarlane (2013), my starting point is that the stewardship of a university requires something different from other institutions. If intellectual leadership is understood as the capacity to create and share powerful ideas that spur scientific, social, technological and institutional revolutions (Macfarlane, 2013), then its centrality to university governance is self-evident, especially during precarious times. With principles of public provision under threat and municipal services being dismantled and privatized, the guidance offered by governing bodies becomes vital. Indeed, for management teams to recognize and fulfil their institution's role as part of a common good – and to see beyond defective metrics, misleading league tables and political pressure to compete for waning resources – they need the explicit backing of their governors. Yet senior staff in the institution have typically been ushered in an opposite direction by governing bodies hyper-aware of short-term financial precarity but less attuned to the longer-term intellectual precarity that stems from their actions. Many senior managers submitted willingly, flattered by the new forms of power invested in them, and by the more generous remuneration packages that usually accompany reform.

This chapter focuses on governance shifts in English higher education. However, the trends that I identify are recognizable internationally, and previous studies have highlighted parallels in other countries as collegial and democratic models of governance are replaced by systems based more on principles of executive power (Austin and Jones, 2015; Lewis, 2013). Though I focus here on the impact of market-based measures, precarity in governance has been shown to emerge in multiple ways, including through the influence of philanthropic organizations and individual donors (Drezner, 2019). I begin by summarizing some of the key contributions in the literature and offering a potted history of university governance before outlining three areas that I suggest are under threat in this new regime: expertise, independence and collegiality. I then conclude by making the case for more transparent and non-corporate forms of governance. Throughout the chapter I show how a flawed model is linguistically sustained at the political and sector level, and how discourses of capitalist realism and market pragmatism keep resistance to a minimum. This discursive strategy has enabled a far-reaching overhaul of governance to be effected without the consent of – and sometimes without the knowledge of – a previously more engaged and informed workforce.

English universities and their governance structures

Governance is a site in which struggles for control over the higher education sector play out at an institutional level, as Rowlands (2017) and others have pointed out. However, changes in university governance have been less noticeable, and therefore less critiqued, than those in university management or in many other sectors. This is partly because governance remains a mainly hidden area of institutional activity; the authoritarian turn has been effected via behind-the-scenes political and regulatory prodding rather through any form of open academic discussion. Consent has either been assumed or else manufactured through disingenuous, and often retrospective, staff and student *engagement* exercises. But the alienation of academic labour comes at a long-term cost to any institution (Hall, 2018), and the associated loss of public trust is even more damaging to the sector (Fitzpatrick, 2021; Jones, 2022).

Shattock (2012) outlined four ages of university governance, from the period in the mid-1950s when governing bodies were a controlling force within the institution, through phases of greater academic self-rule, to a shift back towards vice-chancellor sovereignty, followed by a further concentration of decision-making authority. Changes were often attended and legitimated by sector-level reviews and government policy directives. The Jarratt Report (1985), commissioned by the *Committee of Vice-Chancellors and Principals* (later rebranded as *Universities UK*), was among the first public reports to recommended greater emphasis on governance, and therefore a lessening in the power of senates. Senates are the authority on academic matters in most universities, so attacks on senates are effectively attacks on staff. The Jarratt Report was followed in 1992 by legislation giving explicit responsibility to governing bodies for 'determining the educational character' of their institution (Schofield, 2009). The Dearing Committee (1997) increased the focus on the *effectiveness* of governance structures, particularly around their financial accountability. In 2019, the replacement of the *Higher Education Funding Council for England* (HEFCE) by the *Office for Students* (OfS) further cemented the notion of university governance as a private and corporate endeavour. Following the *Higher Education and Research Act 2017* (e.g. see section 8.1.(a)–(c)) the OfS, a more politically interventionist regulator than HEFCE, increased the duties held by governing bodies. For example, boards became charged with 'ensuring that their provider's access and participation strategy is put into practice at all organisational levels, through a whole provider strategic approach' (OfS, 2020). Governing bodies thus assumed a greater level of influence and accountability, in this case being required to give assurances that fair admissions principles were embedded throughout the institution. Boards were also handed legal responsibility for an increasing range of complex risk and value-for-money returns (Office for Students, 2020).

On many governing bodies, there is a requirement for lay members to be in the majority. Lay members are those from outside the higher education sector who are assumed to bring a more detached perspective to the work of the university. Following suggestions in the Jarratt Report, they are mostly drawn 'from industry, commerce and the professions' (1985, p. 23). This means that few lay governors have sensitivity to the very particular needs of institutions that serve to enrich their host society in multifaceted and non-economic ways. Many governors are alike in terms of social class, gender and race, and fall into a similar age bracket. The Higher Education Statistics Agency notes that only 2.6 per cent of governors are Black, with a further 9.1 per cent belonging to other ethnicities (Higher Education Statistics Agency, 2022). Fifty-seven per cent are aged 56 or older, with only 9% under 36, and a further 9% in the 36–45 bracket. University governors are significantly older than their peers in the NHS, charities and sports organizations (Kakabadse, Morais, Myers and Brown, 2020). The gender split is about 60:40 in favour of men. Some of these distributions are not dissimilar from those within the academic workforce; for example, only 2.8 per cent of academics are Black, with a further 12.7 per cent belonging to other ethnicities. However, while awareness of the lack of diversity among academics has grown and is being robustly challenged (Arday, 2018), among governors the problem remains under-acknowledged. This is particularly unsatisfactory in the context of a power shift from academics to governors and inevitably leaves the institution in a more precarious position: prone to group-think, lacking in fresh ideas and sometimes unable to grasp the implications of its own research. Kakabadse et al. (2020) bluntly suggested that governing bodies are largely composed of individuals who are semi-retired, who do not understand the sector and who lack basic critical competencies, such as understanding the digital world.

Lay governors from a corporate background tend to align themselves with top-down visions of the sector – entrepreneurial; outcome-focused; globally competitive – rather than with public university principles (Shattock and Horvath, 2019). Most are individually well-intentioned, but the system falters because, as Scott put it, it denies that the democratic principle has any serious role to play in the governance of higher education (2021, p. 180). In-groups of business-minded governors conspire with senior managers to hold firmer lines on negotiations around pay and pensions, performance monitoring and compulsory redundancies, while expediently overlooking the damage to staff and student welfare. Their clandestine and mostly unproblematized empowerment reflects the widespread but untested ideological assumption that corporatizing *disruption* within the sector was necessary.

Discourses of university governance

The *gold standard* for governance in higher education increasingly emulates that associated with the private sector: smaller, more closed board composition; limited transparency; an emphasis on commercial and financial proficiency. Academic members are often the first to be squeezed out when chairs decide to *streamline*, and meetings of university governing bodies and their sub-committees mostly remain unrecorded, with ambiguous, delayed and 'sanitized' minutes often the only retrospective clue to how discussions unfolded and who said what (Scott, 2021, pp. 183–4). A superficially convenient distance is thus maintained between the governing body and the wider institution, and opportunities for scrutiny or interaction are minimized. This separation requires a discursive strategy that justifies and naturalizes the shift to corporate governance, and shuts down debates about the extent to which it is appropriate for a higher education sector. On issues like pay and pensions, governors tend to position themselves as the grown-ups in the room, advocating restraint and prudence. Newly appointed *comms* teams cheerily cascade messages to university staff, who are assumed to be less financially literate, even if eminent academic names in germane disciplines. For a fee, external auditors stand ready to write reports for governing bodies to assure them that their approach is the right and proper one. The method favoured by these profit-making consultants is invariably to benchmark governance *effectiveness* against norms elsewhere in the sector. Though areas of possible improvement are sometimes identified, a business model reliant on similar commissions makes direct criticism of any individual institution unlikely. In such ways, self-congratulatory discourses echo around the sector's chambers, smoothing the passage for further market-based interventions, and normalizing a faulty underlying conceptualization of university governance.

The *Committee of University Chairs* (CUC) is the representative body for chairs of UK universities, and the group's code of governance (2020) captures much of how authority is discursively maintained. Some stated objectives of the code – such that governors 'promote excellence in learning, teaching and research' (CUC, 2020) – involve a remit that appears to go beyond historical understandings of governance and step instead into management territory. With no background or training in pedagogy or academic research, many lay governors would understandably struggle to know what *excellence* in these areas looks like. At the same time, the code simultaneously marginalizes staff and students, with Section 5.2 "Effectiveness" illustrating how the qualities they bring are assumed to be secondary to those of lay members:

> The governing body needs the appropriate balance of skills, experience, diverse backgrounds, independence and knowledge to make informed decisions. Some constitutional documents specify governing bodies must include staff and student members.
>
> (CUC, 2020)

The claim here is that staff and students sometimes 'must' be admitted to the governing body by virtue of historical statutes and ordinances, but the code elaborates no further on what those members might bring to the table. Instead, there are vague allusions to opportunities for 'engagement' (CUC, 2020, section 6.1) and 'liaison' (CUC, 2020, section 6.4). Throughout the code, the language of the company boardroom is unthinkingly borrowed, with the senior management team referred to as 'the Executive' (CUC, 2020, sections 1.6, 2.4, 2.11 and 5.1), distinctions drawn between 'executive' and 'non-executive' governors (CUC, 2020, section 5.3), and the vice chancellor branded the university's 'Chief Executive' (CUC, 2020, appendix 2).

On issues that matter both substantively and to the public perception of universities, like senior pay or free speech, the code remains silent. This sets the tone for governing body discussions, where all members – though particularly staff and student representatives – can find it difficult to speak out. The chair's reminders about how full the day's agenda is, or how important the financial items and reports are, serve to proscribe wider debate. The code thus works discursively both to narrow the boundaries of what university governance is for, and to flatter lay members of the board into believing that they are the only true members. Sector discourses are reinforced at the political level by calls to *professionalize* university governance, as though any non-corporate approach is inherently amateurish. The rhetoric is eagerly ingested by institutional managers keen to self-identify as slick executives and to rationalize widening pay gaps between themselves and frontline staff.

Unaccountable individuals communicating in coded language within opaque environments provide the ideal conditions for corporate group-think. Principles of confidentiality and collective responsibility trump any commitment to transparency or inclusiveness, and maintaining board anonymity allows *difficult decisions* to be reached and implemented less contentiously. Over time, deficit discourses emerge around academic staff: exchanges between governors and managers insidiously 'other' scholars and their scholarship in stereotypical terms. This is not unlike the longstanding tropes perpetuated about leaders who are female (Fitzgerald, 2013) and/or from ethnic backgrounds (Arday, 2018). It becomes easy for lay governors, many of whom do not personally know any academics (Kakabadse, Morais, Myers and Brown, 2020), to be persuaded that university staff are incalcitrant, idealistic or wedded to a golden age of self-rule. Many lay governors emerge from industries in which pension schemes were already brutally dismantled. For them, the perceived absence of performance management and surveillance culture is a sign of weakness (Ball, 2012). Self-soothing discourses emerge about doing what is right for the institution in the long term even if it means taking painful or unpopular decisions in the short term. Gradually, models of university governance grow indistinguishable from those within private sector enterprises.

During early phases of reform, policy discourse fantasized about *light-touch* sector regulation and governance of English universities, imagining that once freed from state interference a high-functioning market would emerge organically. But education is not a naturally market-like product, despite the rhetoric of ministers, and university applicants do not behave rationally according to simple cost-benefit economic principles. This led to more interventionist approaches, consistent with authoritarian turns elsewhere in government policy. Though the language of *arms-length* guidance persisted, firmer lines were taken by the OfS: the sector became talked about almost exclusively through the instrumental lenses of *employability* (Arora, 2015), *graduate outcomes* (Fryer, 2020) and *value-for-money* (Jones, Vigurs and Harris, 2020), and closure became a much-vaunted threat for under-recruiting or under-performing institutions. Behind the tough political rhetoric was a belief that *risk* should be devolved. Instead of financial sustainability being a sector-wide concern, it became the responsibility of individual governing bodies (even though, in a competitive internal environment, the only way for one university to win was for another to lose). Governors, readily co-opted by the discourse and sometimes excited by the prospects of institutional competition, ploughed resources into hip advertising campaigns and glassy new-builds rather than into the human resources that would more directly sustain teaching, learning, research and public engagement. They therefore became complicit in a commercial agenda, hoping that student-consumers would begin to focus on individually acquiring *experiences* (sports facilities, catering, accommodation, etc.) rather than seeing themselves as co-creators of academic knowledge, members of scholarly communities or even learners.

Far from offering intellectual leadership, the danger is that new forms of governance are fundamentally *anti*-intellectual. Governors may be able to avoid critical attention by staying in the campus shadows, and turn to discourses that privilege their authority as corporate heavyweights and *real-world* pragmatists. However, the lack of staff and student input leaves them vulnerable to an environment with which they have little familiarity or understanding. In such a context, even the business decisions they take can be poor ones. Precarity spreads and takes hold as the identities and values of the university workforce drift further from the actions of those that govern them, as the following sections explain.

A sector under threat

According to Scott, many of the 'major flaws' (2021, p. 179) in university governance emerge from the tensions arising between the status of the modern university as publicly funded and accountable in principle, yet quasi-private and commercially motivated in practice. Scott draws attention to shifts in who is perceived to have the right to manage universities, noting that academic collegiality and disciplinary independence are challenged by a new class of governors and senior administrators whose authority is largely self-determined. Scott calls for the current oligarchic pattern of university governance to be abandoned and replaced with something bolder (2021, p. 184). Naturally, those at the helm would question whether the flaws that Scott talks about are genuine shortcomings, or whether his is simply foreseeable employee critique of an overdue reconfiguration and modernization. Larger institutions now have an annual turnover exceeding £1bn, chairs of governors may point out, and oversight for compliance, finance, audit and a range of other complex regulatory demands cannot continue to be delegated to clusters of well-meaning community members, institutional alumni or time-pressed academics. I now explore precarity in the university with reference to three specific areas in which I suggest that currently dominant governance models are creating intellectual deficits: expertise, independence and collegiality.

Expertise under threat

Intellectual leadership matters more than ever at a moment when anti-intellectualism and post-truth discourses are undermining the very notion of the university (Nichols, 2017), and populist strategies contest the nature of knowledge, the sites of knowledge ownership and the legitimacy of knowers (Gunter, 2005). As part of the move to marketization and corporate, anti-expert rhetoric seeks to privilege business interests and thwart regulation. In such a context, one might reasonably expect intellectual leadership that vigorously defends the sector. Instead, there is timidity on the part of individual institutions and representative bodies like *Universities UK*, and an inexplicable reluctance to re-assert the value of robust research and evidence-based policymaking.

There are two ways in which university governance is part of this problem. The first is that the modern university has accepted the positioning of academic knowledge as a commodity to be digitized, metricized and traded. At the same time, performance has become measured against – and therefore determined by – crude metrics like the National Student Survey (NSS) and the Research Excellence Framework (REF). Rather than push back against market-based trends that monetize learning and destabilize professional trust, governors have embraced the board-level empowerment ostensibly associated with new surveillance models. A dashboard of performance indicators now track disciplinary and individual achievement, and all kinds of internal reconfigurations, restructures and even redundancies can be justified on the back of suboptimal outcomes (Ball, 2012). But governing bodies are generally unable to recognize the limitations of the scorecards placed before them. With academic input curtailed, an informed critique of the mostly flawed indicators is no longer available. Governors are therefore unable to contextualize NSS data as a snapshot of students' fleeting *satisfaction*, subject to all kinds of conscious and unconscious biases (Sabri, 2011) and often no more than a distant proxy for underlying teaching quality (Gunn, 2018). Nor can they see that the REF relies on often inexpert grading of scholarship and has a scarring effect on collegiality, as well as making research more formulaic and narrowing its scope (Sayer, 2014). In such ways, the distance between on-the-ground academic activity and university governance widens further. Those doing the teaching and research wonder how their contribution can be so misunderstood and undervalued by those charged with protecting it; those in the governing body are bemused by academic resistance to decisions finally being based on ostensibly objective assessment across multiple datasets.

A second, more direct way through which academic expertise is devalued involves its rejection *within* governance, as staff are systematically marginalized by a system that prizes external know-how over that of its own workforce. The role of staff in university governance has been simultaneously restricted and controlled (Rowlands, 2017), with representation minimized and tightly managed on the sub-committees at which key decisions are made. Academic membership on the governing body can soon grow tokenistic (Shattock and Horvath, 2019, p. 163). Rarely are questions asked about which kind of individuals are best placed to contribute and what kind of input is needed, other than by expensive private consultants with a vested interest in maintaining the status quo. Analysis of *skills gaps* undertaken by bought-in auditors usually identifies a need for further audits, or else focuses on openings for additional financial and business proficiency. However, would-be governors with experience in these areas tend not to be from diverse backgrounds, nor to live in the campus neighbourhood. Often they are wealthy white men who have taken early retirement. Their instinct to *give back* is usually sincere, even if they are also attracted by the prestige of association with an elite sector. However, their understanding of higher education, and how it might differ from the sectors in which they enjoyed their own professional success, is usually limited.

It is not only academic expertise that it marginalized in university governance: schools and colleges, charity sectors and civic institutions increasingly lack representation. Local communities have fewer governors than in previous generations, even though institutional activity can affect them fundamentally, for better and worse. There is also the question of students' expertise (usually coded as *student voice* to homogenize it and down-play its significance); most governing bodies have a representative or two, but it can be difficult for those individuals to make themselves heard, surrounded not only by highly successful lay members but also by academic representatives who may well be directly involved with their teaching and supervision. This results in governance systems that are precarious because they draw on shallow pools of established knowledge, something that should be unacceptable to a sector in which intellectual progress is often fuelled by non-authorized and counter-hegemonic thinking.

Independence under threat

For lay governors more familiar with private sector practices, the intellectual independence of academics can be baffling. How does one comprehend, let alone accommodate, the peculiar principle of *academic freedom*? The temptation is to see the special privileges associated with the profession as a historical quirk and the intellectual independence of academics as a barrier to *effective* governance. Institutional discourses tend therefore to repurpose *freedom* as the autonomy to maximize market share at the expense of rival providers. Independence can be similarly reframed in individualistic terms, as *agility* or *resilience*. Academic freedom as a fundamental moral protection for staff to research or teach ideas that may be inconvenient to external authorities without fear of censure thus becomes obscured.

Within the governing body, independence and diversity of thought are also diminished. Lay governors are often chosen through opaque processes, with institutional managers and senior administrators closely involved in appointments. Those governors then themselves become responsible for overseeing *executive* hires, usually in conjunction with firms of head-hunters, and for setting senior pay through renumerations committees of which vice chancellors are sometimes themselves members. Despite the rhetoric about providing *robust challenge* and holding management teams to account, conflicts of interest are unavoidable. Scott warns of particularly 'close and collusive' relationships between chairs of governors and institutional managers (2021, pp. 184–5), with the latter group typically surrounded by a clique of biddable senior officers.

Recent examples of intellectual independence coming under threat in England include one institution placing at risk of redundancy numerous staff who worked in the area of Critical Management Studies (Morrish, 2021). The perceived *quality* of their research was not the problem; the work was simply an inconvenience, and perhaps a threat, to a managerial agenda. For the governing body that signed off on the redundancies, it probably made good business sense to shut down an area of activity that was apparently undermining the direction of travel in which the institution planned to go. Appeals to historical freedoms were dismissed as naive or nostalgic. Morrish (2021) reported similar cases at other universities, both in England and overseas, offering a taste of what may lie ahead unless intellectual independence once again becomes a cornerstone of university governance.

Governing bodies were never known for their transparency, but the recent turn towards secret operations and, in some extreme cases, an instinct to shut down academic research, is more sinister. Discursive slippage is rife around notions of *autonomy, freedom* and *independence*. Governors obstinately focus on the financial precarity of the institution rather than on threats to the well-being of the sector as a whole, or the rights of disciplines or academics to conduct research free from political pressure and employer interference. They also tend to prefer *soft power* strategies to taking a public stance, with vice chancellors keen to reassure staff that they *have the ear* of ministers without putting forward the kind of arguments that might actually change government thinking or policy. As such, market imperatives become paramount; educational imperatives fall by the wayside and are sometimes dismissed as the indulgence of an over-entitled workforce.

Collegiality under threat?

Where institutions are run as though private enterprises, the notion of collegiality becomes precarious. By *collegiality*, I here refer to the idea of the campus as a community of scholars, researchers, learners and other workers in pursuit of broadly aligned intellectual goals. While there is undoubtedly a tendency to romanticize the notion of collegiality, it is difficult to dispute that current governance models militate against a spirit of collaboration. Externally, this is the result of a funding model that rests on competition between providers. Internally, it is the result of a top-down economistic culture that seeks to expose under-performing areas, usually without appropriate contextualization, and create suspicions of excessive cross-subsidy. Often, *bottom line* accountancy indicators are privileged by governors over more holistic indicators of disciplinary success. In such a context, even academic areas with a long-standing record of inspiring teaching and substantial strategic value to society (such as modern languages) become under threat when their financial *contribution* is felt to be wanting. The impact of governance decisions ripples across the campus, as so-called *high-value* disciplines with *high-value* (usually international) students begin to feel exploited, dividing academics and paving the way for boards to take drastic measures without widespread pushback.

The move away from collegiality as an underlying principle of university governance is also felt across the sector because models focused so heavily on institutional one-upmanship do not sit well with the kind of arguments sometimes needed to defend higher education more broadly. A divided university sector is a gift for any government seeking to execute a programme of structural change, and policymakers have been quick to recognize that sympathetic governing bodies can grease the wheels of reform. Indeed, governors who see their role in terms of financial judiciousness ahead of public leadership make excellent foils for market-based policy. The approach is one that sets the wider campus adrift of decision-making activity, with bogus consultations engineered for decisions already taken, and charismatic or masculine individual leadership implicitly favoured over more democratic forms of institutional administration.

Again, corporate discourses are available and often deployed; governance by consensus would be very nice, senior managers and chairs of governors might allow, but to democratize decision making would require bridges to be built across disciplinary boundaries and between headstrong individual academics. Moreover, campus consensus is not reached easily or quickly, and faced with a demanding regulator and hostile policy environment, governing bodies need to act decisively. However, the problem with unchecked board sovereignty, and autocracy in governance more generally, is that it wears away at the collaborative fabric on which universities are built. Without collegiality, the merchandise that governors believe themselves to be producing and trading ceases to exist. To think otherwise is to misinterpret the fundamental contribution that universities make within societies and to deny any principle of common good (Nixon, 2010).

If the sector is to confront the challenges that lie ahead in the next decade, a genuine partnership between governing bodies, senates and other academic forums needs to be re-established (Jones and Hillman, 2019; Scott, 2021; Shattock and Horvath, 2019). Questions about whose knowledge counts, and what should be done with that knowledge, cannot be ignored. Staff are excluded from governance systematically, their contributions suspected of being ideologically driven. Stripped of the power to bring collective intellectual leadership, senates can become inflexible and awkward, at which point they are easily dismissed by chairs of governors as a *block* to progress, a *blob* of unreconstructed lecturers harbouring a *political* agenda. With the discursive frame established, institutional policy can soon seek to repurpose senates as rubber-stamping sub-committees rather than sites for the co-development of institutional strategy. Such actions are considered necessary by governing bodies wanting to enact internal policy without protracted debate, but inflame tensions further within academic and student communities, and incubate long-term institutional precarity. If expertise is diminished or discounted within the university's own governance structures, how can it hold its value in public discourses when derided by politicians and media commentators?

Reclaiming university governance as a site of intellectual leadership?

Contemporary conceptualizations of university governance are implicitly premised on the idea that the primary threat to higher education is economic. Precarity is baked in to multiple internal narratives of fiscal calamity that seek to position governing bodies as safe-guarders of institutional sustainability, and sometimes seek to position university staff as a barely affordable indulgence. At the same time, in the cultural realm, a right-wing media targets universities and their students daily with accusations of cancel culture, wokeness and political correctness (Jones, 2022). In some respects, the exaggerated narratives of financial crisis that circulate within the university parallel the confected *culture wars* waged from outside. Both serve to muddy moral waters and distort the core value of higher education. Shattock (2019) suggests that too much expectation is placed on the powers and capacity of lay-dominated governing bodies, acting as pseudo-company boards, to understand the wider political environment in which the university sector operates. However, a more cynical interpretation is that governing bodies embrace and exaggerate financial crises to maintain discursive authority, and tolerate campuses becoming battlefields for *culture wars* because they know that the reputation of staff and students will be dented more than their own. The distractions can form part of a marketization playbook, sowing confusion among and beyond university communities, and prove advantageous to those seeking to deliver a market agenda.

Some analyses of university governance, such as Schofield's (2009), have commended its *effectiveness*. Trakman even argued that 'universities need to be "corporatised" to some degree if they are to be governed properly' (2008, p. 71). However, a body of literature is emerging that asks why, under the stewardship of current governing bodies, the sector has grown so compliant with ministerial directives (Scott, 2021) and so reluctant to speak out on behalf of staff who undertake core academic activity (Shattock and Horvath, 2019). Scholarly critiques of university governance sometimes reflect an academic predisposition to resent any form of perceived authority, and even the most piercing of critical analyses can be dismissed as employees yearning for an era of self-determination discordant with the time-consuming and complex demands of modern university governance. Where this happens, staff can be framed as exceptionalist in their thinking, somehow considering themselves above the kind of accountability regimes that are now commonplace in other professions. However, the trends that I report above represent more than an occupational irritation; they form part of a structural problem for a higher education sector that is being steered in a direction incompatible with its status as a public good (Nixon, 2010). Within this context, governance becomes a site of short-term pragmatism, where common-sense narratives mask a top-down ideological agenda. Market-reformist governments and politicized regulators see new waves of university governors as agents of reform, and forces for modernization in a freshly liberated sector.

Some commentators, including Trakman (2008), warn against a one-size-fits-all model of governance. While different institutions within diverse higher education systems have different governance needs, the danger is that a lack of uniformity leads to a denial of sector-level accountability and an inability to speak with a unified voice. Governing bodies need autonomy to act in the best interests of their individual institution, but they also need to operate in principled and interconnected ways, recognizing that they each play their part in an important, larger-scale public provision. One size of governance may not fit all, but without a collective approach the danger is that a fragmented and disunited sector becomes unable to repel the ideologically driven imposition of an artificial market. Macfarlane noted that the notion of intellectual leadership is inherently collaborative, and therefore far removed from the macho image of the individual 'great leader' (2013, p. 5). He attributed the crisis of leadership in universities to the suspicion that professionals can no longer be trusted to lead themselves (Macfarlane, 2013, p. 8). Yet governing bodies continue to fall into the corporate trap of thinking that *efficiency* and *competitiveness* can be improved only through harsher and less democratized forms of leadership, and that inflated senior remuneration packages are needed to attract and keep *top talent*.

Can university governance be reclaimed as a site of intellectual leadership, even where universities are relentlessly positioned by policy as drivers of a *knowledge economy* whose primary role is to gain competitive advantage across various marketplaces? The first step may involve recognizing – indeed, celebrating – the differences between educational and non-educational sectors. Progress could then be accelerated by broadening the composition of governing bodies in terms of social class, gender and race. Senior managers could begin to position themselves as a bridge between academic communities and university governors. This could in turn trigger more sustained and concerted pushback against a political programme intended to hollow out a crucial public provision by effectively maintaining precarity across multiple fronts. However, the market offers few incentives for managers to question political and regulatory frameworks that tend to empower them and disempower their workforce. In-house expertise is kept at a safe distance, with staff and student input micro-managed and decision-making processes rarely troubled by scholarly knowledge.

Conclusion

The imitation of private sector boardroom practices in higher education can easily be mistaken for *professionalization*, and self-generated discourses can frame governors as the responsible defenders of institutional balance sheets against the insatiable demands of ivory towered academics. Clearly, financial and regulatory oversight for institutions with substantial annual turnovers is essential, and universities must draw upon the skills of individuals with the necessary experience and aptitude, regardless of whether their professional background is academic or not. The sector gains immeasurably from the time invested, mostly for free, by lay members. However, many governors lack awareness of – or are even threatened by – the non-instrumental, non-financial and less readily measurable contributions that higher education makes in society. University governance demands something more than importing performance management tactics from profit-driven sectors. It requires sensitivity to an environment in which workers are not motivated primarily by salary and often bring strong personal values to their professional role. Alternative forms of governance are thinkable, and more open models need not be anything to fear, potentially challenging some of the corporate assumptions on which governance principles currently rest, and offering ways for custodians of the institution to work more constructively with an academic workforce whose expertise has for too long been underused.

In this chapter, I have framed the governance deficit as one of intellectual leadership, arguing that the sector requires the confidence to embrace collegiality over rivalry and to reclaim universities as sites of independent research expertise and non-authorized forms of thinking. My argument is not merely that contemporary understandings of university governance as a form of intrusive corporate administration tread on hard-won academic freedoms, but rather that the model fails in practice (despite the associated and relentless *what works* rhetoric). To see universities as businesses, as commercially trained lay governors are inexorably minded to do, is to disregard the monumental breadth of their potential contribution. Higher education is uniquely placed to change lives; freed from an expectation to generate profit or gratify shareholders, universities can drive societies forward through their research, teaching and community partnerships, creating generations of better informed, more civically engaged citizens with enhanced and optimized capabilities. Universities can also help people to think critically about power relations, stand up for more marginalized members of their communities and challenge dominant political ideologies where appropriate. A new social contract is needed between higher education sectors and their host societies, and a fundamental reimagining of university governance is an overdue first step.

References

Arday, J. (2018). Understanding race and educational leadership in higher education: Exploring the Black and ethnic minority (BME) experience. *Management in Education*, 32(4), 192–200. https://doi.org/10.1177/0892020618791002

Arora, B. (2015). A Gramscian analysis of the employability agenda. *British Journal of Sociology of Education*, 36(4), 635–48. https://doi.org/10.1080/01425692.2013.838415

Austin, I., & Jones, G. A. (2015). *Governance of higher education: Global perspectives, theories, and practices*. Routledge.

Ball, S. J. (2012). Performativity, commodification and commitment: An I-spy guide to the neoliberal university. *British Journal of Educational Studies*, 60(1), 17–28. http://dx.doi.org/10.1080/00071005.2011.650940

Committee of University Chairs (2020). *The higher education code of governance*. https://www.universitychairs.ac.uk/wp-content/uploads/2020/09/CUC-HE-Code-of-Governance-publication-final.pdf

Dearing, R. (1997). *The report of the National Committee of Inquiry into Higher Education, under the chairmanship of Lord Dearing*. http://www.educationengland.org.uk/documents/dearing1997/dearing1997.html

Deem, R., Hillyard, S., & Reed, M. (2007). *Knowledge, higher education and the new managerialism: The changing management of UK universities*. Oxford University Press.

Drezner, N. D. (2019). The global growth of higher education philanthropy and fundraising. In N. Y. Ridge & A. Terway (Eds), *Philanthropy in education* (pp. 90–104). Edward Elgar Publishing.

Fitzgerald, T. (2013). *Women leaders in higher education: Shattering the myths*. Routledge.

Fitzpatrick, K. (2021). *Generous thinking: A radical approach to saving the university*. Johns Hopkins University Press.

Fryer, T. (13 September 2020). Value, graduate outcomes and the post-pandemic university: A scoping review and alternative way forward. *The post-pandemic university: Building the post-pandemic university*. https://postpandemicuniversity.net/2020/09/13/value-graduate-outcomes-and-the-post-pandemic-university-a-scoping-review-and-alternative-way-forward/

Giroux, H. A. (2014). *Neoliberalism's war on higher education*. Haymarket Books.

Gunn, A. (2018). Metrics and methodologies for measuring teaching quality in higher education: Developing the Teaching Excellence Framework (TEF). *Educational Review*, 70(2), 129–48. http://dx.doi.org/10.1080/00131911.2017.1410106

Gunter, H. M. (2005). Conceptualizing research in educational leadership. *Educational Management Administration & Leadership*, 33(2), 165–80. https://doi.org/10.1177/1741143205051051

Gunter, H. M. (2018). *The politics of public education: Reform ideas and issues*. Policy Press.

Hall, R. (2018). *The alienated academic: The struggle for autonomy inside the university*. Springer.

Higher Education Statistics Agency (17 February 2022). *Who's working in HE? HE Staff Data*. https://www.hesa.ac.uk/data-and-analysis/staff/working-in-he#governors

Jarratt, S. A. (1985). *Report to the Committee of Vice-Chancellors and Principals Steering Committee for Efficiency Studies*. CVCP. http://www.educationengland.org.uk/documents/jarratt1985/index.html

Jones, S. (2022). *Universities under Fire: Hostile discourses and integrity deficits in higher education*. Palgrave Macmillan.

Jones, S., & Hillman, N. (2019). *University governance in a new age of regulation*. HEPI report 119. https://www.hepi.ac.uk/wp-content/uploads/2019/08/HEPI-University-governance-in-a-new-age-of-regulation.pdf

Jones, S., Vigurs, K., & Harris, D. (2020). Discursive framings of market-based education policy and their negotiation by students: The case of 'value for money' in English universities. *Oxford Review of Education*, 46(3), 375–92. https://doi.org/10.1080/03054985.2019.1708711

Kakabadse, A., Morais, F., Myers, A., & Brown, G. (2020). *Universities governance: A risk of imminent collapse*. Henley Business School. https://www.kakabadse.com/uploads/universities-governance_final_13-10-2020.pdf

Lewis, J. (2013). *Academic governance: Disciplines and policy*. Routledge.

Macfarlane, B. (2013). *Intellectual leadership in higher education: Renewing the role of the university professor*. Routledge.

McCaig, C. (2018). *The marketisation of English higher education: A policy analysis of a risk-based system*. Emerald Group Publishing.

Morrish, L. (2020). Academic freedom and the disciplinary regime in the neoliberal university. In S. Dawes & M. Lenormand (Eds), *Neoliberalism in context* (pp. 235–53). Palgrave Macmillan.

Morrish, L. (2021). Academic freedom is in crisis: Free speech is not. *Council for the Defence of British Universities*. http://cdbu.org.uk/academic-freedom-is-in-crisis-free-speech-is-not/

Nichols, T. (2017). *The death of expertise: The campaign against established knowledge and why it matters*. Oxford University Press.

Nixon, J. (2010). *Higher education and the public good: Imagining the university*. Bloomsbury Publishing.

Office for Students (27 July 2020). *Topic briefing: Governing bodies*. https://www.officeforstudents.org.uk/advice-and-guidance/promoting-equal-opportunities/effective-practice/governing-bodies/

Rowlands, J. (2017). *Academic governance in the contemporary university*. Springer.

Sabri, D. (2011). What's wrong with 'the student experience'? *Discourse: Studies in the cultural politics of education*, 32(5), 657–67. https://doi.org/10.1080/01596306.2011.620750

Sayer, D. (2014). *Rank hypocrisies: The insult of the REF*. Sage.

Schofield, A. (2009). *What is an effective and high performing governing body in UK higher education?* Leadership Foundation for Higher Education.

Scott, P. (2021). *Retreat or resolution?: Tackling the crisis of mass higher education*. Policy Press.

Shattock, M. (2006). *Managing good governance in higher education*. McGraw-Hill Education (UK).

Shattock, M. (2012). *Making policy in British higher education 1945–2011*. McGraw-Hill Education (UK).

Shattock, M. (2019). *University governance in a new age of regulation* (foreword). HEPI report 119. https://www.hepi.ac.uk/wp-content/uploads/2019/08/HEPI-University-governance-in-a-new-age-of-regulation.pdf

Shattock, M., & Horvath, A. (2019). *The governance of British higher education: The impact of governmental, financial and market pressures*. Bloomsbury Publishing.

Smyth, J. (2017). *Toxic university*. Palgrave Macmillan.

Tomlinson, M. (2017). Student perceptions of themselves as 'consumers' of higher education. *British Journal of Sociology of Education*, 38(4), 450–67. https://doi.org/10.1080/01425692.2015.1113856

Trakman, L. (2008). Modelling university governance. *Higher Education Quarterly*, 62(1–2), 63–83. https://doi.org/10.1111/j.1468-2273.2008.00384.x

Whitchurch, C. (2012). *Reconstructing identities in higher education: The rise of 'third space' professionals*. Routledge.

4

The Geopolitics of International Higher Education, Transnational Intellectual Collaboration and Leadership

Ly Thi Tran, Jill Blackmore and Diep Thi Bich Nguyen

Introduction

Political, institutional and intellectual leadership has taken on new significance in the uncertain high-risk times of Covid-19, climate change, financial crisis and rapidly changing geopolitics marked by rising authoritarianism such as China and Russia (Blackmore, 2022). China's rising authoritarianism and power in military, economic and soft diplomacy have become a threat to the rule-based world order and security, challenging the United States' traditional domination. The emergence and growth of middle powers like India, South Korea, Iran and Brazil expose the world to a multipolar system (Tran, Phan & Bui, 2022). Geopolitics, exacerbated by Covid-19, impacts on transnational flows of students and academics and intellectual collaborations, with international border closures and, more recently, Russia's invasion of Ukraine.

Internationalization in higher education operates in a transnational space, entailing the integration of international, intercultural or global dimensions into multi-faceted institutional operations (Knight, 2015), thereby being subject to the relationships and collaborations between individuals and across institutions, nations and regions which are embedded in political contexts. This chapter discusses how the Australian higher education sector responds to the changes associated with rising geopolitical tensions between Australia and China and the Russian invasion of Ukraine specifically. It considers how political and university leaders seek to balance national security needs, transnational partnerships and international research collaborations, all of which directly impact on intellectual leadership and knowledge generation by academics. It analyses how knowledge production generated through transnational research collaborations, student and staff mobilities, and internationalization of higher education has changed in times of precarity and rising geopolitical conflicts. Finally, we consider the new social reality within which the mobilities of transnational knowledge, ideas and research are located given rising geopolitical tensions and the implications for intellectual leadership.

The geopoliticalization of international education

Internationalization of higher education involves multiple dimensions, ranging from student and staff mobilities, internationalization of the curriculum, teaching and learning, transnational education and offshore delivery, and international research collaborations. These dimensions play a critical role in diversifying, enriching and transforming knowledge production, intellectual leadership and the university. Ideally, internationalization aspires to enhance intercultural understandings, empathy, people-to-people connections and transnational intellectual collaboration (Tran, 2020a). However, international education is increasingly seen as a tool for nation states to exercise and increase their soft power (Altbach & de Wit, 2017; Byrne & Hall, 2013; Tran et al., 2023). Multiple motives underpin international education programmes ranging from aid and developmental support, cultural enhancement, commercialization, international collaboration, reciprocal learning, to public diplomacy and geopolitical purposes (Tran, Bui & Nguyen, 2021; Tran & Rahimi, 2018; Tran & Vu, 2018).

International education was largely shaped by dual means for both aid and soft power until the early 1980s. On the one hand, international education programmes like the Colombo Plan by Australia, the Fulbright programme by the United States and development programmes for socialist countries by the Soviet Union were designed to support knowledge and technical transfer and capacity building for developing countries (de Wit, 2013; Rizvi, 2011), drawing on the intellectual expertise of developed nations and academic commitment to make a difference. On the other hand, these programmes were also driven by geopolitical motives and used as a vehicle by developed countries as aid providers to exercise soft power on receiving countries as aid recipients. International education programmes are equally a mechanism for the elites in postcolonial states and former colonial powers to build relationships and exert influence on developing and poorer countries and for developed nations to attract talent (Tran & Nguyen, 2023). For example, in Australia, the Colombo

Plan, an inbound mobility programme sponsoring more than 20,000 Asian scholars studying in Australia (1951–85) (National Archives of Australia, 2022), linked to aid, nation building and cultural liberalism (Rizvi, 2005), and aimed to develop human resources in the Asia-Pacific.

The mid-1980s witnessed a shift of international education from aid to commercialization in Australia and the UK (Rizvi, 2005; Tran, 2020c) and from aid to academic and intellectual exchange in Continental Europe (de Wit, 2013), in part due to the cost of sustaining international education as aid programmes to developing countries. This shift also resulted from policy changes and significant social, economic and political developments in background contexts influencing international education. In Australia, the shift from international education as an aid to the development of an education export industry accompanied national policy reforms (often referred to as the Dawkins reforms) of 1988 which corporatized the higher education sector, introducing market and managerial drivers facilitating increased executive power (Blackmore, 2022). The development of the business model underpinning international education in Australia resulted from the Commonwealth government's policy moves which over time reduced public funding for higher education and met the rising demand for overseas education from middle-class families in source countries, especially in Asia, which accelerated people and knowledge flows (Tran, 2020b).

Regardless of the move of international education from aid to trade or academic exchange, the internationalization of HE is often viewed as part of a nation's public diplomacy (Tran & Vu, 2018). Public diplomacy goals embedded in international education programmes are concerned with using international education as an instrument to strengthen global ties, stimulate peace and enrich mutual understanding between nations, and foster international development via educational exchange opportunities for students and academics from home and host countries, as well as nurturing intellectual leadership cross-culturally. Examples of these programmes are the US Fulbright foundation, the EU ERASMUS+ programme, FUS Institute of International Education, Deutscher Akademischer Austauschdienst and the British Council (de Wit, Hunter, Howard & Egron-Polak, 2015). Primary education exchange and learning-abroad programmes such as ERASMUS and the recent ERASMUS+ by the European Union have been developed to foster intercultural understandings and learning through cooperation with non-European countries (de Wit, Hunter, Howard & Egron-Polak, 2015). In Asia, international education has been used to drive national political agendas; educational hubs have been created in China, Malaysia, Singapore and Hong Kong seeking to increase each nation's geopolitical influence through expansion into the international education market to develop intellectual capital regionally (Lee, 2015).

Government commitments to creating an alignment between outbound mobility and economic and political goals have influenced the choices of targeted destinations for study-abroad and exchange programmes (Gribble & Tran, 2016). In Australia, the New Colombo Plan launched in 2014 was driven by the Commonwealth government's aspiration to use student mobility to enhance Australia's regional engagement and position with the Indo-Pacific region and therefore enhance Australia's social, diplomatic and economic development, as well as develop intellectual networks and connection with the region (e.g. Foreign Policy White Paper, Global Alumni Strategy 2016–20). This outbound mobility scheme positions Australian students at the centre, facilitating the humanization of foreign policy objectives (Lowe, 2015) and the implementation of public (soft) diplomacy goals (Tran & Vu, 2018) while enabling them to develop international networks. Similarly, the UK's programmes such as 'Generation UK-China' and 'Generation UK-India', and the United States's '100,000 Strong China' have embedded geopolitical imperatives into student mobility even though their targeted destinations (China and India) are not as diverse as those of the New Colombo Plan, which stretches to forty locations in the Indo-Pacific (Tran & Rahimi, 2018).

The weaponization of international education: The Sino-Australia relationship

Despite continuing debates and efforts at institutional, federal, state, territorial and local government levels to diversify international student bodies and move away from Australia's overdependence on China as a source country, the international education relationship between Australia and China was described as productive and positive prior to Covid-19 (CIE Working Group, 2019, p. 24). China and Australia have a fruitful relationship regarding the two-way flows of inbound and outbound mobility students and academics. China has been the top source country for Australia with around 30 per cent of all international students in Australia before Covid-19 (DESE, 2019) and by the end of 2021 (DESE, 2022). Reciprocally, China was the most popular study-abroad destination for Australian students prior to Covid-19, accounting for 15 per cent (AUIDF, 2020). Additionally, Sino-Australian research collaboration progressed from 'minimal engagement' to China overtaking the UK to be Australia's second research partner after the United States prior to Covid-19 (CIE Working Group, 2019;

Ross, 2022). Between 2016 and 2021, the number of journal articles co-authored by Chinese and Australian researchers increased by 84 per cent based on the Scopus database of indexed research (Ross, 2022), indicating the mutual benefits of such collaborations and the nurturing of intellectual leadership.

Despite these fruitful collaborations, the Sino-Australian international education relationship has been weaponized, especially since Covid-19. Neighbouring nations in the Indo-Pacific region and Western higher education providers such as Australia, Canada, the United States and UK have expressed concerns over territorial expansion of China over a decade, such as the building of militarized islands strategically in the South China Sea and the Belt and Road Initiative. However, Sino-Australian tensions escalated with Covid-19 with the Australian government's call for an independent investigation into the origins of Covid-19 and then their opposition to China's responses to Hong Kong's Security Law, Taiwanese autonomy and China's escalation in the South China Sea (Heydarian, 2020; Walden & Choahan, 2020). In particular, following Australia's precedence of offering 42,000 Chinese international students residency after Tiananmen Square (Fang & Weedon, 2020), and with the Hong Kong National Security Law, the Australian government offered a five-year extension post-study visa and pathway to permanent residency for Hong Kong students, leading to a surge in applications (Lo, 2020) and Australia gains intellectual capital through HE and skilled migration (Lehmann, 2020). Most recently, an agreement between the Solomon Islands government and China brings the potential for a Chinese military presence even closer to Australia, causing significant concern also for the United States, leading to the AUKUS agreement between Australia, the UK and United States in 2021.

In response, China has discouraged students from selecting Australia as a study destination, citing threats of increasing anti-Chinese racial attacks, violence and discrimination (Kuo & Murphy, 2020; Tran, 2020b), diverting thousands to the UK if Australia refuses to change its political position (Bagshaw et al., 2020). In 2020, less than half of Chinese students planned to return to their study in Australia (Zhang, 2020). A further escalation occurred with China making public a list of fourteen complaints against the Australian government on 20 November 2020 issued to the Australian press which included funding for 'anti-China' research, raids on Chinese journalists, academic visa cancellations, Australia 'crusading' in multilateral forums on China's affairs in Taiwan, Hong Kong and Xinjiang, calling for an investigation into the origins of Covid-19, banning Huawei from the 5G network and blocking Chinese foreign investment in Australia. These significant demands impacted on Australian sovereignty and were rejected immediately by the Australia government.

Russia–Ukraine war and intellectual collaboration

The geopolitical context has again shifted with the Russian invasion of Ukraine in February 2022. Russian universities had been developing closer teaching and research collaborations with Western universities (e.g. Manchester University), research collaborations on climate change, space exploration and so on, and established campuses in previous Soviet countries (Burakovsky, 2022). But Putin had become concerned about the Westernization of higher education and had restricted collaborations with foreign agents and undesirable organizations, scrutinized funding, outlawed think tanks and in 2021 required all Russian scholars meeting with foreign scholars to be approved by the government (Burakovsky, 2022). Controlling intellectual leadership is a primary concern of authoritarian leaders.

Transnational intellectual collaboration was disrupted due to a global wave of condemnation against the invasion. Globally, universities have applied restrictions on Russian institutions and individuals and condemned this 'unprovoked and unjustified' attack on Ukraine. With regard to political leadership, in Australia, the government adopted a dual-policy approach of sanctions on Russia and aid to Ukraine. In addition to existing sanctions since 2014 following Russia's annexation of the Ukrainian territory of Crimea (Parliament of Australia, 2022), 476 further sanctions have been imposed on specific Russian individuals and entities deemed responsible for the unprovoked war (Prime Minister, 2022). Meanwhile, Australia committed a significant aid package to Ukraine, including financial, humanitarian and military aid along with a supportive visa policy for Ukrainian individuals who want to leave their country (Prime Minister, 2022).

Many Australian universities, as with universities globally, have condemned Russia's attack on Ukraine's people and sovereignty. The Group of Eight research-intensive universities in Australia have reconsidered collaboration with Russian counterparts to stand in solidarity with the global research community. The Australian National University (ANU) executive (Chancellor, Vice Chancellor and Chair of Academic Board) stated: 'Russia's invasion of Ukraine threatens the peace, freedom and democracy on which freedom of inquiry and academic collaboration is based' (ANU, 2022). Accordingly, ANU suspended all ties with Russian institutions and urged other universities to act likewise. Deakin University and Western Sydney University have officially suspended existing academic ties or have not entered new agreements with Russia while providing support to Ukrainian scholars and students where needed (Campus Morning

Mail, 2022). Nonetheless, not all Australian universities have made similar public statements, indicating a lack of institutional leadership.

Individual interactions and collaboration with Russian colleagues, in adhering to the principles of academic freedom, have not ceased but have been discouraged (Deakin University, 2022) or restricted, for example, at ANU, in relation to publications in Russian journals and funding for Russian colleagues or other costs that could potentially be borne by Russian institutions. Obviously, Russian academics, many of whom condemn the Ukrainian wars (Kampmark, 2022), are increasingly disadvantaged in the global research community. Networks have been established by academics internationally to support those Russian academics fleeing from Russia as they envisage increased censorship. Some Australian universities welcome Russian students (e.g. ANU) on the condition of being funded from non-Russian competitive grants. However, generally Australian universities stand with universities worldwide to support Ukrainian scholars and students wanting to leave Ukraine such as through the Charles Darwin University Ukrainian Assistance Scholarship (CDU, 2022), counselling services (e.g. University of Melbourne) and other support areas (e.g. Monash University).

Such policies have received criticism and opposition. A group of academics of largely Russian background urged the ANU leadership to reconsider its suspension of all ties with Russian institutions, arguing that this will 'have a devastating effect on those academics in Russia who strive for international collaboration and thus slow down the country's descent into the dark ages' (Lansdown, 2022). At the same time, decisions to cut ties with Russian institutions by universities in Australia and overseas in relation to research, teaching, or staff and student exchange activities can potentially deny Russian institutions and individuals the opportunity to engage in the global knowledge community as well as benefit from global education and funding. In addition, freezing connections with Russian institutions can be counterproductive as it feeds Russia's isolationist propaganda machine rather than making the Russian government aware of the long-term consequences of their actions (Putnins, 2022). Furthermore, boycotting Russia will punish the innocent academics and damage the prospects of a peaceful future as the intellectual leaders become disengaged from Western ideas and relations (Kampmark, 2022). Academics are often the last source (other than journalism) of resistance to authoritarianism as public intellectuals speaking out for the public good (Daniels. & Thistlewaite, 2019; Hil, Lyons & Thompsett, 2022). Some academics argue being public intellectuals means keeping communications open with Russian academics that will 'help Russians see what the rest of the world sees' (Putnins, 2022). Intellectual leadership is, many academics argue, critical in a world which is facing decreased trust in expertise and institutions and increased disinformation and political propaganda.

Intellectual leadership and research collaboration in a politicized context

The shifting terrain of geopolitics globally has arguably been driven by a form of masculinist authoritarianism (not leadership) characterized by narcissistic personalities and their imaginaries of past empires that needed to be reclaimed or invented (e.g. China, North Korea, Russia). Political leadership by conservative governments in Western nation states has also been lacking in the United States, the UK and Australia (Altbach & de Wit, 2017), adding to a growing concern that core democratic principles and institutions are under threat in the wider context of anti-science conspiracy theories and misinformation circulating through social media with the rise of state authoritarianism. This distrust has been escalated as Western governments have been perceived to be less accountable and lacking (Quiggin, 2021).

Intellectual leadership can be understood in the context of internationalization and loss of trust in leaders, expertise and democratic institutions (Palmer, 2017). Forging international collaborations have always been central to academic intellectual work. Universities play a key role in such debates as a source of scientific evidence and research-informed debate (Felt, 2018). With the escalation of competition in the international education field, internationalization policies of governments and university management have encouraged international research collaboration because it enriches research practices and outcomes, attracts funding and improves university rankings and research impact (Epseland & Sauder, 2016) and is complementary to other dimensions of internationalization such as offshore delivery, international student recruitment and outbound mobility. Consequently, university executive leadership is hypersensitive about reputational damage because international students seriously consider university rankings in selecting study destinations.

While research collaborations have been more the norm in the natural and physical sciences, they are increasingly so in the humanities and social sciences, although more often undertaken by more senior or productive scholars. Gender also plays a key role in who collaborates, with women less likely to undertake international collaborations, or be editors and first authors in international journals (Langmann, Fahrleitner-Pammer, Pieber & Zollner-Schwetz, 2011). Greater disciplinary specialization by individual academics together with the pressure for interdisciplinarity have also made international collaborations more important, as is the need to develop international networks, engagement and impacts as evidence of an academic's intellectual leadership for promotion. International research collaborations are also expected to arise from institutional internationalization programmes such offshore campuses and student mobilities.

Intellectual leadership is therefore understood by university management and governments as being a good thing both for the nation state and the university which accrue financial and reputational benefits from academics leading research projects transnationally. As Marginson (2018, p. 1) argues, 'research intensive universities ... now operate as a single network, one that is increasingly integrated and also produces a positive sum with leading research nations fostering emerging science countries through collaboration ... "Flat" cooperative science works differently from markets and command structures'. Intellectual leadership therefore works through different collegial networks and logics of practice based on norms of peer review, collegiality and professional ethics.

But such collaborations are becoming more difficult with the changing geopolitics. Australian governments have responded to the exertion of soft power on Chinese international students, state-sponsored cyber-attacks on universities (e.g. Australian National University) and political interference through soft diplomacy (e.g. Confucius Institutes in thirteen host universities). The Foreign Influence Transparency Scheme aims to increase government control over universities' international collaborative research with any collaboration having to be registered, including Confucius Institutes (Hunter, 2019). The Australian foreign minister has the power to veto public universities' international collaboration agreements with foreign governments and organizations. A recent change requires international student doctoral theses to be registered and the seeking of ministerial approval if they wish to change their thesis topic due to concerns about 'unwanted transfer of critical technology' (Hare, 2022). Universities view this as interference with their autonomy and intellectual leadership, discouraging student flows and impeding valuable transnational research collaborations (Campus Review, 2020).

University management, in the competitive global anxiety-driven environment of university ranking, has viewed partnerships with elite Chinese universities as one way of improving their rankings. Therefore. international research collaborations continue with China, despite increased tensions between the nations. China was outside the top 10 international research partners, downgrading from its position among the top 5, for Australian universities under the Australian Research Council's latest Discovery scheme 2022. This is a decline from about fifty to eighty collaborations with China in each year's grants to twenty-three in the latest funding round (Ross, 2022). China also dropped from being among the top 3 international partners for Australian universities to being outside the top 8 and also became outside the top 10 for the latest Linkage funding round and Linkage Infrastructure, Equipment and Facilities funding round, respectively (ibid). The declines show that international education and transnational intellectual collaborations have become weaponized within bilateral and regional geopolitics, a trend that is not new but has exacerbated recently.

The paradox with regard to intellectual leadership is that while academics have been encouraged to undertake transnational research collaborations, universities have not protected academics' work conditions that nurture international collaboration: intellectual freedom and security of employment. Covid-19 illuminated the vulnerability of the higher education sector in Australia with up to 70 per cent of academics casual or on contract, and international student numbers comprising up to 30 per cent of students in some universities cross-subsidising research as government funding of research and universities generally was in decline (Blackmore, 2020). Student–staff ratios have trebled over decades, the academic job has expanded and employment has become precarious. Various Australian universities are being charged for underpayment of casual staff (Fenton & Kane, 2021). Furthermore, university workload models (Kenny, 2018) and research priorities echo national government policies' focus on commercialization (Hancock, 2020). Consequently, there is a narrowing focus on STEM and quantifiable outcomes such as research assessment, graduate employability and commercial outputs, and by default a neglect of the arts, humanities and social sciences (Belfiore, 2015).

In the highly corporatized Australian higher education sector, market, managerial and commercial drivers and measures impact on academic work in terms of what research is done, who with, how it is done and how it is assessed (Hancock, 2020; Rowlands, 2019). Serial organizational restructuring in Australia has undermined the capacity of academics to do their core intellectual work of teaching and research (Connell, 2006) and failed to recognize and value intellectual leaders in decision making (Evans, 2018; Macfarlane, 2012). This has produced significant academic disenchantment and a loss of trust in university executive managers (Blackmore, 2022; Woelert & Yates, 2015). There is no coherent mechanism to protect the security and well-being of academics affected by geopolitical tensions related to their transnational research collaborations and transnational research fieldwork in conflicted areas.

International research collaborations occur because academics have always had an international disposition motivated by the desire to expand their research across different contexts, cultures and populations. Academics also consider they can be both critic and conscience in a democracy and as a global citizen (Williams, 2016). Intellectual leadership is conditional on academic freedom not only to profess about their expertise but also more widely as public intellectuals (Jameson, 2019). Hence, academics as journalists are the first to be targeted in authoritarian states (e.g. China, Russia). Yet even in Western democracies, academic freedom is under threat (Brown, 2015). University management has failed to utilize intellectual leadership, with academics excluded from core decision making and university executives rejecting critical analysis of their management (Blackmore, 2022; Jameson, 2019; Jones, Lefoe, Harvey & Ryland, 2012). The exertion of executive power over decades in Australian universities symbolizes a shift from intellectual to managerial capital (Macfarlane, 2012; Rowlands, 2011). Successive industrial agreements and codes of conduct have intensified academic work and also restricted academics speaking outside their expertise, for example, as whistle-blowers over international student recruitment. The pressure for international collaboration fuelled by policies focusing on commercialization has undermined academic engagement as public intellectuals (Hancock, 2020). Academics are discouraged from speaking publicly unless it improves the reputation of their university. Intellectual leadership is increasingly justified in terms of economic benefits for the university and not for the public good (Hil et al., 2022).

Concerns over academic freedom in the international sphere are occurring within the context of domestic debates over academic freedom in Australia as to the role of externally funded institutes (e.g. Ramsay Centres for Western Civilization, Confucius Institutes), with university management acting against whistle-blowers who publicly state that international students are being used as cash cows (Knaus, 2019). Conservative and far-right politicians and media continually reignite the culture wars and create divisions over gender fluidity, climate science, feminism, multiculturalism and Indigenous rights while simultaneously arguing freedom of speech on campuses has been restricted, despite parliamentary reviews concluding the opposite. In the context of the conservative Australian government ramping up defence talk against China prior to the 2022 election, there have been political interventions in national research grants schemes on projects in the humanities and social sciences because they were not in the national interest. While such conservative interventions are not new in the humanities, in 2022 the Minister rejected a project investigating student activism against climate change and two projects focusing on Chinese culture and history, indicating the impacts of geo-politics and the politicization of research (Jayasuriya & McCarthy, 2021).

The public purpose of the university, many academics argue, is now in crisis (Connell, 2019; Shore & Taitz, 2012). The legislative requirements together with overt censorship therefore make academics reconsider whether they will undertake international research collaborations with China. Yet in the context of the global pandemic, climate change, geopolitics *and* the crisis of relations between knowledge, state and society, intellectual leadership and transnational research collaborations have become even more critical.

The changing geopolitics of research have also emerged in more vocal forms of collective intellectual leadership in the community of global scholars (Dovey, Burdon & Simpson, 2017). Transnational intellectual leadership was displayed in the pandemic as scientists worked through their international research collaborations, for example, sharing of the genetic code to establish the DNA by Chinese and other scientists of the virus regardless of their national citizenship. Chief health officers and epidemiologists advised government on pandemic responses and continue to draw from their international networks to develop 'living evidence' of the patterns of each virus (Blackmore, 2020; Ross, 2021). This was made possible because of temporal and geographical differences and the variety of policy and civic responses. Similarly, the intergovernmental reports on climate change have driven governments to respond, even if reluctantly, as the evidence has mounted for the need for urgent action. Academics have also engaged through their international and national collegial networks to defend academic freedom, for example, with the formation of the Australian Association of University Professors in 2019. AAUP joined in 2022 with the student associations and tertiary education union to create Public Universities Australia which argues there is need to reform university governance. Many academics consider that universities have lost focus on their responsibility to the public, that they have become commercial, not knowledge-oriented enterprises and that academic freedom to speak as public intellectuals is under threat, which leads them to mistrust their executive leaders (Hancock, 2020; Jameson, 2012). These activities signify the powerful role of intellectual leadership in democracies.

Conclusion

This chapter provides insights into how international education has been used as a vehicle of politics to foster bilateral and regional relationships and serve national political agendas. It underscores the importance of situating international education, transnational intellectual exchanges and international research collaborations at the intersection of education, public diplomacy and politics to have nuanced understandings on the policies and practices shaping university operations and academic activities in precarious times characterized by escalating geopolitical crises. International education and transnational intellectual collaborations, as well as the role of academics as intellectual leaders, play an important role in enriching our knowledge and outlooks, nurturing research and scientific developments, and enhancing institution-to-institution partnerships and country-to-country relationships.

The Covid-19 crisis illustrated that intellectual leadership and international collaboration offer potential to address the impending climate crisis. However, international education and transnational intellectual collaborations are also highly vulnerable, as are individual academics, to political turbulences and interventions. Any debates about intellectual leadership therefore need to address the geo and national political context as well as take into account how mobilities of knowledge and ideas originating from transnational intellectual leadership can be generated through research collaborations and student and staff mobilities or academic diplomacy. Geopolitics impacts on Australia's positioning by government and institutional policies in ways that also influence academics' work and vulnerability. Intellectual collaboration and enquiry can be disrupted or even ruined by government-to-government tensions, yet universities' responses can improve or exacerbate the geopolitical relationship between countries.

References

Altbach, P. G., & de Wit, H. (2017). Trump and the coming revolution in higher education internationalization. *International Higher Education*, 89(Spring), 3–5. https://doi.org/10.6017/ihe.2017.89.9831

AUIDF (Australian Universities International Directors' Forum) (2020). *Australian Universities learning abroad 2019*. Canberra. https://info.i-graduate.org/blog/more-australian-students-studying-overseas-pre-pandemic

Australian National University (ANU) (3 March 2022). *ANU statement on Ukraine.* https://www.anu.edu.au/news/all-news/anu-statement-on-ukraine

Bagshaw, E., Hunter, F., & Liu, S. (10 June 2020). Chinese students will not go there: Beijing education agents warn Australia [Online]. *The Sydney Morning Herald.* https://www.smh.com.au/politics/federal/chinese-students-will-not-go-there-beijing-education-agents-warn-australia-20200610-p55151.html

Belfiore, E. (2015). 'Impact', 'value' and 'bad economics': Making sense of the problem of value in the arts and humanities. *Arts & Humanities in Higher Education,* 14(1), 95–110. https://doi.org/10.1177/1474022214531503

Blackmore, J. (2020). The carelessness of entrepreneurial universities in a world risk society: A feminist reflection on the impact of Covid 19 in Australia. *Higher Education Research and Development, Special Issue,* 39(7), 1332–6. https://doi.org/10.1080/07294360.2020.1825348

Blackmore, J. (2022). *Disrupting leadership in the entrepreneurial university: Disengagement and diversity in higher education.* Bloomsbury Academic.

Brown, W. (2015). *Undoing the demos. Neoliberalism's stealth revolution.* Zone Books.

Burakovsky, A. (1 April 2022). The war in Ukraine ruins Russia's academic ties with the West. *The Conversation.* https://theconversation.com/the-war-in-ukraine-ruins-russias-academic-ties-with-the-west-180006

Byrne, C., & Hall, R. (2013). Realising Australia's international education as public diplomacy. *Australian Journal of International Affairs,* 67(4), 419–38. https://doi.org/10.1080/10357718.2013.806019

Campus Morning Mail (10 March 2022). Deakin University and WSU stand-up for Ukraine. https://campusmorningmail.com.au/news/deakin-u-and-wsu-stand-up-for-ukraine/

Campus Review (14 October 2020). Universities baulk at foreign deal laws. *Campus Review.*

Charles Darwin University (CDU) (1 March 2022). CDU announces new scholarship fund Ukrainian students. https://www.cdu.edu.au/news/cdu-announces-new-scholarship-fund-ukrainian-students

CIE Working Group (2019). *The Australia-China relationship: Diversity, complexity and maturity.* CIE. https://www.dese.gov.au/download/4813/australia-china-education-relationship-diversity-complexity-and-maturity/7174/document/pdf

Connell, R. W. (2006). Core activity: Reflexive intellectual workers and cultural crisis. *Journal of Sociology,* 42(1), 5–23. https://doi.org/10.1177/1440783306061350

Connell, R. W. (2019). *The good university: What universities actually do and why it's time for radical change.* Monash University Publishing.

Daniels. J., & Thistlewaite, P. (2019). *Being a scholar in the digital era: Transforming scholarly practice for the public good.* Bristol University Press.

de Wit, H. (2013). Internationalization of higher education, an introduction on the why, how and what. In H. de Wit (Ed.), *An introduction to higher education internationalization* (pp. 13–46). Center for Higher Education Internationalisation, Universita a Cattolica Del Sacro Cuore.

de Wit, H., Hunter, F., Howard, L., & Egron-Polak, E. (2015). *Internationalisation of higher education*. European Parliament Committee on Culture and Education.

Deakin University (8 March 2022). *Deakin University statement on Ukraine*. https://www.deakin.edu.au/about-deakin/news-and-media-releases/articles/deakin-university-statement-on-ukraine

DESE (2019). *International student data monthly summary December 2019*. https://internationaleducation.gov.au/research/International-Student-Data/Documents/MONTHLY%20SUMMARIES/2019/Dec%202019%20MonthlyInfographic.pdf

DESE (2022). *International student data monthly summary December 2021*. https://www.dese.gov.au/download/12716/international-student-data-full-year-data-based-data-finalised-december-2021/25844/international-student-data-december-2020-monthly-info-graphic/pdf/en

Dovey, K., Burdon, S., & Simpson, R. (2017). Creative leadership as a collective achievement: An Australian case. *Management Learning*, 48(1), 23–38. https://doi.org/10.1177/1350507616651387

Epseland, W., & Sauder, M. (2016). *Engines of anxiety: Academic rankings, reputation, and accountability*. Russel Sage Foundation.

Evans, L. (2018). *Professors as academic leaders: Expectations, enacted professionalism and evolving roles*. Bloomsbury Publishing.

Fang, J., & Weedon, A. (9 June 2020). China's Tiananmen generation reflect on how Bob Hawke gave them a permanent Australian home. *ABC*. https://www.abc.net.au/news/2020-06-09/china-tiananmen-square-massacre-bob-hawke-australian-asylum/12332084

Felt, U. (2018). Responsible research and innovation. In S. Gibbon, B. Prainsack, S. Hilgartner, & J. Lamoreaux (Eds), *Handbook of genomics, health and society* (pp. 108–16). Routledge.

Fenton, E., & Kane, L. (18 March 2021). Casual wage theft in the corporate university. *Arena Online*. https://arena.org.au/casual-wage-theft-in-the-corporate-university/

Gribble, C., & Tran, L. T. (2016). *International trends in learning abroad: Information and promotions campaign for student mobility*. Universities Australia & IEAA.

Hancock, L. (2020). Commercialization and corporatization: Academic freedom and autonomy under constraints in Australian Universities. In Z. Hao & P. Zabielskis (Eds), *Academic freedom under siege: Higher education in East Asia, the U.S. and Australia* (pp. 219–46). Springer.

Hare, J. (8 April 2022). Foreign researchers will need ministerial approval to change course. *Australian Financial Review*. https://www.afr.com/work-and-careers/education/foreign-researchers-will-need-ministerial-tick-to-change-course-20220408-p5ac44

Heydarian, R. (27 October 2020). The Quad and China: A new rivalry in the South China Sea. *China and US Focus*. https://www.chinausfocus.com/peace-security/the-quad-and-china-a-new-rivalry-in-the-south-china-sea

Hil, R., Lyons, K., & Thompsett, F. (2022). *Transforming universities in the midst of global crisis: A university for the common good*. Routledge.

Hunter, F. (21 March 2019). Foreign influence showdown as universities decline to register China-funded Confucius Institutes. *Sydney Morning Herald*.

Jameson, J. (2012). Leadership values, trust and negative capability: Managing the uncertainties of future English higher education. *Higher Education Quarterly*, 66(4), 391–414. https://doi.org/10.1111/j.1468-2273.2012.00533.x

Jameson, J. (Ed.) (2019). *Critical university leadership: International perspectives on leadership in higher education*. Routledge.

Jayasuriya, K., & McCarthy, G. (2021). Australia's politics of research funding: Depoliticization and the crisis of the regulatory state. In R. Eisfeld & M. Flinders (Eds), *Political science in the shadow of the state* (pp. 119–44). Springer Nature.

Jones, S., Lefoe, G., Harvey, M., & Ryland, K. (2012). Distributed leadership: A collaborative framework for academics, executives and professionals in higher education. *Journal of Higher Education Policy and Management*, 34(1), 67–78. https://doi.org/10.1080/1360080X.2012.642334

Kampmark, B. (18 March 2022). The West should not freeze out Russian academics. *Times Higher Education*. https://www.timeshighereducation.com/blog/west-should-not-freeze-out-russian-academics

Kenny, J. (2018). Re-empowering academics in a corporate culture: An exploration of workload and performativity in a university. *Higher Education*, 75(2), 365–80. https://doi.org/10.1007/s10734-017-0143-z

Knaus, C. (15 October 2019). Academics condemn harassment of whistleblower by Murdoch University. *The Guardian*. https://www.theguardian.com/australia-news/2019/oct/15/academics-condemn-harassment-whistleblower-murdoch-university-schroeder-turk

Knight, J. (2015). Moving from soft power to knowledge diplomacy. *International Higher Education,* 80(Spring), 8–9. https://doi.org/10.1007/978-94-6351-161-2_82

Kuo, L., & Murphy, K. (9 June 2020). China warns students to reconsider travel to Australia for study. *The Guardian*. https://www.theguardian.com/world/2020/jun/09/china-warns-students-to-reconsider-travel-to-australia-for-study

Langmann, A., Fahrleitner-Pammer, A., Pieber, T. R., & Zollner-Schwetz, I. (2011). Women underrepresented on editorial boards of 60 major medical journals. *Gender Medicine*, 8(6), 378–87. https://doi.org/10.1016/j.genm.2011.10.007

Lansdown, S. (8 March 2022). Academics criticise Australian National University's decision to suspend ties with Russia. *Canberra Times*. https://www.canberratimes.com.au/story/7648439/academics-speak-out-against-anus-decision-to-suspend-ties-with-russia/

Lee, J. T. (2015). The regional dimension of education hubs: Leading and brokering geopolitics. *Higher Education Policy*, 28, 69–89. https://doi.org/10.1057/hep.2014.32

Lehmann, A. (10 August 2020). What we have lost: International education and public diplomacy. *The Interpreter*. https://www.lowyinstitute.org/the-interpreter/what-we-have-lost-international-education-and-public-diplomacy

Lo, W. (2020). A year of change for Hong Kong: From east-meets-west to east-clashes-with-west. *HE Research & Development*, 39(7), 1362–6. https://doi.org/10.1080/07294360.2020.1824210

Lowe, D. (2015). Australia's Colombo plans, old and new. *International Journal of Cultural Policy*, 21(4), 448–62. https://doi.org/10.1080/10286632.2015.1042468

Macfarlane, B. (2012). *Intellectual leadership in higher education: Renewing the role of the university professor*. Routledge.

Marginson, S. (2018). *The new geopolitics of higher education. Global co-operation, national competition and social inequality in the World Class University sector*. Centre for Global Higher Education.

National Archives of Australia (2022). *The Colombo Plan*. https://www.destinationaustralia.gov.au/stories/work-play/colombo-plan

Palmer, C. (2017). Help us restore trust in expertise. *The Conversation*. https://theconversation.com/help-us-restore-trust-in-experts-73059

Parliament of Australia (28 February 2022). Sanctions imposed on Russia in response to aggression against Ukraine – how are they imposed under Australia's sanctions laws? *Parliament of Australia*. https://www.aph.gov.au/About_Parliament/Parliamentary_Departments/Parliamentary_Library/FlagPost/2022/February/Sanctions_on_Russia

Prime Minister (20 March 2022). Additional support for Ukraine. https://www.pm.gov.au/media/additional-support-ukraine#:~:text=In%20response%2C%20Defence%20has%20developed,so%20far%20to%20%2491%20million

Putnins, T. (11 March 2022). Why universities need to open the lines of communication with Russians, not close them. *The Conversation*. https://theconversation.com/why-universities-need-to-open-the-lines-of-communication-with-russians-not-close-them-179080

Quiggin, J. (2021). Dismembering government: New public management and why the commonwealth can't do anything anymore. *The Monthly*. https://www.themonthly.com.au/issue/2021/september/1630418400/john-quiggin/dismembering-government#mtr

Rizvi, F. (2005). Rethinking 'brain drain' in the era of globalisation. *Asia Pacific Journal of Education*, 25(2), 175–92. https://doi.org/10.1080/02188790500337965

Rizvi, F. (2011). Student mobility and the shifting dynamics of internationalization. In D. Davis & B. Mackintosh (Eds), *Making a difference: Australian international education*. UNSW.

Ross, J. (2021). Pandemic research must prioritize human and political behaviour. *Times Higher Education*. https://www.timeshighereducation.com/cn/news/pandemic-research-must-prioritise-human-and-political-behaviour

Ross, J. (17 February 2022). Australia-China research collaboration nosedives. *Times Higher Education*. https://www.timeshighereducation.com/news/australia-china-research-collaboration-nosedives

Rowlands, J. (2011). Academic boards: Less intellectual and more academic capital in higher education governance? *Studies in Higher Education*, 38(9), 1274–89. https://doi.org/10.1080/03075079.2011.619655

Rowlands, J. (2019). The domestic labour of academic governance and the loss of academic voice. *Gender and Education*, 31(7), 793–810. https://doi.org/10.1080/09540253.2017.1324132

Shore, C., & Taitz, M. (2012). Who 'owns' the university? Institutional autonomy and academic freedom in an age of knowledge capitalism. *Globalization, Societies and Education*, 10(2), 201–19. https://doi.org/10.1080/14767724.2012.677707

Tran, L. T. (2020a). Teaching and engaging international students: People-to-people empathy and people-to-people connections. *Journal of International Students*, 10(3), xii–xvii. https://doi.org/10.32674/jis.v10i3.2005

Tran, L. T. (20 June 2020b). How to secure recovery of international student mobility. *University World News*. https://www.universityworldnews.com/post.php?story=20200620071618800

Tran, L. T. (20 August 2020c). Understanding the full value of international students. *University World News*. https://www.universityworldnews.com/post.php?story=20200820103708349

Tran, L. T., Nguyen, D. T. B., Blackmore, J., He, B., & Vu, H. Q. (2023). COVID-19, geopolitics and risk management: Towards framing a reciprocal, coordinated, responsive and empathetic international education sector. Policy Futures in Education, 14782103231163480.

Tran, L. T., & Nguyen, D.T.B. (2023). Global processes: Global trade in international education and the international education-migration nexus. In R. J. Tierney, F. Rizvi, & K. Erkican (Eds), *International Encyclopedia of Education* (Vol. 1, pp. 250–9). Elsevier.

Tran, L. T., & Rahimi, M. (2018). *New Colombo Plan: A review of research and implications for practice: Research Digest, No. 14*. International Education Association of Australia (IEAA). https://www.ieaa.org.au/documents/item/1448

Tran, L. T., & Vu, T. T. P. (2018). Beyond the 'normal' to the 'new possibles': Australian students' experiences in Asia and their roles in making connections with the region via the New Colombo Plan. *Higher Education Quarterly*, 72(3), 194–207. https://doi.org/10.1111/hequ.12166

Tran, L. T., Bui, H., & Nguyen, D. (2021). *National report: Australian student mobility to the Indo-Pacific region through the New Colombo Plan*. Deakin University.

Tran, L. T., Phan, H. L. T., & Bui, H. (2022). Geopolitics and internationalisation of higher education in Vietnam. In S. Marginson & X. Xu (Eds), *Changing higher education in East Asia* (pp. 165–84). Bloomsbury.

Walden, M., & Choahan, N. (27 July 2020). China is pushing its South China Sea claims during the coronavirus pandemic – this is what the tensions are about. *ABC News*. https://www.abc.net.au/news/2020-07-27/south-china-sea-what-tensions-with-us-australia-are-about/12492432?nw=0

Williams, J. (2016). *Academic freedom in the age of conformity: Confronting the fear of knowledge*. Palgrave Macmillan.

Woelert, P., & Yates, L. (2015). Too little and too much trust: Performance measurement in Australian HE. *Critical Studies in Education*, 56(2), 175–89. https://doi.org/10.1080/17508487.2014.943776

Zhang, M. Y. (6 July 2020). Students in China heed their government's warnings against studying in Australia – less than half plan to come back. *SBS News*. https://www.sbs.com.au/news/students-in-china-heed-their-government-s-warnings-against-studying-in-australia-less-than-half-plan-to-come-back

5

On the Abolition of Intellectual Leadership

Richard Hall

Introduction

The lived experiences of university labourers (students, professional services' staff and academics) in the institutions of the Global North are increasingly described and analysed as being precarious. Discussions of academics quitting, or *quit lit* (McKenzie, 2021), and 'the great resignation' from universities (Gewin, 2022), have unfolded against existing critiques of these institutions as places of ongoing risk and marginalization for some bodies and identities. Moreover, such critiques situate precarious existences against decades of marginalizing, material practices. For instance, sexual violence on campus has been examined in relation to silencing, secrecy, questioning credibility and denial (Mellgren & Ivert, 2019). Cultures of silencing and secrecy, underpinned by policies of using non-disclosure agreements (Weston, 2020) and shutting-down complaints (Ahmed, 2021), have exacerbated the peril felt by many inside these institutions.

Examinations of these experiences situate them against *both* institutional structures *and* the agency of those in leadership positions. Thus, there have been descriptions of the disconnect between academics and leaders (Erickson, Hanna & Walker, 2020); 'a macho agenda', in which narcissism, psychopathy and Machiavellian activity mix (Perry & Miller, 2017); the desire for new markets, cost-reduction and erecting capital-intensive infrastructure projects, and an obsessive focus upon performance metrics and league tables as a kind of fantasy sports league (Spooner, 2017); and the tolerance given to patriarchal, white and value-driven positions (Inge, 2022). Disconnections are also situated against cultures in which precarity has been normalized for certain groups as a colonial matrix of power (Mignolo & Walsh, 2018), through leadership that catalyses restructuring, the loss of tenure, performance management, workplace monitoring and workload intensification (Advance HE, 2021).

The structural precarity of working inside these institutions, described as anxiety machines (Hall & Bowles, 2016), demands constant adaptation and intensification. As a result of overwork and negative performance management, extreme levels of acute and chronic anxiety and depression in PhD students have been reported (Nature Editorial, 2019), alongside student and staff suicides (Parr, 2014). Constant adaptation and intensification require intellectual leadership that privileges particular worldviews and modes of knowledge production (Tuck, 2018). However, a richer unfolding of our understanding about how these institutions reproduce the world, based on specific matrices of power, runs into the brutal, political economic realities that shape higher education (HE) for-value. These realities are increasingly conditioned through culture wars that centre a dominant model of economic growth, based upon the common sense of meritocracy and work-based efficiencies, and in opposition to the legacies of the Rhodes Must Fall and Black Lives Matter movements (Hall, Gill & Gamsu, 2022).

Universities are situated as a site of struggle between: first, a dominant political economy that is pathological in the search for value-for-money, impact, excellence, entrepreneurship and efficiency; and, second, the humane values that make lives liveable. In this struggle, working lives in the University are shaped against pathological cultures, which are imminent to practices that have a methodological rhythm, imposed in relation to the desires of academic commodity production, hierarchical divisions of labour, intellectual property rights and the market (Hall, 2021). Those who govern, regulate and fund higher education demand the measurement, sorting and separation of individuals, disciplines, institutions and national sectors, based upon imposed norms. Measurement feeds into performance management that is designed to mitigate the risks to the productivity of the institution and its partner organizations, increasingly based upon particular techno-financial futures (Williamson & Komljenovic, 2023).

This chapter describes one tendril of these pathological cultures, in relation to the experiences of the notionally most privileged of all academic workers, the professor. It is acknowledged that *Professor* contains a multiplicity of entangled and complicated identities and meanings. Increasingly, there are pathways describing the work of professors as research and innovation, teaching and scholarship, or knowledge exchange and practice. There are also conflicts between professors in senior management roles and those leading within scholarly communities, networks and teams. Moreover, whilst the ideal of the professor may stand for some as the apogee of academic labour, it has also been described in relation to: struggles for representation for women (Varpio et al., 2021); increasing stress catalysing a lack of morale (Evans, 2018); invisibility and a lack of respect for professors who are Black, Indigenous and People of Colour (EagleWoman, 2022); and the negative cultures associated with accelerating performance pressures (Pace, D'Urso, Zappulla & Pace, 2021).

In this chapter, the argument is framed around a professorial ideal that stands at the intersection of intellectual leadership and precarious existence, experienced differentially. It is positioned in relation to an idealized view of the professor-as-leader in the formation of knowledge or in regimes of knowledge production. The context for this is England, with a specific governance, regulatory and funding regime for HE. Here, the professor is entangled: first, as the alleged epitome of academic privilege and position, with access to institutional resources; second, as a crucial, entrepreneurial, organizational node enabling institutional managers to reproduce particular forms of academic labour; third as a carrier of disciplinary and occupational values, often framed around authority/reliability and methodological validity; and fourth, as a precarious identity, shaped through competition and the need for self-exploitation inside what is described as the academic peloton.

In developing this focus upon self-exploitation, the second section of this chapter focuses upon the competitive, HE environment inside which the self-exploitation of the professor is incubated and reproduced. In the third, such reproduction is situated against the idea of the peloton, a term from professional cycling, in order to demonstrate how the entangled identities of these idealized knowledge workers are imminent to cultures of silence or *omertà*, and overwork. In the fourth section, this precarious, generalized, academic experience and its compulsive tendencies to over-perform are framed against the reproduction of hegemonic knowledge production for-value rather than authentic human knowing. Thus, the final section argues that this is a hopeless position, contending that intellectual leadership needs a new way of being, knowing and doing in the world, predicated upon the abolition of the professor-as-entrepreneurial-knowledge-producer. Crucially, without such abolition, intellectual work has no way of engaging meaningfully with intersecting crises. Such engagement, enriched through intergenerational, intercommunal and intersectional ways of knowing, pushes beyond the markets, private property, divisions of labour and commodities that enable the professor to flourish.

Competition and self-exploitation

The existence of professors in the University tends to be framed by competition. This is exacerbated because the University is a core node in the reproduction and expansion of economies in the Global North. Increasingly, the cultures and practices of these institutions are governed and regulated in relation to specific forms of transnational finance capital, which demands forms of new managerialism (Carchedi & Roberts, 2018). Crises of capitalism, revealed financially as austerity or epidemiologically through Covid-19, intersect and flow through lines of institutional fear about economic sustainability. In this, universities are folded into transnational responses to the permanent scarring caused to economies and societies by negative events, like the global financial crash of 2007/8. In the case of the financial crash, there has been an inability to re-establish stable systems of social reproduction through economic growth and rates of profitability through capital accumulation, in spite of ongoing austerity programmes and calls for increased productivity.

As economies tend not to be able to make up for lost value, and face a re-set, this questions the validity of business-as-usual for universities and enables policymakers to push for more efficiencies rather than public spending. In England and Wales, in response to the pandemic, sector leaders linked government-backed support to their commitment to 'reduce costs, increase efficiency and moderate certain behaviours to increase stability and sustainability' (Universities UK (UUK), 2020). The desire to recover demands new modes of performance within and across institutions, although it is important to note the differential rates of recovery amongst universities, predicated upon: the ability to draw down on reserves of financial capital or access relatively liquid assets; the level of exposure to high/strict debt or other fixed costs that need to be serviced; and the diversification of income streams. *In extremis*, those institutions with higher social and intellectual or cultural capital are demonstrably better able to leverage resources, in order to maintain position and compete.

In England, government policy and ministerial statements during the pandemic demanded that universities connect economic growth to personal opportunities, within a competitive structure 'designed to ensure those providers make changes that will enable them to make a strong contribution to the nation's future' (Department for Education, 2020, p. 3). Such socio-economic leadership is reinforced by short-term, regulatory consultations that are determined by performance data, efficiency and specific student outcomes (e.g. OfS, 2021). Within universities, this tends to worsen conditions of labour, reduce access to research and teaching resources, and intensify workloads, especially where competition is structured inside relations of collaboration (not liberatory cooperation) through which teamwork is enacted for private interest, predicated upon the production of commodities within hierarchical divisions of labour.

It is here that the idealized role of the professor-as-entrepreneurial-knowledge-producer noted above becomes fundamental, in looking to transform the forces and relations of production inside universities. This role demands excellence in research and innovation, teaching and scholarship, knowledge transfer and/or practice-based activity. It tends to demand alignment with University strategy, in order to generate demonstrable impact inside and outside the institution. For instance, national research assessments that serve as comparative judgements on performance, like the Research Excellence Framework in the UK, enable units of assessment across universities to be sorted and ranked based upon measurements of outputs, impact and environment. Here, measurable international outputs and success in grant capture (commensurable with the level of the role) are matched by the demand for innovative leadership and academic citizenship. International communication and dissemination also underpin the desire for knowledge transfer, spin-outs and commercialization, alongside policy impacts.[1]

These desires for intellectual leadership are reproduced through the drive to generate surpluses, and such drives widen the gap between intellectual life and the ability of collective, intellectual labour to solve capitalism's reproduction crises. Instead of such labour using its skills, ways of knowing and expertise to reveal new paths through intersecting emergencies, it finds itself compelled to respond in relation to processes like commodification, commercialization and knowledge transfer. The only way to respond appears to be by constantly renewing the productive powers of labour, for-value, through the mediations of the market, private property, commodity-exchange and the division of labour. This is shaped through a particular value-frame, which requires ongoing self-exploitation, and the demonstration of such through overwork, overproduction and the denigration of self-care as a collective activity.

For Marcuse (1974), such value-frames are imminent to: first, accepted behavioural norms and values, embodied in institutions, relationships, technologies and policies; and, second, performativity, locked into ideas of efficiency, value-for-money and competition. At this aggressive, acquisitive intersection, sit white, male, ableist modes of conditioning institutional structures, cultures and practices for-value. This is not to fetishize the construction of masculinity and femininity, rather to note that in the competitive University, performance takes on particular, capitalist identity-formation. As Marcuse

(1974, p. 282) argued, the alternative, 'socialism, as a *qualitatively* different society, must embody the *antithesis*, the definite negation of the aggressive and repressive needs and values of capitalism as a form of male-dominated culture'.

This is a competitive culture which reproduces progression around (self-) exploitation and (communal) expropriation and the ability to engage in 'the game of excellence', through which externally defined forms of measurement rooted in quantity act as proxies for quality (Butler & Spoelstra, 2020). Measurements are predicated upon the ability to overwork; place family, self and caregiving as secondary; access and leverage networks and resources; and reflect back to those doing the measuring what they are looking for. Increasingly, such reflections of an individual's essence are defined hegemonically, through institutional promotions pathways and criteria, and also national research excellence assessment regimes, through the professor who embodies racialized and patriarchal norms of behaviour, language, impact, excellence, entrepreneurship and performance. These norms unfold overwork and a lack of self-care across the class of University labourers, whose work is also recalibrated and measured against such recalibrations.

As a result, we witness fewer Black, female professors or leaders in HE (Rollock, 2019); Black, female and non-cisgender professors achieving lower citation levels (Odic & Wojcik, 2020); BIPOC women professors being discriminated against in the sciences (Prescod-Weinstein, 2021); discrimination against certain forms of knowledge produced from intersectional groups or the South as 'invisible colleges' (Walker & Boamah, 2019); and structures that militate against progression for mothers and caregivers (Amsler & Motta, 2017). Intellectual leadership is entangled with structures conditioned through settler-colonial practices, which reinforce racial-patriarchal cultures of academic work. This questions whether it is possible to transcend an unsustainable, precarious, crisis-ridden life. Or, as Davis et al. (2022) and Andreotti (2021) have noted, is this work of transcendence predicated upon abolishing or hospicing the competitive, self-exploitative world, as-is?

An important question is whether new and collective value-frames might emerge within individuals, including those with privilege like professors. This accepts the huge intersectional diversity in professorial lived experiences noted above. It also recognizes the concrete reality that these positions are explicitly embedded in relation to institutional and national competitive desires requiring intellectual leadership for-value and the generation of surpluses. Such desires tend to homogenize these lived experiences and place intellectual production in imminent relation to the illogic of competition in a prestige economy. In turn, this modulates University work around modes of leadership that are productive and generative of knowledge that can be commodified and exchanged, rather than for new ways of knowing the world. In this prestige economy intellectual leadership mirrors the dynamics of the *peloton* in professional cycling (Hall & Bowles, 2016; Hall, 2021), and its toxic cultures of self-harm, endless self-sacrifice and overwork.

The academic *peloton*

The metaphor of the *peloton*, a key structure within professional cycling, enables us to explore the cultures, structures and practices that attempt to shape the subjectivity of the professor, in relation to knowledge production for-value alone. This is a one-sided subjectivity, developed solely against economic value, rather than communal, humane values. The *peloton* is the collection of teams on the road at any point in a day or stage race, and depending on the racing conditions, weather, geography and strategic demands, those teams have to adapt tactics, including who is sacrificed to do specific jobs for the benefit of the whole team. This means that, for some, existence in the *peloton* is more precarious than others because of the demands made of them on a daily basis (Megoran & Mason, 2020).

In cycling, teams are constructed around: team leaders looking to win races or place on the podium; team managers and *Directeurs Sportifs* organizing teamwork to maximize returns; (*super*)*domestiques* who ride in the service of the team and its leader rather than their own success; specialists hunting for success, for instance, in sprints or one day events; and professional services like coaches, doctors, *soigneurs* and mechanics. In the University, they might be professors looking to win grants or place towards the top of excellence ratings; vice-chancellor's or Research Offices organizing to maximize returns; teaching and research staff who work in the service of the team and its leader, with their own success a by-product; early career researchers hunting for success, for instance, in tenure; and professional services' staff, like research and teaching administrators, librarians and technicians.

The culture of the *peloton*/HE sector, as the collection of competing teams, is reinforced by social forces and relations of production, as cycling teams/research groups/teaching units/universities compete against each other for scarce resources (such as wins, bonuses, impact and ratings). Crucially, such cultures, both across the *peloton* and the University, demand *omertà* or codes of silence as a means of maintaining control. This includes hiding, denying or individualizing anxiety over conditions of labour; the lack of transparency over decision making for reward, recognition and restructuring; and the quiet compulsion to accept overwork in the name of an allegedly, higher cause, like the student experience or societal impact (Jaffe, 2021).

In both fields, *omertà* normalizes the cognitive dissonance required to hold *both* social collaboration *and* pathological competition as organizing principles within and across teams. Collaboration binds teams together inside institutions because they are competing for scarce resources, like time and recognition. In generating shared disciplinary and problem-based contexts for future-funding and impact, this also binds together teams in cognate fields in different institutions. In spite of the potential for cooperation, externally imposed, quality and risk-based measures normalize the habitual compulsion to compete for private gain, and this drives hopelessness precisely because it prioritizes economic obligations over humanity (Lashuel, 2020). As such, the duality of collaborate/compete is represented in academia's imaginaries that inspire resilience/overwork, empowerment/inferiority, engagement/burnout and enlightenment/isolation.

Here, the leadership role of the professor in the University *peloton* is fundamental in pivoting these entanglements around an idealized historical and material form of intellectual life. Access to relative forms of privilege, status and resources rests upon the ongoing exploitation of a hierarchy with the professor at its apex. Emerging from particular measures, the valorization of intellectual life is grounded in impact, knowledge exchange/transfer, commercialization, public engagement and entrepreneurship, recalibrated around particular modes of performance. Such leadership, implicated in how the University generates power and prestige, casts professors as 'a specifically academic ideal' that is distinct from intellectual life in society (Bourdieu, 1988, p. 37).

The concrete existence of intellectual workers is grounded in the abstract and reified labour of professors, for whom fears of the transience and scarcity of power ensure that it is hoarded or defended, individually or inside research teams. This then amplifies and transmits anxiety throughout the academic *peloton* because its sustainability is calibrated against externally mediated and internally governed performance management. Outcomes of this include redundancies and restructuring, but also ill-being (Hall & Bowles, 2016), demands to overwork, or bullying and harassment (Goodboy, Martin, Mills & Clark-Gordon, 2022). These are then experienced differentially, in relation to positionality in *both* the academic environment *and* society.

For Marcuse (1969) this constrains the leadership potential of the professor around the dependency of the University on 'the financial and political goodwill of the community and of the government', which shapes its (non-)place 'in the larger struggle for change'. As the University stands for 'an ever more methodical creation of conformist needs and satisfactions', the result is 'mutilated, crippled and frustrated human existence' (Marcuse, 1969) shaped through divisions and separations. The measures that pivot around professorial performance become exclusive and contain a negative character for individuals who cannot attain the exclusivity they define. Yet, inside the *peloton*, the struggle remains for position, rather than for liberation from it, and this subsumes human being and knowing under the needs of capital for knowledge that can be commodified for-value. Thus, the intellectual leadership of the professor is reduced to the mediation of particular methodological impulses, for modes of hegemonic measurement, the development of a performative essence and the desire for objectified knowledge production.

Intellectual work as knowledge production

The collapse of intellectual work around measurements calibrated against ideals of excellence tends to work against meaningful solutions to the causes of a range of intersecting emergencies. These include those of political economy, environment and epidemiology. Instead, the focus for such work is upon short-term, symptomatic responses, predicated upon the production of commodified knowledge. As such, packets of disciplinary knowledge can be brought into relation with risk-management centred upon the defence of business-as-usual, with the aim of generating surpluses.

These packets or photons are shaped against the gravitational pull of knowledge production in the Global North, which is imminent to the reproduction of capitalism. Thus, the validity of knowledge work in generating a meaningful existence for intellectual workers *both* in the institution *and* in the world is reduced. As knowledge work is alienated and commodified, an explosion of negative metaphors about the University follows: zombie; hopeless; in ruins; psychotic; and so on (Hall, 2021). These metaphors and the concrete practices that characterize them cast a shadow over conceptions of leadership, such that it tends to be constructed around cultures and practices for the production of knowledge-as-commodity.

Here, the idealization of the professor points towards inauthentic desires, in the sense that they are only obliquely a reflection of a many-sided human essence, and are conditioned by institutional requirements for specific kinds of intellectual leadership that deliver surpluses. Within a system that demands the production of academic commodities, the roles and communities with which individuals identify situate the self as a partial, social being. This partial nature is reinforced through academic labour because the potential for solutions to socio-economic and socio-environmental emergencies (be they climate forcing, ocean acidification, a collapse in the nitrogen cycle, secular crises of capitalism or epidemiology) is reified as more efficient knowledge production, mediated in the market and reinforced through disciplinary divisions. Thus, social problems emerging from an interconnected web of practices and conditions of life remain hidden below the surface, under the fetish of impactful disciplinary control within an allegedly closed, capitalist system.

Intellectual leadership in the entrepreneurial, empowering or enabling University reinforces such fetishes by deliberately separating individuals from each other, and disciplines from meaningful scholarly activity in a historical and material totality. In working to shape outputs, impact and environments that can be monitored and sorted against externally mediated measures, this works to fragment teaching, research and scholarship into micro-subjects that can be credentialized and exchanged. Notwithstanding the differential experiences of those who work as professors, the overall motor of competition shapes intellectual leadership that reinforces bureaucratic control over University labour: by reproducing disciplinary separations and divisions of labour; through specific regimes of peer review; and in cultures of reward and recognition that reflect hegemonic types of performance judged as excellent.

In pushing beyond separations of self and other, Lukács (1968, p. 230) argued for the reintegration of disciplines, mindful of their historical and material contexts, in order to bring apparently independent systems of thought and practice into a comprehensive whole. Such independent, disciplinary systems are integral to the institutional privilege of the professor-as-expert, and are further witnessed in the various pathways for professorial appointments. In refusing this, leading as a process of reintegration demands that the categories of the social world be defined intersectionally, intercommunally and intergenerationally, rather than hegemonically and methodologically. Moreover, it demands a focus upon ways of knowing that lie beyond the commodity, in the communal facilitation of questioning and storytelling (Andreotti, 2021). Intellectual leadership for new ways of knowing cannot reduce the world to logical categories, impact or new knowledges, predicated inside a closed system of capitalist reproduction. Yet, this is an issue for competitive institutions because in them leadership is conditioned less by influencing and more by specific modes of managerial accountability, hierarchical performativity, mentoring and developing positional agency.

The denial of reintegration and the maintenance of disciplinary separations underpins the idealized roles of professors, reflected in the many and varied titles for chairs that exist inside HE institutions. This remains a sign of alienation and fetishisation of sub-disciplinary expertise, and reproduces an alienated subjectivity that is predicated upon the reproduction of singular disciplines and their particular methods and measures. In turn, this shapes a limited activity, *for-value* (Hall, 2018), and reinforces a limited development of skills, knowledge and capabilities in relation to the production of life. One outcome is that knowledge production methodologies tend to collapse understanding into the disciplinary positivism of outputs, impact and entrepreneurialism, validated from the Global North as world class (Sheehan, 2017). As a result, commodified knowledge production trumps socially useful ways of knowing the world in-flux.

Rather than fetishizing the role of experts over closed systems of knowledge production, there is a desperate need to focus collectively upon a new, socially useful unfolding of society (Nail, 2020). This is a refusal of evidence-based practice or the knowledge of facts, which cannot know reality unless situated against a historical, material totality, through a dynamic, dialectical relation (Sheehan, 2017). In response, this demands: first, that knowledge production, represented through the leadership of the professor, acknowledges its relation to ruling class ideology; and, second, that intellectual leaders reflect upon their existence and ways of knowing, being and doing, in relation to their mediations (Dunayevskaya, 1991).

A renewed, dialectical unfolding, or of knowing the world otherwise, catalyses reflection upon gendered and racialized knowledge production, the denial or co-option of indigenous practices, and of 'invisible colleges' as vehicles for survival-pending-revolution (Austin, 2013; Walker & Boamah, 2019). This uncovers how the privilege of knowledge production from institutions in the Global North excludes, marginalizes and erases, for instance, through the politics of citation, underrepresentation and ontological certainty. Thus, hegemonic positions are reproduced through constrained leadership cultures and practices, like capacity-building; role modelling and coaching; and performance management and evidence-based, peer review (Prescod-Weinstein, 2021). As a result, ideas of intellectual leadership in relation to the development of capabilities through trust-based relationships, accountability and positive impact, and influence and professional agency, are refracted contextually *in situ*. However, this stands in relation to the dominant, capitalist mode of social reproduction, which demands specific kinds of knowledge work.

There is a material history to this critique of the privilege of such knowledge and its professorial prophets. In discussing Milla Granson's night-school project in Kentucky, Hull and Smith (1982, p. xix) argue: 'The act of a black person teaching and sharing knowledge was viewed as naturally threatening to the power structure. The knowledge she conveyed had a politically and materially transforming function, that is, it empowers people to gain freedom.'

This is one of the reasons why Ahmed's (2006) cry for queering what is socially useful is important. It brings us back to the role of the professor, and the question of what types of intellectual leadership might contribute to revolutionary science, in order to address critical issues of social importance dialectically and from multiple perspectives. Or can such intellectual work merely contribute to the development of academic commodities (non-revolutionary science) by reinforcing hegemonic norms (Neary, 2020)?

It is important to remember that such norms emerge from settler-colonialism and racial-patriarchal disciplinary constructions (e.g. see Downs, 2021; Mbembe, 2017), which operate through logics of dispossession and displacement. These questions of revolutionary and non-revolutionary science require an alternative set of imaginaries located against-and-beyond the centres of knowledge production for-value and their settler-colonial and racial-patriarchal, intellectual leadership. Instead, they are predicated upon decolonizing the role of the professor, such that new, transgressive sensibilities might emerge (Darder, 2018). This returns us to a consideration of intellectual leadership as professorial privilege inside capitalist universities. Such a consideration also reveals an imminent potential for abolishing the pathological cultures and methodological practices that underpin such leadership, in order to unfold a more socially useful process of leading-as-knowing.

Conclusion: Leading through abolition and eldership

Bourdieu (1988, p. 19) is clear about the screwed-up nature of academic labour symbolized by the professor, who is complicit in being led by positional privilege to accept the 'effort to persevere in a social identity which they recognize as their own', in spite of its illusory reality. In part, this is reinforced because this positional privilege is predicated upon cultural capital, 'a subordinate form of capital' (Bourdieu, 1988, p. 36), even though there is more pressure for innovations in impact, commercialization and knowledge transfer, in order to generate commodity or money capital. Through these shifting pressures, Bourdieu (1988, p. 88) argues:

> By making visible strategies of domination and structures that render impossible and effective: it is no less evident that the powers conferred by mastery of the strategic positions which give control over the progress of the competitors will only have an effective impact on the new entrants ... On condition that they are willing to play the competitive game, and accept its objectives.

Thus, professorial privilege, accumulated over the deep time of the disciplinary life of the University, demands the reproduction of complicity throughout the academic *peloton*. In turn, this requires the annihilation of life through control of academic time, and is one strand of 'the great resignation'. Moreover, the internalized compulsion for impact, excellence, spillover, entrepreneurship and surplus has a solvent effect on academic autonomy, and recalibrates performance management both inside and outside the institution. Here, leadership pivots around accountability for the performance management of intellectual work, which is presented as a scientific reality and acts as a form of domination. This is a new form of academic subsumption (Hall & Bowles, 2016), through which such work is constantly recalibrated for-value. Academic existence is thereby implicated in the essence of the institution, which has a particular appearance or value-frame. This reinforces the idea that the University might be a family in which, if one only has faith, one might become 'consecrated academically' (Bourdieu, 1988, p. 155).

In articulating a struggle against the professor-led, academic *peloton*, which prioritizes singular forms of knowledge in the struggle for position, is it possible to generate intellectual liberation through authentic modes of knowing, doing and being at the level of society (Dunayevskaya, 2002)? Is it possible to struggle against institutionalized work that is increasingly shaped by heteronormative and colonial quantification? Might answers to these questions be influenced by communities struggling for decoloniality and indigeneity, as ways of engaging with global, social emergencies (Andreotti, 2021)? There are multiple other ways of knowing existence and essence, which are always at risk of being othered, co-opted and colonized, but that acknowledge people's rights to exist in relation to their material history. These tend not to recognize the validity of onto-epistemological matrices of power, reflected in coloniality (Fanon, 1961/2001), and instead provide multiple positions for critiques of normative modes of quantifying existence.

Beyond this, there are opportunities to uncover the worlds buried under imposed modes of methodological knowledge production, and to ask new questions that shape meaning-making, rather than fetishizing scientific, evidential truth (Yazzie Burkhart, 2004). A collective renewal of analysis, grounded in the tools of abolition as enabling an opening-out rather than a foreclosing or incarceration of ways of knowing, is an experimental journey through safety, accountability and healing. This points towards community accountability and transformative justice, in which understanding is generated compassionately at the level of society, rather than from within institutions calibrated around value production.

The truth of this is in the ability 'to make space for what we have not yet been able to imagine, but at the same time to amplify that the practice is grounded, every day, and already unfolding – now' (Davis, Dent, Meiners & Richie, 2022, p. 15). Abolition is a refusal of intellectual work reified inside professorial characteristics that seek to measure the world. Instead, abolition works towards 'being able to live a true humanism – the humanism made to the measure of the world' (Césaire, 1972/2000, p. 73). Inside increasingly precarious institutions, the potential for such a true humanism is constantly being subsumed under responses to crises of capitalist reproduction. In this, the idealized professorial role embodies the precarity demanded by a value frame that demands constant surplus.

In denying this true humanism, the idealized professor sits in dialectical relation to the 'constant revolutionising of production, uninterrupted disturbance of all social conditions, everlasting uncertainty and agitation' (Marx & Engels, 1848/2002, p. 13). Yet, in response, institutional performance management and re-engineering ensure that the material existence of those in the academic *peloton* 'with their train of ancient and venerable prejudices and opinions, are swept away', such that all intellectual workers are 'at last compelled to face with sober senses [their] real condition of life and [their] relations with [their] kind' (Marx & Engels, 1848/2002, p. 13). There is no escape from the gravitational pull of precarity inside capitalist institutions.

It is in this moment of precarious, material existence that the possibility for engaging with alternative ways of knowing self, other and the world, and of generating an essence that is beyond one-sided (as worker) might emerge. The hope of socially useful, intellectual work is that through the generalization of precarity and its toxic modes of anti-life, those with privilege look to question the stunted essence of their own status. We do not need a life or work inside institutions that are becoming more efficiently unsustainable. Rather than reproducing competition, commodification, division and private property, the hope of socially useful, intellectual work is that it opens out into the abolition of our false needs. This includes the anti-humanism of privileged knowledge production and its mediations.

A starting point is to question why we need the professor, and what dissolving professorial privilege into the fabric of society might enable us to do, to be and to become? In addressing the crises that make existence precarious, our desires must turn to the urgency and possibility of living otherwise (Andreotti, 2021), and how this might be reconstituted as a new beginning. In its abolition, intellectual leadership negates commodity production, the division of labour, private property and the market by letting go of a privileged existence. This is the starting point, less a formal *constituo libertatis* (Arendt, 1963), or a new beginning with a new constitution, and more a recognition of the potentiality of *preguntando caminamos*, or *asking, we walk* (Marcos, 2002). Through abolition, intellectual leadership dissolves into leading, guiding, storytelling, advising, in- and-through community. It takes the form of eldership that is able to help others with rites of passage, and to develop hindsight, insight and foresight, for the benefit of individuals and communities (Andreotti, 2021, p. 196).

The abolition of intellectual leadership is a world beyond competition, commodity-exchange and surpluses. Through reflexivity, alongside the ability to hold space for others to recognize their own and their community's needs, it recovers the idea that we make our own history and our own paths through collective dialogue, based upon where we find ourselves. Here, leading sees intellectual work as socially – and communally – constructed, as a process predicated upon: first, abolishing separation, for instance, between teacher and student; second, transcending roles, such that each individual articulates their intellectual capabilities as a social activity; and, third, on knowing rather than measurable knowledge. Through abolition, leading as a process of eldership celebrates wisdom that transcends intellectual leadership as a reified practice designed to solve or fix. As it constantly unfolds through knowing, empathising, holding, storytelling, questioning and healing, eldership is knowing how to show up for ourselves, others and ecosystems (Andreotti, 2021, p. 199). This is leading as a social process that is against-and-beyond the present state of things.

Note

1 Characteristics listed here are taken from an analysis of eleven professorial person specifications from institutions in Australia, Canada, Germany, Switzerland, the UK and United States. The roles are based in Aerospace, Digital Education, Education, Entrepreneurship, Health Systems, History of Architecture, Information Systems, Innovation, Media and Cultural Studies, Nursing, and Psychiatry.

References

Advance H. E. (2021). *Equality in higher education: Statistical report 2021*. https://www.advance-he.ac.uk/knowledge-hub/equality-higher-education-statistical-report-2021

Ahmed, S. (2006). *Queer phenomenology: Orientations, objects, others*. Duke University Press.

Ahmed, S. (2021). *Complaint!* Duke University Press.

Amsler, S., & Motta, S. (2017). The marketised university and the politics of motherhood. *Gender and Education*, 31(1), 82–99. https://doi.org/10.1080/09540253.2017.1296116

Andreotti, V. (2021). *Hospicing modernity: Facing humanity's wrongs and the implications for social activism*. North Atlantic Books.

Arendt, H. (1963). *On revolution*. Penguin.

Austin, D. (2013). *Fear of a Black nation: Race, sex, and security in sixties Montréal*. Between the Lines.

Bourdieu, P. (1988). *Homo Academicus* (P. Collier, Trans.) Polity Press.

Butler, N., & Spoelstra, S. (2020). Academics at play: Why the 'publication game' is more than a metaphor. *Management Learning*, 51(4), 414–30. https://doi.org/10.1177/1350507620917257

Carchedi, G., & Roberts, M. (2018). *A world in crisis: A global analysis of Marx's law of profitability*. Haymarket Books.

Césaire, A. (1972/2000). *Discourse on colonialism*. Monthly Review Press.

Darder, A. (2018). Decolonizing interpretive research: Subaltern sensibilities and the politics of voice. *Qualitative Research Journal*, 18(2), 94–104. https://doi.org/10.1108/QRJ-D-17-00056

Davis, A. J., Dent, G., Meiners, E. R., & Richie, B. E. (2022). *Abolition. Feminism. Now.* Hamish Hamilton.

Department for Education (DfE) (2020). *Higher education restructuring regime*. HMSO. https://www.gov.uk/government/publications/higher-education-restructuring-regime

Downs, J. (2021). *Maladies of empire: How colonialism, slavery, and war transformed medicine*. Harvard University Press.

Dunayevskaya, R. (1991). *Philosophy and revolution: From Hegel to Sartre, and from Marx to Mao*. Aakar Books.

Dunayevskaya, R. (2002). *The power of negativity: Selected writings on the dialectic in Hegel and Marx*. Lexington Books.

EagleWoman, A. (2022). Trailblazing and living a purposeful life in the law: A Dakota woman's reflections as a law professor. *Southwestern University Law Review*, 51(2), 227–39.

Erickson, M., Hanna, P., & Walker, C. (2020). The UK higher education senior management survey: A statactivist response to managerialist governance. *Studies in Higher Education*, 46(11), 2134–51. https://doi.org/10.1080/03075079.2020.1712693

Evans, L. (2018). *Professors as academic leaders: Expectations, enacted professionalism and evolving roles*. Bloomsbury.
Fanon, F. (1961/2001). *The wretched of the earth* (C. Farrington, Trans.) Penguin.
Gewin, V. (31 May 2022). Has the 'great resignation' hit academia? *Nature*, 616, 211–13. https://www.nature.com/articles/d41586-022-01512-6
Goodboy, A. K., Martin, M. M., Mills, C. B., & Clark-Gordon, C. V. (2022). Workplace bullying in academia: A conditional process model. *Management Communication Quarterly*, 36(4), 664–87. https://doi.org/10.1177/08933189221103625
Hall, R. (2018). *The alienated academic: The struggle for autonomy inside the university*. Palgrave Macmillan.
Hall, R. (2021). *The hopeless university: Intellectual work at the end of The End of History*. MayFly Books.
Hall R., & Bowles, K. (2016). Re-engineering higher education: The subsumption of academic labour and the exploitation of anxiety. *Workplace: A Journal for Academic Labor*, 28, 30–47. https://doi.org/10.14288/workplace.v0i28.186211
Hall, R., Gill, R., & Gamsu, S. (2022). 'Whiteness is an *immoral* choice': The idea of the University at the intersection of crises. *Higher Education: The International Journal of Higher Education Research*. https://doi.org/10.1007/s10734-022-00855-3
Hull, G. T., & Smith B. (1982). Introduction: The politics of Black women's studies. In G. T. Hull, P. Bell Scott, & B. Smith (Eds), *All the women are white, all the blacks are men, but some of us are brave: Black women's studies* (pp. xvii–xxxiv). The Feminist Press.
Inge, S. (6 June 2022). Manchester vice-president told to apologise over racism row. *Research Professional*. https://www.researchprofessionalnews.com/rr-news-uk-universities-2022-6-manchester-vice-president-told-to-apologise-over-racism-row/
Jaffe, S. (2021). *Work won't love you back: How devotion to our jobs keeps us exploited, exhausted and alone*. Hurst Publishers.
Lashuel, H. A. (2020). Mental health in academia: What about faculty? *eLife*, 9, e54551. https://doi.org/10.7554/eLife.54551
Lukács, G. (1968). *History and class consciousness*. Merlin Press.
Marcos, S. (2002). *Our word is our weapon: Selected writings*. Serpent's Tail.
Marcuse, H. (1969). An essay on liberation. *Marxists Internet Archive*. https://www.marxists.org/reference/archive/marcuse/works/1969/essay-liberation.htm
Marcuse, H. (1974). Marxism and feminism. *Women's Studies*, 2(3), 279–88.
Marx, K., & Engels, F. (1848/2002). *The Communist manifesto*. Penguin.
Mbembe, A. (2017). *Critique of Black reason* (L. Dubois, Trans.). Duke University Press.
McKenzie, L. (18 August 2021). Reading academic quit lit – How and why precarious scholars leave academia. *LSE Impact of the Social Sciences blog*. https://blogs.lse.ac.uk/impactofsocialsciences/2021/08/18/reading-academic-quit-lit-how-and-why-precarious-scholars-leave-academia/
Megoran, N., & Mason, O. (2020). Second class academic citizens: The dehumanising effects of casualisation in higher education. *UCU Report*. https://www.ucu.org.uk/media/10681/second_class_academic_citizens/pdf/secondclassacademiccitizens

Mellgren C., & Ivert, A.-K. (2019). Is women's fear of crime fear of sexual assault? A test of the shadow of sexual assault hypothesis in a sample of Swedish university students. *Violence against Women*, 25(5), 511–27. https://doi.org/10.1177/1077801218793226

Mignolo, W. D., & Walsh, C. E. (2018). *On decoloniality: Concepts, analytics, praxis.* Duke University Press.

Nail, T. (2020). *Marx in motion: A new materialist Marxism.* Oxford University Press.

Nature Editorial (13 November 2019). The mental health of PhD researchers demands urgent attention. *Nature.* https://www.nature.com/articles/d41586-019-03489-1

Neary, M. (2020). *Student as producer: How do revolutionary teachers teach?* Zero Books.

Odic, D., & Wojcik, E. H. (2020). The publication gender gap in psychology. *American Psychologist*, 75(1), 92–103. https://doi.org/10.1037/amp0000480

OfS. (2021). *Consultation on regulating quality and standards in higher education: Analysis of responses.* https://www.officeforstudents.org.uk/media/617ca48b-4a5b-4bf5-9154-50565d94c264/analysis-of-consultation-responses-final-for-web.pdf

Pace, F., D'Urso, G., Zappulla, C., & Pace, U. (2021). The relation between workload and personal well-being among university professors. *Current Psychology*, 40, 3417–24. https://doi.org/10.1007/s12144-019-00294-x

Parr, C. (3 December 2014). Imperial College Professor Stefan Grimm 'was given grant income target'. *Times Higher Education.* https://www.timeshighereducation.com/news/imperial-college-professor-stefan-grimm-was-given-grant-income-target/2017369.article

Perry, C., & Miller, C. (2017). Dysfunctional leadership in universities: Identifying and dealing with sociopaths. In D. Hall & G. Ogunmokun (Eds), *Management, leadership and marketing of universities and colleges of higher education* (pp. 70–96). Global Publishing House International.

Prescod-Weinstein, C. (2021). *The disordered cosmos: A journey into dark matter, spacetime, and dreams deferred.* Bold Type Books.

Rollock, N. (2019). *Staying power: The career experiences and strategies of UK Black female professors* [Project report]. Universities and Colleges Union. https://www.ucu.org.uk/media/10075/Staying-Power/pdf/UCU_Rollock_February_2019.pdf

Sheehan, H. (2017). *Marxism and the philosophy of science: A critical history: The first hundred years.* Verso.

Spooner, M. (2017). Qualitative research and global audit culture: The politics of productivity, accountability, and possibility. In N. Denzin & Y. Lincoln (Eds), *Sage handbook of qualitative research* (5th ed., pp. 894–914). Sage.

Tuck, E. (2018). *I do not want to haunt you but I will: Indigenous feminist theorizing on reluctant theories of change.* Faculty of Arts: University of Alberta.

Universities UK (UUK) (2020). *Achieving stability in the higher education sector following COVID-19.* UUK Policy and Analysis, Reports. https://universitiesuk.ac.uk/news/Documents/uuk_achieving-stability-higher-education-april-2020.pdf

Varpio, L., Harvey, E., Jaarsma, D., Dudek, N., Hay, M., Day, K., Bader Larsen, K., & Cleland, J. (2021). Attaining full professor: Women's and men's experiences in medical education. *Medical Education*, 55(5), 582–94. https://doi.org/10.1111/medu.14392

Walker, M. A., & Boamah, E. F. (2019). Making the invisible hyper-visible: Knowledge production and the gendered power nexus in critical urban studies. *Human Geography*, 12(2), 36–50. https://doi.org/10.1177/194277861901200203

Weston, M. A. (2020). Buying secrecy: Non-disclosure agreements, arbitration, and professional ethics in the #MeToo era. *Pepperdine University Legal Studies Research Paper*, 2020/5. http://dx.doi.org/10.2139/ssrn.3542590

Williamson, B., & Komljenovic, J. (2023). Investing in imagined digital futures: The techno-financial 'futuring' of edtech investors in higher education. *Critical Studies in Education*, 64(3), 234–49. https://doi.org/10.1080/17508487.2022.2081587

Yazzie Burkhart, D. (2004). What Coyote and Thales can teach us: An outline of American Indian epistemology. In A. Waters (Ed.), *American Indian thought: Philosophical essays* (pp. 15–26). Blackwell Publishing.

6

Irish Academia: Nirvana for Gender Equality and Female Leadership?

Pat O'Connor

Introduction

The academy is one of the most enduring institutions and has a taken-for-granted institutional legitimacy (Meyer, Ramirez, Frank & Schoffer, 2007). However, beyond saying that universities are concerned with knowledge (its creation, use, application, credentialization and conservation), it is impossible to adequately describe what their purpose is (O'Connor, 2014). This lack of clarity has enabled them to become part of wider social projects which have legitimated their activities, provided funding for them and influenced the profile of their leadership positions. These wider projects to date have been little concerned with gender equality. Thus, for example, traditionally universities were concerned with the education of a (white) male elite and this influenced the profile of their leaders. There has been a reluctance by such leaders to reflect on their position of privilege as elite (white) men so as 'to fully comprehend how they are perceived and how they represent particular forms of leadership that may "other" some forms of masculinity, most forms of femininity and indigenous ways of being and leading' (Blackmore, 2013, p. 147; see also Hearn, 2021).

Across the EU positional power is currently overwhelmingly held by men in universities. The most obvious locus of such power is the president/rector/vice chancellor position, although full professorial positions may also be a locus – not least because they are frequently underpinned by positional resources. Those who hold such positions can be seen as intellectual leaders because they have the possibility of re-envisioning higher education and/or its disciplines. The Covid-19 pandemic was a global crisis that impacted on all aspects of life. Leadership in this kind of 'glass cliff' situation (Ryan, 2022; Ryan & Haslam,

2007) has been seen as 'risky, precarious and even doomed to failure'. Women may access positions of leadership in these challenging contexts, but the extent to which they can transform higher education (HE) is questionable, even if they wish to do this.

Neoliberalist managerialism is overwhelmingly endorsed by higher educational institutions (HEIs) in Western society and it is highly unlikely that men or women who gain access to leadership positions in them will be opposed to it. In such contexts those holding positional power may 'continue to see their role as implementers rather than leaders ... focused less on change and more on doing the same tasks more efficiently, effectively or accountably' (Power, 2021, p. 144). Furthermore, even when the proportion of women in leadership positions increases, those women may be chosen from the same class and cultural backgrounds as their male counterparts (Carvalho & Machado-Taylor, 2017), so that the only change may be a symbolic one.

This chapter is concerned with exploring the transformation of the gender profile of some senior positions in Irish universities. It is located in the context of recent work on critical leadership studies which include a focus on power (Collinson, 2019) and feminist institutionalism (Krook & Mackay, 2011; Mackay, Kenny & Chappell, 2010). The evidence base used is scholarship based on academic texts, policy documents and biographical data from HEI websites. Core concepts will first be discussed, followed by a description of the national context and the characteristics of those accessing academic leadership positions, and finally conclusions will be drawn.

Leadership, neoliberalism and glass cliffs

Leadership in general, and intellectual leadership in particular, has been defined as a process of influence (Gunter, 2010). Leadership involves the articulation of values, and of a related strategic vision, with a willingness to identify priorities and to take action to reflect these, often in complex situations. Although, at one level, everyone knows what leadership is, at another level, its content is so unclear that it has been suggested that it is necessary: 'to take seriously the possibility of the non-existence of leadership as a distinct phenomenon' (Alvesson & Sveningsson, 2003, p. 359), with Blackmore (2013, p. 140) arguing that 'leadership is discursively overworked and theoretically underdone in policy and in much of the literature'. The role of academic leaders with positional power in enacting leadership in crisis situations initially involves shaping the construction of reality, so that change is defined as necessary, articulating the vision and identifying and legitimating the subsequent processes, procedures and allocation of resources in these difficult and challenging situations.

Frequently leadership is presented in unambiguously positive terms so that it 'fits nicely into a culture of grandiosity' (Alvesson, 2019, p. 27). Heroic ideas about leadership behaviour, styles and characteristics break down when those in leadership positions in HE are asked to describe what they actually do. Behaviour such as listening, which might be seen as quite unremarkable (or even typically female) if it was done by non-leaders, becomes transformed when it was enacted by those with positional power. Critical leadership studies suggest that the crucial element is not the characteristics, style nor behaviour of the leader, but their power.

With a small number of exceptions (e.g. Collinson, 2019; Lumby, 2019; O'Connor et al., 2019) little recent attention has been paid to the relationship between leadership and power. For Alvesson and Sveningsson (2003, p. 365) in an organizational context, leadership 'has something to do with asymmetrical relationships, influencing processes, and where people in some kind of formal dependency relationships are targeted'. Thus, in their construction of leadership an implicit link is made to positional power. Those who occupy such positions typically have material and organizational resources and an ability to use them to shape reality, to set agendas, to effectively obscure certain options and to create structures which purport to be decision making but which lack any real power. They can also create a culture that endorses legitimating discourses (around individual excellence, choice, 'nature' and gender neutrality: O'Connor & White, 2021b) which justify the status quo. Finally, they can offer inducements and positions to those who support their agendas: in other words, they can exert stealth power (O'Connor et al., 2019; Webb, 2008, p. 127).

Some form of neoliberal managerialism has become a taken-for-granted reality in most Western HE systems (Deem, Hillyard & Reed, 2007; Lynch, Gummell & Devine, 2012). Neoliberalism is defined as a political ideology that favours market deregulation, reduction in government spending and performativity as reflected in a focus on key performance indicators. Lynch (2014, p. 1) suggested that 'New Managerialism represents the organisational arm of neoliberalism' with Shepherd (2018, p. 1668) recognizing that managerialism remains 'a slippery and under-theorized concept'. Under managerialism there is an intensification of the 'pace, intensity and moral legitimacy' of the marketization and commodification of HE, with global league tables indicating that market values have been incorporated into the sector (Lynch, 2006, p. 6). Global rankings have become part of a new mode of market governance (Lynch, 2015). STEM disciplines in particular are seen as having market value (Lynch, 2006). Thus, the focus is on 'the quantifiable use value of knowledge', particularly research which is 'metricized, audited' and used in global rankings (Morley, 2016, p. 29) on the assumption that these are objective and gender-neutral (Felt, 2016; Morley, 2016). This meritocratic myth is still the taken-for-granted norm in STEM, although it has begun to be challenged (Campbell, 2018; Nielsen, 2016; O'Connor & Barnard, 2021; Van den Brink & Benschop, 2012). The prioritization of peer-reviewed journal articles in a neoliberal managerialist context (Lynch, 2006) devalues and potentially undermines the role of academics as public intellectuals: i.e. transforming private troubles into public issues (Wright Mills, 1970). Paradoxically those who are inside the academy may be so consumed by attempts to make marginal changes there that they have little energy to tackle broader social issues (Gallagher, 2012).

Neoliberalist managerialism in HE is also characterized by a centralization of power in the rector/president/vice chancellor (Blackmore, 2014; Lynch, Gummell & Devine, 2012; O'Connor et al., 2019). Ryan & Haslam (2007) put forward the concept of the 'glass cliff' (i.e. where women or members of a minority group ascend to a leadership position in challenging circumstances where the risk of failure is high). Even before the pandemic, only 22 per cent of senior leaders in Irish HE thought that institutional management capability was appropriate to meet the challenges and responsibilities facing HE (BH Associates, 2019; see also O'Connor, 2020b). During the Covid-19 pandemic the demands on those in senior leadership positions increased exponentially as teaching moved online overnight, with 'normal' revenue streams (such as international education, student accommodation and conference activities) totally disrupted and responsibility for the health of students and staff increasing dramatically.

The pandemic has been depicted as heightening the links between society and HE. In Ireland, in practice, research in a narrow range of medical and biological sciences was valorized (Hazelkorn, 2021), supplemented by non-specialist civic engagement by other staff (Gallagher & Munck, 2021) – activities that are often gender-stereotyped and unlikely to lead to career progression. International research (Andersen, Nielsen, Simone, Lewiss & Jagsi, 2022; Finkel, 2020; Matthews, 2020; NASEM, 2020) highlighted the impact of Covid on women's research output in a context where globally they were bearing the brunt of home schooling and other caring responsibilities.

National context

The Irish university system has been undergoing a period of rapid and substantial change. A new Department of Further and Higher Education, Research, Innovation and Science was established in August 2020, with a full minister. Legislation is in train to increase the regulatory power of the Higher Education Authority which provides oversight, funding, policy advice and implementation. The state has focused on continuing/initiating developments, almost regardless of the consequences of the pandemic for academic staff.

Thus, for example, the creation of new Technological Universities (TUs), formed by combining at least two existing Institutes of Technology (IOTs), has continued apace. The first of these emerged in 2019 (before the pandemic), and by 2022, there were five of them. The new TUs are seen as different from the existing universities in that they 'will address the social and economic needs of their region and will engage in industry-focused research ... [and a] focus on science and technology programmes that are vocationally and professionally oriented' (HEA, 2022a). There was mission drift among the IOTs, reflected in the development of programmes at PhD level (BH Associates, 2019) and it is not clear if this or the decline in staff numbers (O'Connor, 2022) will be reversed in the multi-campus TUs.

In Ireland the Protection of Employees (Fixed-Term Work) Act 2003 implemented the EU Directive (99/70/EC), which states that an employee who has contract(s) totalling more than four years is entitled to a contract of indefinite duration (CID). Following the recommendation of the Cush report (2016), this was shortened to two years for academic positions, although specific purpose, fixed-term contracts are used to avoid giving CIDs. The State Employment Control Framework during the economic recession limited the number of permanent staff that could be employed by each university: a cause of considerable irritation to the sector (BH Associates, 2019).

The Covid pandemic which started in March 2020 occurred in a context that was already under serious pressure because of under-resourcing, at least partly reflecting the 2008–11 economic crisis, and the very substantial increase in student enrolment (mirroring, in part, the unavailability of jobs) during that period. Thus, whereas in 2010, 200,000 students attended HE in Ireland, by 2020, 245,000 had enrolled in publicly funded HE (DFHERIS, 2022a) – an increase of more than a fifth. Despite this increasing demand, from 2008 to 2015, public funding to HE decreased from €1.4 billion to €923 million (DFHERIS, 2022b) – a decrease of roughly one-third. The cumulative effect of this increase in numbers and decrease in public funding was partly offset by increases in the student contribution, by international recruitment and commercial activities. However, there was an impact on staff/student ratios. Thus, whereas the 2018 Eurostat figures (excluding Ireland) showed an average academic staff student ratio of 15.3:1, the HEA figures showed that the Irish figure was 19:1 (DFHERIS, 2022b).

In theory, fees are not paid by full-time students, but a student contribution (of E2,000 pa, November 2023: effectively a fee) has been levied on them. A recent major policy document on the funding of HE (DFHERIS, 2022b) rejected the UK solution of loans to students. That document includes only one glancing reference to Covid, around reskilling those who lost employment due to it (DFHERIS, 2022b, p. 18) – thus implicitly depicting HEs as the solution, rather than focusing on the impact of Covid on them. Thus, in Ireland the state's role is seen as involving control and accountability, with the HE leaders being expected to deal with Covid.

The requirement to move lectures online with immediate effect in 2020 posed considerable challenges to Irish academic staff who identified concerns about this and about the impact of Covid on research productivity and culture, exacerbated by managerialism and the impact of the 2008 economic crisis (Shankar et al., 2021). There were additional difficulties for women since many of them were simultaneously juggling paid work with caring responsibilities and home schooling (Copeland, 2021). The Irish government's decision to close all schools for an extended period starting in March 2020 (combined with, in the first phase, the 'cocooning' (i.e. the effective imprisonment) of the over seventies who as grandparents might have helped with child care) created high levels of exhaustion among mothers who were the main home schoolers, particularly if they were in paid work, parenting alone or had multiple children (Flynn et al., 2021).

A €168 million funding package was provided by the state to help meet the additional costs to HE associated with Covid-19 (DFHERIS, 2020). Almost a quarter of this (€48m) was to deal with the disruption caused to research students and contract researchers because of inability to access labs/facilities, subjects, archives, etc. (Copeland, 2021). Other funds were directed at increasing HEIs' ability to deliver lectures online (€34m); to provide personal protective equipment for limited face-to-face teaching (€14m); to facilitate student access to laptops (€15m); to improve students' financial and mental well-being; for disability (€19m) – with a further 1.2m being allocated for research. No funding was provided by DFHERIS to reduce the workloads of those with expanded caregiving demands, e.g. reducing their pastoral care and course administration responsibilities, activities for which women are stereotypically assumed to be suited but which are not typically seen as important for promotion. Neither was there even any exhortation to HEIs to reallocate such work among their academic staff in the interests of maintaining progress towards gender equality.

The closing down of international travel and the impact of Covid on commercial activities (including student accommodation) had implications for the funding of HE – although since only 10 per cent of the Irish student body consisted of international students (Cox, 2020), this was less of a problem than in other countries such as the UK or Australia (Copeland, 2021). Furthermore, in the Irish situation the financial impact of the loss of international students was offset by an increased intake of national students because of an attempt to ameliorate the impact of grade inflation consequent on the abandonment of the written Leaving Certificate examination because of Covid and political pressure (previously, students with extremely high scores could still be denied access to university because of shortage of places). Thus, in the Irish HE system the issue of Covid-related academic staff job losses simply did not arise.

Women and positional leadership in HEIs

The academy in most countries is a masculinist institution, where the structures, criteria, procedures and processes are created by men for men: 'academia remains predominantly a site of men's power, privilege and mutual support' (Hearn, 2021, p. 101). Some women seek or accept formal leadership positions 'out of a sense of duty to their gender', trying 'to make a difference – as managers and as women' (Peterson, 2016, pp. 123 and 122, respectively; see also O'Connor, 2015). Others seek such positions in the hope that they can influence the long-term strategic plans in their organizations; improve women's position in academia and challenge its masculinist structure and culture. Yet others see any involvement in formal leadership positions as essentially collusion with an exploitative and misogynistic structure (Blackmore, 2014; Harford, 2018; Morley, 2014).

Up to 2020, no woman had ever headed up a public university in Ireland. Across the EU, women make up 18 per cent of those at rector/president/vice-chancellor level in universities and just under 24 per cent of the heads of all HEIs (EC, 2021). Similar patterns exist outside the EU. Women constitute 34 per cent of those in these positions in universities in the United States; 24 per cent in Australia; 17 per cent in India and 15 per cent in South Africa (O'Connor and

White, 2021a). Sweden and New Zealand are notable exceptions: with roughly half of those in these positions being women there – illustrating the importance of context.

The patterns are broadly similar in the case of those in full professorial positions. Across the EU, women are less likely than their male counterparts to be in these positions, comprising 26 per cent of those in the equivalent of full professor (Grade A: EC, 2021), despite making up 47 per cent of academic staff in starter positions (Grade C) and 40 per cent in mid-level ones (Grade B). These patterns are not peculiar to the EU. Thus, women make up 34 per cent of full professors in the United States; 30 per cent in Australia; 24 per cent in India and 28 per cent in South Africa (see O'Connor & White, 2021a). In Ireland, the proportion of women in such positions is 31 per cent (HEA, 2023).

The European Union through its funding of research and broader policy support has relentlessly promoted gender equality over the past twenty years (Rosa, Drew & Canavan, 2021). Even it, however, has recognized that 'progress has been particularly slow and insufficient in the area of gender equality in leadership positions' (EC, 2021, p. 176). Pressure for change in this area has also come from international organizations such as the OECD (OECD, 2012) and the United Nations, through its identification of gender equality among its Sustainable Development Goals (UN, 2021). THE Impact Ranking (THE, 2021) measures university performances against these goals. This is useful in moving forward a gender equality agenda in a performativity, image-driven context, although only just over 15 per cent of the marks for Goal 5 (Gender Equality) measure the proportion of senior leadership positions held by women, with no reference to targets or quotas.

For women in HEIs who want to access positional leadership there are three interrelated cultural and structural hurdles to overcome: that of gender, organizational location and discipline. In terms of gender, men overwhelmingly occupy positions of power in academia, reflecting and reinforcing male stereotypes as regards leadership (Fitzgerald, 2018, 2021; Schein, Mueller, Lituchy & Liu, 1996), with the construction of leadership and its enactment being male dominated and masculinist (Blackmore, 2014; O'Connor, 2020a). Secondly, women are disproportionately located at the lower levels of the organizational hierarchy, frequently in career cul-de-sacs, undertaking low-profile 'housekeeping' activities (such as teaching, pastoral work and undergraduate course administration: Lynch, 2006). In a neoliberal perspective these activities are not seen as of strategic importance or as areas from which 'next level' people are selected. Thirdly, with the possible exception of medicine, many women are coming from devalued disciplinary knowledge bases (Becher & Trowler, 2001) such as languages, education and nursing (as compared with engineering, mathematics or information communications technology). The latter male-dominated disciplines are not only more highly valued but are also (paradoxically) seen as 'naturally' leading to leadership positions, despite being less likely to involve people-oriented interactions. Other factors which reduce women's chances of accessing such positions include the valorization of geographical mobility; risk avoidance, which impacts on candidates who are more diverse, and the homosociability of the predominantly male vice chancellors/rectors/presidents (who identify with, favour and sponsor other men: Parsons & O'Connor, 2023; Shepherd, 2017).

These studies (which reflect work done pre-pandemic) suggest that women's under-representation in positional leadership can be described as 'choices' only in the context of a very narrow and decontextualized definition of the concept of choice (Linková, Atay & Zulu, 2021).

The gender profile of academic leaders in Irish higher education

The transformation of the gender profile of the presidents/rectors of Irish universities has been much more extensive and sudden than the change in the gender profile of the professoriate.

From the sixteenth century up to 2020, no woman had ever headed up an Irish public university. Women head up eight of the now thirteen public universities (including the Royal College of Surgeons). To some extent at least this can be seen as reflecting a 'glass cliff phenomenon', i.e. women's access to these positions increasing dramatically during the Covid pandemic – an extremely difficult period for all of society, including the universities. Indeed, two of the male presidents/rectors of the then seven universities retired three years into their ten-year appointment during Covid, with a third man retiring two years before the end of his term.

Shepherd (2017) found that while men and women were equally likely to have applied for a pro-vice chancellor position in their own institution, men were more than twice as likely to have applied for such a position in another institution. There is no data available on applications for president/rector positions in Irish HEIs. However, four of the original seven universities are now headed by women – including the oldest, most highly ranked and most prestigious university – Trinity College Dublin, in addition to University College Dublin, the largest university, and two of the younger universities (University of Limerick and Maynooth University). Three of the five TUs (Munster Technological University, Atlantic Technological University and South East Technological University) are also headed by women, despite the expected dominance of male-dominated STEM disciplines in these HEIs. (There had been occasional women in these positions in the IOTs prior to this – a pattern that arguably reflected their lower status: EC, 2021.) In the Royal College of Surgeons these appointments are only for two years (and under a very different system) and hence they are excluded from the subsequent discussion.

Prior to the onset of the Covid crisis in 2020, universities had received a strong message that the predominantly male profile of their management and governance structures needed to change, consequent on, among other things, the setting up of the Expert Group (HEA, 2016) which recommended linking core funding to the gender profile of senior positions and the adoption of the Athena SWAN award system, with the recommended linking of research funding to the institutional achievement of such awards (O'Connor & Irvine, 2020). To varying degrees this had begun to happen before the onset of Covid (O'Connor, 2020b).

Feminist positional leadership can enhance the profile of the HE institution (Pereira, 2012). However, when leadership is female rather than feminist there is likely to be little substantive change, although it may be symbolically important. It is impossible to assess the feminist orientations of the seven female university presidents who took up their positions in Irish universities during the period 2020–23. Four of these seven women have had no formative higher educational experiences here (i.e. doing neither their undergraduate or postgraduate degrees here): the presidents of Maynooth, University of Limerick, Munster Technological University and South East Technological University.

The disciplinary backgrounds of five of the seven women are in the Science, Technology, Engineering and Mathematics areas (i.e. engineering, pharmacology, bio-chemistry/mineralization, mathematical physics/computer science). These are seen as higher status and predominantly male academic staff disciplines. The two exceptions here are the President of the University of Limerick from humanities and the President of Maynooth from linguistics and psychology. Both of these were born outside Ireland and are presidents of relatively new universities (but not TUs).

Four of the seven female presidents had held management positions in the institution that they subsequently headed: in Trinity College Dublin as Dean of Research; in University College Dublin as Vice-President for Research, Innovation and Impact; University of Limerick as Vice President Academic Affairs; Athlone Technological Institution as President of the IOT that it subsumed (GMIT). In two other cases their appointment as president was their first contact with the Irish HE system: the President of Maynooth was born in Finland and was previously Vice Chancellor and President of Murdock University in Perth; while the President of the Munster Technological Institute was born in the UK and prior to her appointment was a faculty Dean in Stirling. The seventh was Bursar and Director of Strategic Innovation in Trinity College Dublin prior to her appointment as President of the South East Technological University.

As a group the dominant pattern of their appointments reflects an implicit devaluing of Irish HE and particularly of non-STEM areas as a source for the recruitment of potential presidents – a valuing of exclusively non-Irish formative educational experiences for women and of STEM, with variation existing in their prior appointments.

There is less publicly available information on the backgrounds of their five male counterparts. None of them had all their formative higher educational experiences outside Ireland, a pattern that contrasts with their female counterparts. The educational backgrounds of three of the five were in STEM – a less extreme pattern than their female counterparts while still reflecting the current valorization of these disciplines.

In contrast to the pattern at presidential level, the proportion of women in the professoriate in Irish HE has increased slowly but steadily since 2013 (from 19 per cent in 2013–15 to 31 per cent in 2022) – i.e. an average of 1–2 per cent per year (HEA, 2016, 2023). The Senior Academic Leadership Initiative (HEA, 2019a) involving the creation of forty-five new and additional senior academic posts over a three-year period, in areas where women are under-represented, reflects a recognition by the state that gender inequality existed in Irish HEIs and that it required a targeted initiative to address it.

Over the period 2018–20 inclusive, women made up just under 29 per cent (598/2,098) of the applicants for full professorships and 46 per cent (58/125) of the appointments (HEA, 2019b, 2021). Woods (2022) noted that the number of professors had risen from 532 in 2015 to 642 in 2020 inclusive (female professors by 69, from 109 to 178; male professors by 41, from 423 to 464: inclusive). Thus, women made up 63 per cent of the 110 additional professors in the system: implicitly suggesting that the proportion of female professors was related to increases in the total number of professors. This was also implicitly suggested by the fact that men's average 'chances' (in contrast to women's) of accessing a professorship in universities in Ireland varied little over time, or between universities (O'Connor, 2020b).

Based on data relating to the recruitment of permanent associate and full professors over a ten-year period in Norway (2007–17), Moratti (2021) found that women were not more reluctant than men to apply, nor were they deterred by the prospect of re-locating. However, there was an external candidate penalty for women there. This may reflect the greater tendency for men to be seen as exceptional – a pattern that was documented in the Netherlands (Van den Brink & Benschop, 2012) and that was evident in US experimental studies (Moss-Racusin, Dovidio, Brescoll, Graham & Handelsman, 2012). It is arguable that similar processes might operate in Ireland. Moratti (2021, p. 927) also suggested that in Norway an internal bonus for women candidates existed and could not simply be attributed to inbreeding but that it reflected 'the current tension between the intensified emphasis on internationalization and external hiring on the one hand, and the equally pressing need to keep departments running with their daily tasks (particularly teaching) on the other'. Thus, 'inhouse' women, even at professorial level, were hired there to do the more mundane, low-profile, less prestigious departmental 'housekeeping' activities. The opposite situation appears to exist in Ireland insofar as promotion although more popular among the women, appeared to be much less women-friendly than open recruitment. Thus, women made up 53 per cent of the applicants for promotion (57/108) and 46 per cent of the appointments (19/41), whereas in open recruitment women made up 27 per cent of the applicants (541/1,990) but 46 per cent of the appointments (39/84) (HEA, 2021). This might reflect variation in the nature of these procedures, the composition of the boards or their chairs. However, given the patterns as regards presidents/rectors, it seems possible to suggest that, unlike Norway, an internal candidate bonus did not for the most part exist for women. National data is not available on this.

Academic women's experiences in HE are frequently fraught (Fitzgerald, 2021; O'Connor, 2015) with subtle informal interactions being used to marginalize and 'other' them. They are typically exposed to a culture which is hierarchical and adversarial, one where male solidarity is reflected in differential gendered access to those with positional power, in 'side deals' favouring men and sponsorship between senior and junior men (O'Connor et al., 2021). Women's performance in leadership roles is more likely than their male counterparts to be negatively evaluated (Fitzgerald, 2018, 2021). Women's materiality, reflected in their physically embodied appearance, is also problematic, as is maternity leave and their culturally constructed caring subjectivities (Lynch, Gummell & Devine, 2012; Sinclair, 2013). Women are also more likely to experience gender-based violence including micro-aggressions and micropolitics (Bondestam & Lundqvuist, 2020; MacNeela et al., 2022; Morley, 1999; Naezer, van den Brink & Benschop, 2019; O'Connor et al., 2021). These are essentially power-related practices and can include devaluation, condescension, disparagement, threats, invisibility, ridiculing, withholding information, scientific sabotage and 'doubt raisers' (i.e. questioning of their intellectual independence and achievements: Ahlqvist et al., 2013), as well as sexual harassment.

Thus, even if women do access positional leadership, they may only remain for a short period. There is no national data available on this in Irish HEIs.

Conclusions and speculations

The sudden and dramatic increase in the proportion of women in presidential/rector positions in Irish universities (from zero to more than half between 2020 and 2023) can be seen as (at least in part) a response to the 'glass cliff' presented by the Covid-19 pandemic. The increase in the proportion of women at full professorial level has been much slower and has occurred over a longer period of time. It seems likely that it reflects less the 'glass cliff' phenomenon and more the pressures towards gender equality within the Irish HE system since 2014, as well as increases in the number of professorial positions.

Although the state has publicly celebrated the change in the gender profile of the university presidents, it has made little attempt to ameliorate the gendered consequences of Covid for academic staff, or even to encourage universities to tackle this in a context where the structural and cultural tendencies towards the normalization of neoliberal managerialism have continued.

The trends emerging as regards the differential gendered patterns in promotion and open recruitment to full professorship could be seen as suggesting that internal female candidates are less likely to be valued than external ones. This is also implicitly suggested by the characteristics of the female presidents, the majority of whom were born outside Ireland, with their own formative higher educational experiences entirely outside Ireland (patterns that contrast with their male counterparts). This implicitly suggests a disruption of the kind of sponsorship relationships which have facilitated the reproduction of the status quo. It also raises questions about the culture in the universities, and the extent to which women in senior positions will be able to transform it. The fact that the majority of the female presidents (like their male counterparts) are from a STEM background is a further indication of the kind of intellectual leadership that is expected of them. However since senior women are under-represented in STEM, the sustainability of this change in gender representation is problematic.

Thus, despite the changes in gender representation in senior positions in Irish public universities, it seems far too optimistic to see them as nirvana for gender equality and female leadership.

References

Ahlqvist, V., Andersson, J., Hahn Berg, C., Kolm, C., Söderqvist, L., & Tumpane, J. (2013). *Observations on gender equality in a selection of the Swedish Research Council's evaluation panels*. Vetenskapsrådet. https://www.vr.se/nyheterpress/nyheter2013/jamstalldhetsobservationerietturvalavvetenskapsradetsberedningsgrupper2012.5.7e727b6e141e9ed702b2b90.html

Alvesson, M. (2019). Waiting for Godot: Eight major problems in the odd field of leadership studies. *Leadership*, 15(1), 27–43. https://doi.org/10.1177/1742715017736707

Alvesson, M., & Sveningsson, S. (2003). The great disappearing act: Difficulties in doing 'leadership'. *The Leadership Quarterly*, 14(3), 359–81. https://doi.org/10.1016/S1048-9843(03)00031-6

Andersen, J. P., Nielsen, M. W., Simone, N. L., Lewiss, R. E., & Jagsi, R. (2022). Meta-research: Covid 19 medical papers have fewer women first authors than expected. https://pubmed.ncbi.nlm.nih.gov/32538780/

Becher, T., & Trowler, P. (2001). *Academic tribes and territories*. Open University Press.

BH Associates (2019). *Learning to succeed: A climate survey of the Irish Higher Educational sector, 2019*. https://prospectus.ie/5651-2

Blackmore, J. (2013). A feminist critical perspective on educational leadership. *International Journal of Leadership in Education*, 16(2), 139–54. https://doi.org/10.1080/13603124.2012.754057

Blackmore, J. (2014). 'Wasting talent'? Gender and the problematics of academic disenchantment and disengagement with leadership. *Higher Education, Research and Development*, 33(1), 86–99. https://psycnet.apa.org/doi/10.1080/07294360.2013.864616

Bondestam, F., & Lundqvist, M. (2020). Sexual harassment in higher education – A systematic review. *European Journal of Higher Education*, 10, 379–419. https://doi.org/10.1080/21568235.2020.1729833

Campbell, P. (2018). Editorial: Science needs to redefine excellence. *Nature*, 554, 403–4. https://doi.org/10.1038/d41586-018-02183-y

Carvalho, T., & de Lourdes Machado-Taylor, M. (2017). The exceptionalism of women rectors. In K. White & P. O'Connor (Eds), *Gendered success in higher education: Global perspectives* (pp. 111–32). Palgrave Macmillan.

Collinson, D. L. (2019). Critical leadership studies: Exploring the dialectics of leadership. In R. E. Riggio (Ed.), *What's wrong with leadership? Improving research and practice* (pp. 260–78). Routledge.

Copeland, R. (2021). Addressing the challenges of the Covid-19 pandemic: A view from the higher education staff. In S. Bergan, T. Gallagher, I. Harkavy, R. Munck, & H. van't Land (Eds), *Higher education's response to the Covid-19 pandemic* (pp. 281–91). Council of Europe Publishing.

Cox, J. (29 September 2020). University challenge: Why higher education faces some tough questions. *RTE.IE Brainstorm*. https://www.rte.ie/brainstorm/2020/0929/1168174-higher-education-third-level-universities-challenges-covid-19-ireland/

Cush, M. (2016). *Report on fixed-term and part-time employment in lecturing in Third Level Education in Ireland*. https://ictu.ie/publications/cush-report

Deem, R., Hillyard, S., & Reed, M. (2007). *Knowledge, higher education and the new managerialism*. Oxford University Press.

DFHERIS (22 July 2020). Minister Harris announces E168 funding package for third level institutions and students [Press release].

DFHERIS (4 May 2022a). Minister Harris publishes landmark policy on funding higher education and reducing the cost of education to families [Press release].

DFHERIS (2022b). *Funding the future: Investing in knowledge and skills: Ireland's competitive advantage*. https://www.gov.ie/en/policy-information/49e56-future-funding-in-higher-education/

European Commission (EC) (2021). *She figures: 2021 gender in research and innovation statistics and indicators*. https://research-and-innovation.ec.europa.eu/knowledge-publications-tools-and-data/publications/all-publications/she-figures-2021_en

Felt, U. (2016). 'Response-able practices' or 'new bureaucracies of virtue': The challenges of making RRI work in academic environments. In L. Asveld, R. van Dam-mieras, T. Swierstra, S. Lavrijssen, K. Linse, & J. van den Hoven (Eds), *Responsible innovation 3* (pp. 49–68). Springer. https://doi.org/10.1007/978-3-319-64834-7_4

Ferretti, F., Guimaraes Pereira, A., Vertesy, D., & Hardeman, S. (2018). Research excellence indicators: Time to reimagine the 'making of'. *Science and Public Policy*, 45(5), 731–41. https://doi.org/10.1093/SCIPOL%2FSCY007%2F4858431

Finkel, A. (2020). *The impact of Covid-19 on women in the STEM workforce*. https://www.chiefscientist.gov.au/sites/default/files/2020-05/rrif-covid19-women-stem-workforce.pdf

Fitzgerald, T. (2018). Looking good and being good: Women leaders in higher education in Australia and New Zealand. *Education Sciences*, 8(2), 54. https://doi.org/10.3390/educsci8020054

Fitzgerald, T. (2021). Mapping the terrain of leadership: Gender and leadership in higher education. *Irish Educational Studies*, 39(2), 221–32. https://doi.org/10.1080/03323315.2020.1729222

Flynn, N., Keane, E., Davitt, E., McCauley, V., Heinz, M., & Mac Ruairc, G. (2021). 'Schooling at home in Ireland during Covid-19': Parents and students' perspectives on overall impact, continuity of interest and impact on learning. *Irish Educational Studies*, 40(2), 217–26. https://doi.org/10.1080/03323315.2021.1916558

Gallagher, M. (2012) *Academic Armageddon: An Irish requiem for higher education*. Liffey Press.

Gallagher, T., & Munck, R. (2021). The local university mission after Covid 19: Two Irish case studies. In S. Bergan, T. Gallagher, I. Harkavy, R. Munck, & H. van't Land (Eds), *Higher education's response to the Covid-19 pandemic* (pp. 303–10). Council of Europe Publishing.

Gunter, H. (2010). A sociological approach to educational leadership. *British Journal of the Sociology of Education*, 31(4), 519–27. http://dx.doi.org/10.1080/01425692.2010.484927

Harford, J. (2018). The perspective of women professors on the professoriate: A missing piece in the narrative on gender equality in the university. *Education Sciences*, 8(2), 50. https://doi.org/10.3390/educsci8020050

Hazelkorn, E. (2021). Some challenges facing higher education in Europe in view of the Covid-19 pandemic. In S. Bergan, T. Gallagher, I. Harkavy, R. Munck, & H. van't Land (Eds), *Higher Education's response to the Covid-19 pandemic* (pp. 53–66). Council of Europe Publishing.

HEA (2016). *National review of gender equality in Irish higher education institutions*. https://hea.ie/assets/uploads/2017/06/HEA-National-Review-of-Gender-Equality-in-Irish-Higher-Education-Institutions.pdf

HEA (2019a). *Senior academic leadership initiative* [press release]. https://hea.ie/policy/gender/senior-academic-leadership-initiative/

HEA (2019b). *Higher education institutional staff profiles by gender*. https://hea.ie/assets/uploads/2019/07/Higher-Education-Institutional-Staff-Profiles-by-Gender-2019.pdf

HEA (2021). *Higher education institutional staff profiles by gender*. https://hea.ie/policy/gender/statistics/higher-education-institutional-staff-profiles-by-sex-and-gender/

HEA (2022a). *New technological universities*. https://hea.ie/policy/he-reform/technological-universities/

HEA (2022b). *Institutional staff profiles by sex and gender*. https://hea.ie/policy/gender/statistics/higher-education-institutional-staff-profiles-by-sex-and-gender/

HEA Institutional staff profiles by sex and gender (2023) https://hea.ie/policy/gender/statistics/higher-education-institutional-staff-profiles-by-sex-and-gender-2022/

Hearn, J. (2021). Men and masculinities in academia: Towards gender-sensitive perspectives, processes, policies and practices. In E. Drew & S. Canavan (Eds), *The gender sensitive university: A contradiction in terms* (pp. 97–109). Routledge.

Krook, M. L., & Mackay, F. (Eds) (2011). *Gender, politics and institutions*. Palgrave Macmillan.

Linková, M., Atay, O., & Zulu, C. (2021). Making the right choice: Discourses of individualised responsibility in higher education. In P. O'Connor & K. White (Eds), *Gender, power and higher education in a globalised world* (pp. 71–92). Palgrave Macmillan.

Lumby, J. (2019). Leadership and power in higher education. *Studies in Higher Education*, 44(9), 1619–29. https://doi.org/10.1080/03075079.2018.1458221

Lynch, K. (2006). Neo-liberalism and marketisation: The implications for higher education. *European Educational Research Journal*, 5(1), 1–17. https://doi.org/10.2304/eerj.2006.5.1.1

Lynch, K. (2014). New managerialism: The impact of education. *Concept*, 5(3), 1–11.

Lynch, K. (2015). Control by numbers: New managerialism and ranking in higher education. *Critical Studies in Education*, 56(2), 190–207.

Lynch, K., Gummell, B., & Devine, D. (2012). *New managerialism in education: Commercialisation, carelessness and gender*. Palgrave Macmillan.

Mackay, F., Kenny, M., & Chappell, L. (2010). New institutionalism through a gender lens: Towards a Feminist institutionalism. *International Political Science Review*, 31(5), 573–88. https://doi.org/10.1177/0192512110388788

MacNeela, P., Dawson, K., O'Rourke, T., Healy-Cullen, S., Burke, L., & Flack, W. F. (2022). *Report on the National Survey of Staff Experiences of Sexual Violence and Harassment in Irish HEIs*. https://hea.ie/assets/uploads/2021/04/Full-report-Staff-Jan-2022.pdf

Matthews, D. (25 June 2020). Pandemic lockdown holding back female academics, data show. *Times Higher Education*. https://www.timeshighereducation.com/news/pandemic-lockdown-holding-back-female-academics-data-show

Meyer, J. W., Ramirez, F. O., Frank, D. J., & Schoffer, E. (2007). Higher education as an institution. In H. Gumport (Ed.), *Sociology of higher education* (pp. 187–221). Johns Hopkins University Press.

Moratti, S. (2021). A woman's place is in the 'home'? Gender-specific hiring patterns in academia in gender-equal Norway. *Journal of Sociology*, 57(4), 916–34. https://doi.org/10.1177/1440783320960530

Morley, L. (1999). *Organising feminisms: The micropolitics of the academy*. St Martin's Press.

Morley, L. (2014). Lost leaders: Women in the global academy. *Higher Education Research and Development*, 33(1), 114–28. https://doi.org/10.1080/07294360.2013.864611

Morley, L. (2016). Troubling intra-actions: Gender, neo-liberalism and research in the global academy. *Journal of Education Policy*, 31(1), 28–45.

Moss-Racusin, C. A., Dovidio, J. F., Brescoll, V. L., Graham, M. J., & Handelsman, J. (2012). Science faculty's subtle gender biases favor male students. *Proceedings* of the National Academy of Sciences, 109(41), 16474–9. https://doi.org/10.1073/pnas.1211286109

Naezer, M., van den Brink, M., & Benschop, Y. (2019). *Harassment in Dutch academia.* Dutch Network of Women Professors.

National Academies of Sciences, Engineering, and Medicine (NASEM) (2020). *Promising practices for addressing the underrepresentation of women in science, engineering, and medicine: Opening doors.* The National Academies Press. https://doi.org/10.17226/25585

Nielsen, M. (2016). Limits to meritocracy? Gender in academic recruitment and promotion processes. *Science and Public Policy*, 43(3), 386–99. https://doi.org/10.1093/scipol/scv052

O'Connor, P. (2014). *Management and gender in higher education.* Manchester University Press.

O'Connor, P. (2015). Good jobs – but places for women? *Gender and Education*, 27(3), 304–19. https://doi.org/10.1080/09540253.2015.1021302

O'Connor, P. (2020a). Why is it so difficult to reduce gender inequality in male dominated higher education organisations? A Feminist institutional perspective. *Interdisciplinary Science Reviews*, 45(2), 207–28. https://doi.org/10.1080/03080188.2020.1737903

O'Connor, P. (2020b). Creating gendered change in Irish higher education: Is managerial leadership up to the task? *Irish Educational Studies*, 39(2), 139–56. http://dx.doi.org/10.1080/03323315.2019.1697951

O'Connor, P. (June 2022). Briefing document for Royal Irish Academy on higher education in Ireland and Northern Ireland.

O'Connor, P., & Barnard, S. (2021). Problematising excellence as a legitimating discourse. In P. O'Connor & K. White (Eds), *Gender, power and higher education in a globalised world* (pp. 47–69). Palgrave Macmillan.

O'Connor, P., & Irvine, G. (2020). Multi-level State interventions and gender equality in higher education institutions: The Irish case. *Administrative Sciences*, 10, 98. https://doi.org/10.3390/admsci10040098

O'Connor, P., & White, K. (2021a). Gender equality in higher education: The slow pace of change. In P. O'Connor & K. White (Eds), *Gender, power and higher education in a globalised world* (pp. 1–23). Palgrave Macmillan.

O'Connor, P., & White, K. (2021b). Power, legitimating discourses and institutional resistance to gender equality in higher education. In P. O'Connor & K. White (Eds), *Gender, power and higher education in a globalised world* (pp. 187–207). Palgrave Macmillan.

O'Connor, P., Martin, P. Y., Carvalho, T., O'Hagan, C., Veronesi, L., Mich, O., Saglamer, G., Tan, M. G., & Caglayan, H. (2019). Leadership practices by senior position holders in HERIs: Stealth power in action? *Leadership*, 15(6), 722–74. https://doi.org/10.1177/1742715019853200

O'Connor, P., Hodgins, M., Woods, D. R., Wallwaey, E., Palmen, R., van den Brink, M., & Kalpazidou Smith, E. (2021). Organisational characteristics that facilitate gender-based violence and harassment in higher education? *Administrative Sciences*, 11(4), 138. https://doi.org/10.3390/ADMINSCI11040138.

OECD (2012). *Closing the gender gap: Act now!* www.oecd.org/gender/closingthegap.htm/

Parsons, C., & O'Connor, P. (19 January 2023). You've heard of mentorship in science, but what about sponsorship? https://www.nature.com/articles/d41586-023-00123-z

Pereira, M. do Mar (2012). 'Feminist theory is proper knowledge, but … ': The status of feminist scholarship in the academy. *Feminist Theory*, 13(3), 283–303. https://doi.org/10.1177/1464700112456005

Peterson, H. (2016). Is managing academics 'women's work'? Exploring the glass cliff in higher education management. *Educational Management Administration and Leadership*, 44(1), 112–27. https://doi.org/10.1177/1741143214563897

Power, A. (2021). Understanding leadership in higher education as a tool for change in gender relations. In E. Drew & S. Canavan (Eds), *The gender sensitive university: A contradiction in terms* (pp. 140–53). Routledge.

Rosa, R., Drew, E., & Canavan, S. (2021). An overview of gender inequality in EU universities. In E. Drew & S. Canavan (Eds), *The gender sensitive university: A contradiction in terms* (pp. 1–15). Routledge.

Ryan, M. (2022). To advance equality for women, use the evidence. *Nature*, 604(21 April), 403. https://www.nature.com/articles/d41586-022-01045-y

Ryan, M., & Haslam, S. (2007). The glass cliff: Exploring the dynamics surrounding the appointment of women to precarious leadership positions. *The Academy of Management Review*, 32(2), 549–72. https://psycnet.apa.org/doi/10.2307/20159315

Schein, V. E., Mueller, R., Lituchy, T., & Liu, J. (1996). Think manager–think male: A global phenomenon? *Journal of Organisational Behaviour*, 17(1), 33–41. https://psycnet.apa.org/doi/10.1002/(SICI)1099-1379(199601)17:1%3C33::AID-JOB778%3E3.0.CO;2-F

Shankar, K., Pheland, D., Ratnadeep Suri, V., Watermeyer, R., Knight, C., & Crick, T. (2021). 'The COVID Crisis is not the core problem': Experiences, challenges and concerns of Irish academia during the pandemic. *Irish Educational Studies*, 40(2), 169–75. https://doi.org/10.1080/03323315.2021.1932550

Shepherd, S. (2017). Why are there so few female leaders in higher education: A case of structure or agency. *Management in Education*, 31(2), 82–7. https://doi.org/10.1177/0892020617696631

Shepherd S (2018). Managerialism: An ideal type. *Studies in Higher Education*, 43(9), 1668–78.

Sinclair, A. (2013). A material dean. *Leadership*, 9(3), 436–43. https://doi.org/10.1177/1742715013485859

THE (2021). *University impact ratings – United Nations sustainable development goals.* https://www.timeshighereducation.com/impactrankings#!/page/0/length/25/sort_by/rank/sort_order/asc/cols/undefined

United Nations (UN) (2021). *Transforming our world: The 2030 agenda for sustainable development*. https://sdgs.un.org/publications/transforming-our-world-2030-agenda-sustainable-development-17981

Van den Brink, M., & Benschop, Y. (2012). Gender practices in the construction of academic excellence: Sheep with five legs. *Organization*, 19(4), 507–24. https://doi.org/10.1177/1350508411414293

Webb, P. T. (2008). Re-mapping power in educational micropolitics. *Critical Studies in Education*, 49(2), 127–43. https://doi.org/10.1080/17508480802040183

Wood, R. (15 March 2022). Gender inequality remains a serious barrier to female progression in academia. *Irish Times*.

Wright Mills, C. (1970). *The sociological imagination*. Penguin.

7

Thinking Plurality: Academic Leadership, Precarious Institutions and Collegial Bodies as Member States in an Epistemic Union

Sharon Rider

Introduction

In a special report in 2020 on the *Internationalization of Universities and the Repression of Academic Freedom*, Tena Prelec, Saipira Furstenberg and John Heathershaw cite a report by the University and College Union in the UK that underscores the deterioration of academic freedoms (freedom in teaching and research, autonomy, shared governance, and employment protection). They note that while in some countries the threats are tangible and immediate (persecution of students and teachers, censorship or even arrest), in others they are more subtle, 'often driven by market dynamics and the increase of a corporate governance model of the university'. The Freedom House report describes, among other things, how an erosion of universities' financial and institutional autonomy has been documented in top liberal democracies, and how the need for funding has brought them to collaborate with authoritarian regimes whose policies severely delimit the space for what can be taught, researched and discussed on campus.

In this chapter, I want to make a conceptual point about how academic freedom reflects, incarnates and contributes to liberal democracy in the first instance by *instantiating* the latter's character of what one might describe as the productive vulnerability of epistemic pluralism. Plurality of thought is the basic assumption of liberal democracy as well as its inevitable result, which would seem to pose an insoluble dilemma, since it would appear to be impossible to ever reach a state of stable equilibrium. In short, liberal democracy is an intrinsically precarious enterprise. The role of higher education, it has been argued, is to ensure the perpetuation of the public sphere by guaranteeing the possibility of maintaining the plurality by socializing its members to accept and even embrace the precariousness of a life lived together with others without a sovereign other than the plurality itself (Honneth, 1995; Ricoeur, 2005), held together through respect for and understanding of its own institutions for guaranteeing due process. Let us call this principle 'republicanism'. A republic is the form of government arrived at when the political sphere is constituted by rational design, rather than merely arising out of historical contingency or a shared belief in teleological necessity. In this sense, republicanism is less an ideology than a hope that the stringent application of rational principles, a rigorous analysis of past experiences and a readiness for experimentation will create better forms of governance. The historical example par excellence is the Constitution of the United States, in which a new republic was set up with this ideal explicitly in mind.

My aim is to sketch the connection between the circumscription of academic freedom within the university and the undermining of its formal institutions for shared governance such as collegial organs as a fundament for its constitution, organization and leadership. I argue that collegial organs are to be distinguished from participatory democracy, on the one hand, and managerialism, on the other. Two distinguishing characteristics of collegial self-determination, traditionally, are the *primus inter pares* principle and the idea of an epistemic community, guild or corporation ('universitas'). In this form of self-governance, the spirit of the epistemic community itself is what justifies and enables the authority of the leadership. These two defining traits, however, have come to be replaced with line management and group representation (discipline, seniority, gender, ethnicity, etc.), respectively. This dissolution of the special formal character of university leadership has weakened the case for upholding autonomy, since it means that academic governance develops into bureaucracy, in the case of line management, and devolves into vested group interests in the case of governing bodies.

The consequence of this sea change is that even where shared governance is maintained, at least in the form of advisory bodies, it is already contaminated with the very elements which its existence, ideally, would keep at arms' length. To the extent that these bodies are primarily involved in asserting, negotiating and pursuing strategies for fulfilling their own interests and agendas, they will suffer the same deficit in legitimacy and recognition as do formal authorities in liberal democracies that fail to live up to the universalist ideals embedded in the formal legal framework of their institutions. For this reason, to rethink the conditions and limitations of collegial governance is also to consider what it would mean to revitalize and reinvigorate derelict or floundering institutions of liberal democratic governance more generally. My proposal in what follows is that the university should instantiate character of the rule of law as a microcosm of the same complex unity in plurality that animates the idea of the European Union and its constitution.

In the first section, I will describe two principles thought to encapsulate the liberal democratic ideals that are built into the governance structure of the European Union. Whatever faults and failings one wishes to ascribe to the EU, many of these would seem to stem from not meeting the challenges posed by a unity in heterogeneity, and replacing genuine participatory governance – so eloquently formulated by Abraham Lincoln in the Gettysburg Address as 'the government of the people for the people by the people', 'conceived in liberty' by the signatories of the Declaration of Independence and 'dedicated to the proposition that all men are created equal' – with technocratic rule by a homogeneous professional class (for a discussion of the 'democratic deficit' in the European Union, see Mair, 2013). I want to draw a parallel with both the principles and the failures of the EU in practice to manifest them with the governance of universities in the Global North. In the second section, I remind the reader of the radicality of the first European universities, and the context out of which they arose. The third section offers a conceptual framework for maintaining and renewing this radicality since the Enlightenment. In the fourth section, treating the university as a microcosm of the society in which it is embedded, I draw together what I take to be important lessons about the relationship between different kinds of governance, and the forms of freedom and rationality pertaining to them. In the fifth and final section, I will also suggest a proposal that attends to the important objections that have been raised against epistocracy, or what Steve Fuller has called 'the epistemic oligarchy' represented by universities, funding agencies and scholarly journals (Fuller, 2020). Finally, in the conclusion, I offer what I take to be the take-home message of the chapter.

Governing plurality: The principles of subsidiarity and proportionality

The principles of subsidiarity and proportionality as defined and enshrined in Article 5 of the Treaty on European Union exist to ensure that decisions are taken as closely as possible to the citizen, in the first case, and that there are continual checks to guarantee that action at the EU level is justified given national, regional or local conditions and possibilities already in place, in the second. More concretely, the principles prohibit the EU from taking action beyond the areas of its exclusive competence, unless the content and form of action taken at the European level are strictly necessary, or at least demonstrably more effective than at the level of the state or region for achieving the prime objectives of the Treaties. In short, they exist to ensure the agency and sovereignty of member states and the democratic participation of its citizens with regard to *how* to implement this, *how* to remedy that and so forth.

Two protocols annexed to the Treaty of Lisbon make it possible for an EU member state to refer an act to the EU Court of Justice for breach of the principle of subsidiarity. Protocol No. 1 concerns member states' rights with respect to transparency and access to information. The protocol requires that the relevant EU documents be forwarded promptly to national parliaments for examination before the Council makes a decision. Protocol No. 2 affirms the rights of national parliaments to review the measures taken by the Commission to assure that all draft legislative acts at the EU level respect the principle of subsidiarity. This provision allows them to appeal any given proposal on the grounds of a breach of principle, which may, after review, result in its being amended, withdrawn or maintained by the Commission, or blocked by the European Parliament. In a case of a breach of the principle of subsidiarity, EU member states may refer an adopted act directly to the Court of Justice of the EU.

Note that the principle of subsidiarity and the principle of proportionality regulate how the European Union exercises its powers. The proportionality principle means that the EU may take only the action required for clearly circumscribed aims and no more. This approach to responsibility and decision making is applied as part of a cohesion policy, the idea of Europe as an indivisible whole, united by commitment to rights and freedoms for its citizens, as well as reciprocal obligations, as equals before and under the rule of law. One might apply similar principles to the management and administration of the university with regard to the conducting of instruction, science and scholarship, or what can be called intellectual leadership. University management at the highest level must make decisions for the institution in all its parts, with consequences for research and teaching all the way down to the individual student, scholar or teacher. But on this aggregated plane, it would be disastrous for decisions regarding how to implement or how to remedy not to take into account differences in 'local' conditions with regard to size (student–faculty ratio, for instance), economy (levels of external funding especially), subject matter (such as advanced laboratory techniques) and culture (in particular, disciplinary standards and norms). A peremptory ukas on excellence or performance, say, regarding appropriate publication venues for humanities scholars, on the one hand, and researchers in pharmacology, on the other, or long-run employment trajectories for those studying mathematics or philosophy rather than professional training in say, law or teacher's education, without reference to the distinct character of the research or teaching unit, is bound to fail for the simple reason that a rule that is not in the spirit of the community ruled cannot serve as a principle of their action and judgement. The only means available to it will then be coercion, which is hardly in harmony with the ideal of a university as a republic of ideas. Thus, there must be some way of appealing and redressing decisions that undermine the cohesion of the university, the idea of it as an indivisible whole of complementary and competing principles, united and animated by a common commitment to the rights and freedoms of anyone pursuing knowledge under its aegis. Without some unifying principle of due process and checks and balance of powers between different spheres of authority, there will be a tendency towards centrifugal dissolution along lines of disciplinary and individual self-interest.

Origins of academic freedom

The idea of academic freedom is said to have its origins in a decree by the Emperor Fredrik Barbarossa, the so-called *Authentica Habita*, also known as *Privilegium Scholasticum*, which is the first document to set out the specific rules, rights and privileges of students and scholars *as such*, which were eventually extended to universities throughout Italy and ultimately served as a model for the establishment of universities throughout Europe in the medieval period. Already by the eleventh century, people were travelling from afar to Bologna to study canon and civil law with the jurist Irnerius, in particular, the newly rediscovered works of Roman law (D. Lindberg, 1992, pp. 206–13; see also Haskins, 1923, pp. 10–18). As foreigners, they were without legal protection. Because the university had no fixed residencies or venues for teaching, students and scholars belonging to the same city-states or regions formed free associations, or guilds, to secure protections that they could not claim as citizens. Among the liberties, immunities and protections granted were freedom of movement and travel for the purposes of study and the right of students to be tried by their masters, rather than by local civil courts. Importantly, the document was an expression of wider trends in society in a historical period characterized by the modernization of social and political institutions within the Norman kingdom of the south Italian peninsula as elsewhere. In particular, there were many similar efforts to reconcile diverse and even divergent legal arrangements and institutions through formal, legal uniformity; the assumed inviolability of local customs and laws was losing traction. Barbarossa saw in Roman canon law a resource for unification. The influence of medieval canon law is still with us, as it was at the forefront of introducing and defining concepts such as 'equity', 'rationality' and 'office'.

Early universities were thus corporations of students and masters, which in time would receive charters from popes, emperors and kings. They were free to govern themselves (provided they did not teach heretical doctrines or advocate atheism). Students and masters together elected their own rectors; as self-governing, they were also self-owning, which is to say, self-funding. Teachers charged fees, and what we today would describe as 'student satisfaction' was decisive for their income. With no permanent buildings and little property, the earliest corporations called universities were constantly under threat that dissatisfied students and scholars would simply pull up their stakes and set up shop in another city. This was particularly the case with the universities that arose out of schools that were not directly associated with the Church (cathedral schools) but were started in increasingly populated and influential urban centra such as Bologna to meet the interests and demands of a burgeoning economy (D. Lindberg, 1992, p. 190). These centres of learning, historian of science David Lindberg (1992, p. 193) points out, 'like European society more generally, saw a marked "rationalistic" turn – that is, an attempt to apply intellect and reason to many areas of human enterprise. There were attempts, for example, to rationalize commercial practices and the administration of church and state through record-keeping and the development of accounting and auditing procedures'. Lindberg cites historian Colin Morris (1972, p. 46), who described this transformation as a 'managerial revolution'.

It is important to bear in mind, then, that 'the idea' of the university originally had two characteristic features. On the one hand, its *content* was the application of reason to all matters, both practical and theoretical. On the other, its organizational form or structure was that of a free or voluntary association, that is, a guild. The term 'universitas' had no scholarly or educational connotations whatsoever at the time, but simply denoted the choice to come together *to pursue a common purpose and promote mutual well-being*. Among the prime aims of these corporations were *self-government*, related to the common purpose, and *monopoly*, that is, a question of promoting mutual well-being, which, Lindberg (1992, p. 208) notes, amounted to control over teaching: 'Gradually, the universities secured varying degrees of freedom from outside interference and thus the right to establish standards and procedures, to fix the curriculum, to set fees and award degrees, and to determine who would be permitted to study or teach' (see also B. Lindberg, 2014, pp. 39–62). Interestingly, because universities were regarded by their patrons (popes, emperors and kings) as valuable assets, they were nurtured, protected and rarely interfered with. They grew exponentially, both in terms of size and influence, which required a carefully considered internal organization (D. Lindberg, 1992, p. 209). Different guilds within the guild, or faculties, were delegated responsibility for their students and masters: the largest was the 'lower' faculty, devoted to preparatory training (liberal arts), which was a prerequisite for students who wished to be admitted into the professional training in the 'higher' studies of the professional schools of law, medicine and theology.

The standardization of structure in the division of faculties together with a unified content (i.e. a common curriculum consisting of the same subjects taught from the same texts) that developed in the transition period between the early and high Middle Ages were combined with the professorial mobility guaranteed by the *ius ubique docendi* (the right to teach anywhere) for those who had completed their master's degree to create an extraordinarily successful enterprise of international scope. At the same time, as the structure and content were relatively uniform and systematized, the teachers themselves, the 'masters', enjoyed what David Lindberg (1992, p. 213) has described as a 'remarkable' freedom of thought and expression: 'There was almost no doctrine (…) that was not submitted to minute scrutiny and criticism by scholars in the medieval university.'

The legitimate interests of the state

What is striking here is that the university arose as a direct response to entirely worldly external interests, while at the same time designing its activities on the basis of internal (intellectual, scientific, scholarly, pedagogical) considerations, the common purpose. The main benefit bestowed upon the guild of students and master by the regent was protection of their sovereignty with regard to the questions falling properly within the competence and jurisdiction of the university, that is, teaching and study (or as we would say today, 'research'). But university science and instruction were from the outset intended to be 'equipment for service'.[1] As such, they had to live up to many of the requirements we consider typically contemporary: student satisfaction, as mentioned, but also competition between schools, mobility of faculty and students, and the internationalization of research and study.

Reviewing the characteristics of this medieval innovation that was to last a thousand years, then, we find, to begin with, the necessity for legal protections. Protection of what and for whom? For the student and the teacher, there are two dimensions. In terms of the 'common purpose' of higher studies, to pursue the course of argument and reason where it will take them. But there was another aspect, namely, 'promoting mutual well-being', a matter of protecting their shared economic and social interests. For what ends? In the case of purpose, for the betterment of science and society. Regarding self-interest and well-being, attracting student fees or securing patronage, for instance. And what form do these protections and provisions take? Most importantly, it was a question of purpose rather than practical interests: the Church or regent would not interfere with the internal ongoings of thinking and studying where not explicitly and strictly required for the sake of the unity and flourishing of the city-state, region, empire or Christendom. Universities were obliged not to undermine papal or royal authority or their institutions. To the extent that restrictions are placed, they are first considered in proportion to the benefits of having a university to begin with. Decisions regarding what is proper to the *universitas* and its guilds were left in the hands of those who were in a position to make them on the basis of their knowledge and within the jurisdictional framework of the entity. Kant later described this ideal in the famous introduction to the first essay of *The Conflict of the Faculties*:

> Whoever it was that first hit on the notion of a university and proposed that a public institution of this kind be established, it was not a bad idea to handle the entire content of learning (really, the thinkers devoted to it) industrially (fabrikenmäßig), so to speak, by a division of labor, so that for every branch of the sciences there would be a public teacher or professor appointed as its trustee, and all of these together would form a kind of learned community called a university (or higher school). The university would have a certain autonomy (since only scholars can pass judgment on scholars as such), and accordingly it would be authorized to perform certain functions through its faculties (smaller

societies, each comprising the university specialists in one main branch of learning): to admit to the university students seeking entrance from the lower schools and, having conducted examinations, by its own authority to grant degrees or confer the universally recognized status of "doctor" on free teachers (that is, teachers who are not members of the university) – in other words, to create doctors.

(Kant 1798/1979, p. 23. Translation slightly altered)

In the essay, Kant insists that the division of the faculties serves an important aim of science by demarcating the training and instruction in the professions (the higher faculties of medicine, law and theology) that the government has a legitimate interest in controlling (primarily, in order to exert influence over the public) from the lower faculty, 'whose function is only to look after the interests of science' (Kant 1798/1979, pp. 25–6). Kant insists that it is 'absolutely essential that the learned community at the university also contains a faculty that is independent of the government's command with regard to its teachings', one that is 'free to evaluate everything' and in which 'reason is authorized to speak out publicly', arguing that lacking a faculty for the unconstrained use of reason and admitting of no command to hold something as true would be detrimental not only to science itself but also to the professions, the state and its subjects (Kant 1798/1979, pp. 27–9). In a footnote to this passage, Kant relates an anecdote about a minister of the French government who summoned eminent merchants to offer suggestions about how best to stimulate trade, adding the acerbic remark, 'as if he would know how to choose the best'. Kant then recounts the discussion of various proposals, in which an older merchant who had been quiet throughout the conversation exclaims: 'Build good roads, mint sound money, give us laws for exchanging money readily, etc.; but as for the rest, leave us alone!' Kant comments that if the government were to consult the lower faculty about what teachings to proscribe in general, it would get a similar reply: 'Just don't interfere with the progress of insight and science' (Kant 1798/1979, footnote pp. 27–9. Translation slightly altered).

One striking feature of the arguments of *The Conflict of the Faculties* is that Kant largely accepts the strictures placed on the medieval university regarding heresy and atheism with regard to professional training, allowing the practical interests of government to direct the work of the higher faculties. The autonomy that he attempts to secure is not general, but specific: the unfettered use of reason to assess and evaluate its own resources, activities and results, that is, institutionalized rational self-reflection. He is arguing for the human faculty of reason to be organizationally realized in an academic faculty of reason. And for that to be possible, those who are not intellectually capable of rendering a discerning judgement with respect to a given matter should refrain from the exercise of the worldly power to do so. At the same time, that means that many, perhaps most, elements of the university are legitimately under the watch and discretion of the sovereign. In today's Europe, the sovereign is the people, through their elected representatives. Applying Kant's laissez-faire economic rationality to our current situation, it could very well mean putting a great deal of science and higher education into the hands of the government and public administration.

But note, it would *not* mean willy-nilly entrusting popular opinion, political trends or vested interests to decide the curriculum or basic research in the humanities, social sciences or natural sciences, for the simple reason that the one and only job of science properly speaking (in contrast to disciplines constructed with the specific purpose of professional training) is to reason *without* taking into consideration anything other than the integrity and further progress of science and scholarship itself. As a matter of principle, science as such is essentially *inconsiderate*. This lack of consideration has three implications. For the one, the customer (student, government funding agencies, taxpayers, donors, commercial or industrial clients) is not always right (which does not mean, of course, that they're never right); second, the imposition of ideological frameworks to achieve democratic goals constitutes a fundamental incursion on freedom of thought and scientific conscience which can inhibit both; finally, the organization of publicly financed universities such as are commonly found on the Continent has structural parallels to other basic institutions of liberal democracy like courts of law, and, applying the subsidiarity principle, we find that there are decisions that can and should be made at the 'lower' level where both formal resources and competence for local decision making are better than at the more global level of university management.

This insight, which, as our brief survey has shown, has taken different forms for centuries, seems to be lost today. Instead of subsidiarity and proportionality, we find the historically unique hybrid of top-down control combined with the academic equivalent of populist movements among the students and scholars themselves to constrain freedom of thought. One might say that 'promoting mutual well-being' has overshadowed or even overtaken the idea of 'a common purpose' as the point of the university.

Democratic governance in the university: Working conditions or conditions of knowledge?

In order to demonstrate what is at stake as concretely as possible, I will make use of a recent study of the trajectory of the governance of the university in Sweden since the 1970s as a case in point. Johan Boberg (2022, pp. 19–67) describes how the system of self-governing academic bodies with decision-making powers and resources was 'democratized' in the 1970s as part of a larger programme to make state public administration authorities and agencies (which Swedish universities, with a few exceptions, became in the 1970s, having since the seventeenth century been corporative bodies under public law) more representative of the people, and responsive to their interests and demands. In this way, organs that were originally constituted with the purpose of ensuring the continuity, advancement and rigour of research and educational programmes within their disciplinary spheres were to be modelled on corporative paradigms of workers' rights. There is an important similarity, of course, namely, collective decision making. But in the latter case, what is essential is that the collective in question is representative of those *affected* by the decision taken, most especially in terms of their working conditions. The questions to be decided have to do with employees' right of co-determination in the workplace and participatory democracy with regard to corporative policy. In the case of collegial bodies, in contrast, the decisions taken are supposed to be of such a kind that what is at stake is not what is better or worse for the individual or group affected, but what is better or worse for the production, maintenance, dissemination and advancement of knowledge in the relevant domain.

In short, it's not employment conditions but the conditions of knowledge, of learning and discovering, that are to be discussed and decided in the collegium, which is why those making the decisions must have requisite experience and understanding of what it's all about. Naturally, the two often overlapped both in the medieval period and during the Enlightenment when Kant was making his case, for the simple reason that human beings cannot be expected to restrain their self-interest in every instance. But Kant's point was that, in the interests of science and society, they *should*. For reasons that will become clear in what follows, the sole legitimate justification for retaining collegial decision-making bodies is the possibility and desirability of maintaining a distinction between judgements about what is good for an individual, group or even society, and what is good for critical thinking and scientific development as such.

Boberg's article analyses how reforms in the public sector, including higher education, in the 1990s coalesced in unexpected ways with the effects of earlier reforms of the 1970s to transform the university system. Smaller divisions and departments were thought to be administratively inefficient and, in the interests of rationalization and good housekeeping of public funds, the universities were strongly encouraged to reorganize so as to merge small units into larger, more flexible and administratively and economically more viable sections or schools. This initiative was also thought to guarantee more innovative and productive research environments. Responsibility for personnel and budget were decentralized from central university management to the sections, faculties or schools, which in turn made it necessary for them to develop some form of line management so that decisions with legal and financial repercussions could be tracked back to a formalized institutional function and thus a functionary who could be held accountable. A novel situation arose wherein the *primus inter pares* system of election of the dean or head of department by peers became legally untenable, since the point and purpose of collegial organs within the modern university were to ensure scientific, scholarly and educational quality within a determinate field of inquiry, and not to make decisions beyond its competence, such as those involved in the operation of the university as an organization.

The more intertwined these two elements became, the more *all* decisions were seen to fall under the competence of higher management. In the end, most ostensibly collegial organs were reduced to consultative assemblies with little or no discretionary mandate, in many cases with representation of students and technical and administrative staff. The idea behind this solution is that the faculty are simply one interest group among others, rather than a corporation with the specific mission of assuring that their academic activities are based in and on scientific, scholarly or educational principles and considerations. And it is natural, then, that the faculty will perceive the function of such organs in the same fashion, which means that they will think, judge and act in that spirit. The mindset of self-interest will ultimately fail to bear up anything like a universal ideal of common purpose for the sake of knowledge, which in turn will further dissolve any rationale for self-governance.

Academic liberalism and the need for checks and balances

There are reasons, of course, to be sceptical of epistemic elites and their institutions, including collegial organs. Steve Fuller (2018) sees them as primarily engaged in 'rent-seeking', or to use the terminology of this essay, 'promoting mutual well-being'. Specifically, Fuller criticizes the cumulative advantage arising out of formal arrangements that ensure perennial dividends to certain groups, institutions and bodies, which he thinks should be contested. Such orchestration of mutual advantage includes some of the sacred cows of the academy, including peer review, specialization and the reification of scientific or scholarly consensus in the form of citation statistics. Analysing the common characteristics of academic gatekeeping at journals and funding agencies, he interrogates how they lean towards consolidation of resources at the expense of risk-taking and, therewith, inhibit opportunities for genuine renewal. On his account, the academic mentality is inclined to think of epistemic achievement in terms of accumulation, the ultimate aim of which is monopoly. And as we saw in the previous discussion of the early universities, there has always been that element in academic thinking.

But we can also view collegial bodies in another way, as expressions of what the Swedish political scientist Sverker Gustavsson (2010, pp. 429–36)[2] has called 'academic liberalism'. Gustavsson's interpretation of what liberalism means in an academic context (as distinct from economic or political liberalism) is neither rational self-interest nor the goal of consensus arrived at through deliberative democracy, but rather the perpetuation of a dynamic sphere aimed at 'strengthening the integrity and courage to stand up for one's convictions (*civilkurage*)'. What the academic liberal wants to protect and defend is 'constructive uncertainty and an openness to whatever the scientific process (*bearbetning*) can lead'. This person, or rather, this ideal type,

> is not certain of any truths, and wishes, in an orderly fashion, to be able to test continuously the tenability of both new and old conceptions. Concretely, this operation consists of lectures, scholarly or scientific writing, seminars, dissertation defenses and the collegially organized editing of books, articles and journals. Via these institutions, the academic liberal arranges and tends to the critique that is integrated into the system.
>
> (Gustavsson, 2010, p. 436)

This all sounds very attractive and is very much in line with John Stuart Mill's ideal of political liberalism, which stressed openness and standing for one's ideas and opinions rather than attaining consensus. On the other hand, Mill's vision placed rather high demands on the *demos* if they were to be worthy of enfranchisement. Fuller observes that the brand of liberal democracy that *On Liberty* sought to provide a philosophical justification for was indeed criticized in its day for being 'antidemocratic' because of 'the high-performance standard it set'. At the same time, as Fuller also notes, Mill's aim was to 'spread the superior sensibility to a wider portion of the population, resulting in an "aristocracy of everyone"' (Fuller, 2021, pp. 351–56).[3] Fuller contrasts Mill's position on this score with that of Bentham, who was not concerned with self-empowerment so much as with the individual's self-interest and self-protection (which is why the latter advocated a majoritarian rule). As Fuller neatly formulates the difference, Mill was a proponent of the *right to speak*, while Bentham promoted *the right to be heard*.

If we compare these liberal ideals, we will notice that Bentham's is very much in harmony with the ideal of democratic participation and consultation to promote mutual self-interest and achieve consensus through deliberation, resulting in some uniform decision affecting everyone; Mill's vision, on the other hand, is closer to that of what Gustavsson terms academic liberalism, the common purpose of perpetuating knowledge, grounded in the optimistic acknowledgement of the inevitable plurality to which freedom and education give rise. Further, it could be argued that the ultimate goal of this kind of liberalism as institutionalized and instantiated in collegial bodies, ideally, is precisely the achievement of an 'aristocracy of everybody' to the extent that the hope and aim are to construct syllabi, course plans, educational programmes and the like which, in the best-case scenario, will equip anybody who chooses to partake of them to take his rightful place among those who can decide for themselves, in conversation with their peers (potentially everyone), through the exercise of critical rationality about the matter at hand.

But even if we were to stress the ideal of the social and economic equity to be achieved through the democratization of decision making rather than the requirements of scientific progress as a guiding principle, we would still find a justification for collegial bodies in the principle of subsidiarity. Where there is a structure in place that can perform the actions that higher-level management deems necessary for cohesion, it is incumbent on the latter to demonstrate the need for overriding that unifying structure. Failing that, there should be a court of appeal within the university system for objections to be raised and adjudicated that is not itself a part of the executive branch of university governance. In short, there should be a division of powers and responsibilities. A university leadership that embraced academic liberalism would champion the notion that the university is a particular kind of institution, that is, one that is committed to the principle that everyone has a right and duty to be able to give an account and provide reasons for their claims and actions as the basis for decision making.

To reduce academic autonomy to a matter of balancing the interests of a variety of stakeholders is to fundamentally misconstrue the idea of the university and the responsibilities of intellectual leadership.

Conclusion

My aim in this chapter has been to shed light on the university as a structure of self-propagating cohesion in plurality that reflects the basic nature both of liberal democracy and of scientific and scholarly thinking, in each case understood as an activity of self-expression and self-realization with and for others, rather than as a principle of manufacture and accumulation for mutual benefit. The latter sensibility is one that, as I have attempted to show, has been part and parcel of the academic community and the personae constituting it since its inception. But this more worldly dimension was always balanced, to a greater or lesser degree depending upon historical circumstance, by a spirit of common purpose for something at once galvanizing and stabilizing. The freedoms guaranteed by patronage or state protection were thought to ensure, above all, the future of the enterprise of thought unfettered by externalities.

This fundamental feature must be understood as the core of academic freedom, which is actually at risk of disappearing as the corporative aspects of collegiality become all the more ingrained, or alternatively, as corporate top-down managerial models replace collegial ones altogether. But while there is a great deal of literature critically examining the latter, the dangers associated with the former tend not to receive the scholarly attention that they should. Concretely, if, for example, faculty want to have control over decision making, not for the greater good, but, say, to ensure departmental income or prestige, then their motives are not primarily scientific, scholarly or pedagogic, but rather exactly the kind of group self-interest that the managerial mindset is inclined to view them as being. The only way out of the dilemma is to accept or even embrace the thought that the aims of science and education are not always necessarily in harmony with the interests of the individual or collective interests of those engaged in its pursuit. Without this honest appraisal of the situation, the faculty have no recourse to arguments of principle, which will just look like 'ivory-washing' of base egoism.

As the analogy with the EU was intended to suggest, managerial overreach has precisely the same consequences. If decisions are made in the form of edicts from above that cannot be redressed through argumentation or informed examination where the case at hand is set before an independent body the purpose of which is to assess and adjudicate impartially, then the whole justification of a university as a specific institutionalization of the coherence of the human faculty of reason in all its infinite variety falters. Mill realized that democracy – popular self-governance – is fragile and difficult to maintain primarily because of the plurality it entails since human reason takes many forms. If it were univocal, there would be no need for legally protected civil liberties. Similarly, a university contains within itself the seeds of its own destruction as well as for its own perpetuation. The EU has tried to accommodate plurality through the principles of proportionality and subsidiarity, which guarantee the sovereignty and agency required for it to be a unity in plurality for the sake of peace, freedom and justice. Comprehensive universities would do well to consider their 'universitas' emblem in a similar light. In the current atmosphere of ever-more bellicose contentiousness and unimaginative self-promotion, one might envision an ideal university leadership that set for itself the aim of a new constitution under a charter and bill of rights for faculty and students in which the rights and obligations of each and all were subsumed under the ideal of common cause of perpetuating knowledge, the capacity for critical examination and discerning judgement.

Notes

1 A reference to the American professor's attitude towards his work in an article by Lyman Abbot praising the president of the then newly founded University of Chicago in 1906, cited in Rudolph (1962, p. 356).
2 All translations from Swedish are my own.
3 Fuller borrows the phrase 'aristocracy of everyone' from Benjamin Barber (1992), who took the term from Thomas Jefferson's idea of nobility understood in terms of virtues and talents rather than of social position.

References

Barber, B. (1992). *An aristocracy of everyone*. Oxford University Press.
Boberg, J. (2022). Lärosätenas interna organisation. Kollegialitet, demokrati och linjestyring [The internal organisation of seats of learning: Collegiality, democracy and line management]. *Statsvetenskaplig tidskrift*, 124(1), 19–67.
Fuller, S. (2018). *Post-truth: Knowledge as a power game*. Anthem.

Fuller, S. (2020). Expertise as a form of knowledge: A response to Quast. *Analyse & Kritik*, 42(2), 431–41. https://doi.org/10.1515/auk-2020-0017

Fuller, S. (2021). Democracy naturalized: In search of the individual in the post-truth condition. *Analyse & Kritik*, 43(2), 351–66. https://doi.org/10.1515/auk-2021-0018

Gustavsson, S. (2010). Akademisk liberalism. *Statsvetenskaplig Tidskrift*, 112(4), 423–33.

Haskins, C. (1923). *The rise of universities*. Brown University Press.

Honneth, A. (1995). *The struggle for recognition: The moral grammar of social conflicts*. Polity Press.

Kant, I. (1798/9). *The conflict of the faculties/Die streit der fakultäten* (M. J. Gregor, Trans.). University of Nebraska Press.

Lindberg, B. (2014). Akademisk frihet före moderniteten [Academic freedom before modernity]. *Lychnos. Swedish Yearbook for the History of Science and Ideas*. Swedish History of Science Society.

Lindberg, D. (1992). *The beginnings of Western science: The European scientific tradition in philosophical, religious and institutional context, 600 B.C. to A.D. 1450*. University of Chicago Press.

Mair, P. (2013). *Ruling the void. The hollowing of Western democracy*. Verso Books.

Morris, C. (1972). *The discovery of the individual 1050–1200*. Harper & Row.

Prelec, T., Furstenberg, S., & Heathershaw, J. (2020). The internationalization of universities and the repression of academic freedom. In N. Schenkkan, I. Linzer, S. Furstenberg, & J. Heathershaw (Eds), *Perspectives on 'everyday' transnational repression in an age of globalization* (pp. 18–22). Freedom House.

Ricoeur, P. (2005). *The course of recognition*. Harvard University Press.

Rudolph, F. (1962). *The American college and university: A history*. Alfred A. Knopf.

8

Enabling Intellectual Leadership in Precarious Times: The Contribution of the Professional Doctorate

Elizabeth Parr, Janet Lord, Stephen M Rayner and Rachel Stenhouse

Introduction

The professional doctorate has, in recent years, emerged in a wide range of academic disciplines including law, social work, medicine, psychology, nursing, pharmacy and business. In the UK, of all professional doctorates, it is the Doctorate in Education (EdD) that has the largest market (Burnard, Dragovic, Ottewell & Lim, 2018). The drivers for this growth include an increased need for professionals to be able to critically analyse their practice, in order to develop it and to address its challenges. In this chapter, we explore the professional EdD as a vehicle for enabling professional intellectual leadership in education. We focus on educational professionals who, while working as experienced practitioners, have undertaken a part-time EdD alongside their employment. The EdD programme requires educational professionals to undertake independent primary research that is original and that makes a contribution to a research field. In addition, the EdD interplays research methodology, methods and analysis with professional identities, practices and agendas, and as such it challenges educational professionals to critically reflect on their daily practices, and so to contribute intellectual leadership within and beyond the organization(s) in which they are employed. Such intellectual leadership is required to engage with: the purposes of education; the design of the curriculum, assessment and pedagogical practices; and relationships between staff. Increasingly, the focus is on organizational positioning within a competitive market, where intellectual leadership is necessary in order to distinguish between opportunities and threats.

Undertaking doctoral work is therefore risky for educational professionals in a number of ways: first, it requires the individual to engage in learning that may challenge accepted professional strategies and tactics within their organization or their profession more generally; second, such learning may make people vulnerable within performance-management processes, and so their employment and livelihood could be in danger. Precarity therefore operates in two ways: it is a productive change process through enabling the professional to think and act otherwise, but it is also deemed to be potentially inefficient because such learning interrupts the high-stakes delivery agendas that educational services are required to comply with. We therefore examine what it means for educational professionals to seek to develop intellectual leadership at a time when it is not required to operate in the market and indeed may actually be unwelcome there. We do so in two main ways. First, we contextualize the issues through examining recent empirical research into the development of professional doctorate student identities, the impact of professional doctorates on organizational change and the imperative of critical reflexivity as a leader negotiating the roles of practitioner and researcher. Second, we present a series of vignettes from our experiences as EdD graduates. These vignettes were developed through our discussions and analysis of our experiences of the EdD, which we have previously written about (see Rayner, Lord, Parr & Sharkey, 2015). We use the vignettes as the basis upon which we examine the complexity, challenges, location and practices of intellectual leadership.

The EdD

If the traditional PhD seeks to prepare students to become 'professional researchers', the professional doctorate prepares them to become 'researching professionals' (Lunt, 2018). The distinctiveness of the professional doctorate then sees experienced professionals, and usually leaders in their organizations, challenged to explore the relationships between research and practice by stepping outside of their usual role, reflecting on their own practice and deepening their understanding. The Quality Assurance Agency for Higher Education proposes: 'In both practice-based and professional doctorate settings, the candidate's research may result directly in organisational or policy-related change' (QAA, 2020, p. 9). The United Kingdom Council for Graduate Education goes further by suggesting:

A professional doctorate is a programme of enhanced study which, whilst satisfying the University criteria for the award of a doctorate, is designed to meet the specific needs of a professional group external to the University, and which develops the capability of individuals to work within a professional context.

(UKCGE, 2002, p. 62)

It is important to note here that the outcomes for a professional doctorate are for the wider professional group as well as for the individual working within it. In the case of the EdD, participants from across the education sector usually research within their own professional context, such as schools, colleges, universities and local authorities, while at the same time working there. This insider, outsider and 'in-betweener' research involves an element of risk-taking, where negotiating new ways of thinking, doing and being is unsettling and potentially risky for the professional (Burnard, Dragovic, Ottewell & Lim, 2018).

The delivery of the EdD programme typically differs from that of a PhD. While EdD students work with a supervisor on their research projects throughout their programme, there is also a taught element in which EdD students engage with their cohort. This taught stage usually lasts between eighteen months and two years. Wellington & Sikes (2006) highlight the value that professional doctorate students tend to place on the cohort experience. Collegiality, support, friendships and social interactions are all cited as important and effective in the programme. This sharing of the journey for professionals suggests that not only is the EdD an opportunity for professional and personal development but is also suggestive of a social perspective on learning with shared processes, languages and regulation (Wenger, 2010). These processes, languages and routines form part of the professionals' identities as researching professionals and how they understand the world around them (Rayner, Lord, Parr & Sharkey, 2015). The professional doctorate therefore facilitates collective intellectual discussions about the thinking and doing of educational leadership, thus providing opportunities for precarity and conflict to be articulated, shared and explored.

Our particular contribution in this chapter is to recognize the distinctive opportunities afforded by an EdD programme to navigate and practise the thinking and doing of professional intellectual leadership. To do this, we review and discuss empirical evidence from published literature and our own experiences. We consider first the development of professional–doctoral student identities, then the impact of professional doctorates on organizational change, and finally the imperative of critical reflexivity as a leader, negotiating the roles of practitioner and researcher. We argue that the EdD extends learning and understanding beyond the functionality of leadership within a single institution, so that EdD graduates, by developing professional identities, understandings of educational change and critical reflexivity, can theorize on purposes and practices in educational leadership. This, to us, is the essence of professional intellectual leadership.

The development of professional doctorate student identities

Each doctoral student brings past experiences with them when they start doctoral study (Paterson, 2021); EdD students bring a current professional experience with them too, often associated with a role label and an internalization of the expectations of that role (Colbeck, 2008). This added complexity of negotiating an existing professional identity alongside a developing student identity means that EdD students' developing identity becomes a nexus of multi-membership (Wenger, 2010). During the doctorate, students must negotiate how to successfully integrate these multiple identities (Dollarhide et al., 2013) and this integration of identities can be risky if it causes the student to challenge their existing professional identity. This integration of identities is far from a linear transformation, but rather a navigation of different terrains. The nonlinearity of EdD student identity and its interplay with the student's professional identity may cause precarity for the student by interrupting the agenda that their professional role requires them to comply with. There is always a risk that these multiple identities may not become integrated but instead fragmented (Colbeck, 2008) and in tension with each other. Professional doctorate students are likely to examine, or at least reflect on, their own professional practice during their doctoral studies. The scrutiny of professional practice, and hence of professional identity, may be problematic (Scott, Brown, Lunt & Thorne, 2004). Whilst some professional doctorate students may overcome this tension by attempting to compartmentalize their multiple identities (Scott, Brown, Lunt & Thorne, 2004), we would argue that it is not so straightforward as this when a student's doctoral research is interlinked with their professional role. It is the relationship with professional practice, and hence with professional identity, that is a defining feature of the professional doctorate (Scott, Brown, Lunt & Thorne, 2004).

EdD students experience a significant change in their professional identity as they progress through the doctorate (Rayner, Lord, Parr & Sharkey, 2015). This can create a sense of loss as a strong professional identity is questioned (Foot, Crowe, Tollafield & Allan, 2014) and as the students become leaders in their academic field and begin to question the assumptions made in their practice which may leave them feeling in a precarious position as a professional. There are moments of unravelling and moments of becoming (Fox & Allan, 2014) as students negotiate their evolving identity and reflect on existing beliefs. Yet, we argue that the critical reflection that professional doctorate students undergo is needed, now more than ever, as the educational landscape evolves.

The impact of professional doctorates on organizational change

Much published research into professional doctorates focuses on their (potential) impact on change in the organization *in which the researcher is currently employed*. Boud et al. (2018), for example, refer to 'employee learning' and 'how [graduates'] doctoral programme had changed their practice and what was the subsequent impact upon the work of their peers and workplace' (p. 916). A similarly functional approach to the evaluation of impact is noted as 'confidence to apply new knowledge to their working practices' (Robinson, 2018, p. 98), 'capacity to promote emancipation within their work environments' (Lundgren-Resenterra & Kahn, 2019, p. 411), and 'insiders trying to look inside and make sense of their own professional workplace' (Burnard, Dragovic, Ottewell & Lim, 2018, p. 50). Following a systematic review of research on professional doctorates, Hawkes & Yerrabati (2018) identify a shortage of 'literature on the wider impact of professional doctorates' (p. 17). Our understanding of intellectual leadership looks beyond the limits of the organization in which the doctoral student is employed and – if it is a different one – of the organization that is the site of the empirical inquiry on which the doctoral project is based. We argue that the professional doctorate facilitates intellectual leadership by enabling *self-awareness*, resulting in membership of a new (and rather different) generation of scholars; *vigilance*, resulting in critical scrutiny of knowledge claims in precarious times; *trust*, resulting in credibility as a public intellectual; and *collaboration*, resulting in greater understanding of the affordances of dialogue between practice and research.

Self-awareness

The professional doctorate prioritizes the notions of 'required reflection' and 'pensive professionalism' (Cunningham, 2018, p. 64), so that students' previous professional knowledge, understanding and assumptions are simultaneously an advantage and a potential hindrance. A student body that brings with it professional experience includes those with understandings and styles of educational leadership that may have been shaped by neoliberal agendas of performance measurement, corporatization and competition. Those understandings and skills may have been effective in a market-oriented educational system, but intellectual leadership requires 'rethinking the existing social, economic and political frameworks' (Oleksiyenko & Ruan, 2019, p. 408).

Vigilance

Intellectual leadership requires thinking that goes beyond managerial competence and organizational performativity. It must recognize how power and privilege operate within organizations. This is an epistemological opportunity for the professional–doctoral researcher. Knowledge can only be generated by the acute observation and attention to detail that are required in order to conduct a robust and ethically sound empirical project (e.g. see Boyce, 2012; Costley & Armsby, 2007; Taysum, 2006). Only trustworthy research can draw attention to organizations and whole systems that are dysfunctional, ethically compromised or struggling to survive.

Trust

In a programme that places value on new empirical research, the doctoral researcher begins by identifying a situation within their domain of practice that requires investigation. For the research to have validity as a doctoral project, it must not only persuade a university supervisor that it will contribute to academic knowledge, it must also address an issue that is 'of pressing concern for peers in their professional field' (Boud, Fillery-Travis, Pizzolato & Sutton, 2018, p. 920). Therefore, the professional doctorate challenges the assumption (e.g. see Malfroy, 2004) that 'the university remains the central pivot for knowledge production and dissemination, whereas the profession and the workplace are perceived as mere vehicles for such actions' (Lundgren-Resenterra & Kahn, 2019, p. 408). The knowledge resulting from a professional doctorate must have credibility for the profession as well as for the academy.

Collaboration

The professional doctorate requires the individual to work in four spaces: the profession, the workplace, the university and the personal (Pratt, Tedder, Boyask & Kelly, 2015). The resulting transdisciplinary work promotes dialogue between those who inhabit those spaces: the researcher, the research participants, other professionals, the university tutors and supervisors. Most importantly, it subjects discourses and assumptions established in those spaces to scrutiny, recognizing consensus while exposing tensions and misunderstandings. Intellectual leadership may not be a solitary activity, but may be 'formed by collaborative influence-makers' who can 'synergise ideas and resources across institutions to solve problems or reshape societies' (Oleksiyenko & Ruan, 2019, p. 407).

Critical reflexivity as a leader negotiating the roles of practitioner and researcher

The professional doctorate is a lengthy and expensive academic programme, undertaken while participants are simultaneously working in professional contexts involving significant leadership and/or teaching commitments. Individuals are predominantly motivated by their own development and, either directly or indirectly, that of their practice (Fox & Slade, 2014). They renegotiate their identity within the ever-changing and precarious context of education. Their reflections and reflexivity enable insights into the development of intellectual leadership.

There are a myriad of tasks, habits and routines associated with leadership; leaders must possess the skills that enable them to operate in a complex system (Eddy & Rao, 2009): a system further complicated by engagement in research, for example, when engaging in doctoral-level academic work. For researchers, reflexivity can be problematic as by its very nature it causes individuals to challenge existing taken-for-granted assumptions, which may result in feelings of inadequacy and discomfort (Finlay, 2002). As well as working in the liminal spaces which are inevitable as doctoral students develop their contributions to knowledge, leaders additionally need to critically reflect on their practice and the practice within the educational setting within which their practice is situated. If the reflexive work of the professional doctorate causes them to critically reflect in a way which is not aligned with that of their educational context, there will be resulting tensions. As both practitioner and researcher, and perhaps with little integration between these two identities, the leader must learn how to negotiate these tensions. The critical reflexivity that the leader undertakes as part of the doctoral research process might cause that leader to break, or wish to break, from the habits and routines that are associated with their leadership; this can be a risk for the leader and potentially too for the educational setting.

Intellectual leaders must implement new policies and practice and be at the cutting edge of new developments in education; research is one tool that can support this. Research can help leaders to overcome challenges faced in schools but research alone is not enough (Akiva, Crowley, Russell & Hecht, 2018). There is therefore a risk in how leaders negotiate their research and translate this into their practice.

Possession of a doctorate may be an asset, distinguishing the graduate among competitors for leadership positions; in the United States, it is historically seen as preparation for educational leadership (Eddy & Rao, 2009). Whilst there is research on professional doctorates and research on educational leadership, there is a gap on the interplay between the professional doctorate and leadership. This is an area that we explore in the next section through the use of vignettes.

Professional doctorate experiences: A series of vignettes

Truly understanding the experiences of professionals who have engaged with the challenges, tensions and vulnerabilities of completing an EdD while working in education is suggestive of an approach that is phenomenological, contextualized and open-ended. Rather than sharing snippets of experiences from interviews or research diaries as EdD students, we wanted to 'convey the authority, wisdom, and perspective of the subjects' (Lawrence-Lightfoot, 2005, p. 6) and therefore what follows is a series of vignettes. The vignettes are stories written by ourselves as four EdD graduates that 'ask readers to relive the experience through the writer's … eyes' (Ellis & Bochner, 2000, p. 905). These vignettes are important in that they are written by us, professionals who have successfully completed an EdD. We were professional practitioners in education when embarking on our EdD and have continued to hold positions in education after graduation. However, our professional leadership roles before and after the EdD are very different in nature, setting, demands and – most importantly – opportunities to make intellectual contributions. We therefore use the vignettes to document the complexities, challenges, locations and practices of intellectual leadership as experienced by us.

In constructing these vignettes, narrative portraiture was used to frame the experiences using detailed description and a rich narrative to reveal the identity and experiences of the EdD graduates (Smyth & McInerney, 2013). By using portraiture, 'the portraitist seeks to document and illuminate the complexity and detail of a unique experience … hoping that the audience will see themselves reflected in it' (Lawrence-Lightfoot, 2005, p. 13). The complexity and detail of the EdD experience as professionals is explored from a range of perspectives, examining the challenge of balancing multiple roles, the shifts in identity, the cruciality of critical reflexivity and the challenges of affecting organizational change. Pseudonyms have been used throughout the vignettes to maintain the anonymity of settings, supervisors and colleagues.

Vignette 1 (Sam): Balancing the roles of practitioner and researcher

I started my professional doctorate (EdD) in 2011 and completed it in 2017. I studied for the EdD part time whilst working as a full-time teacher. I had been teaching since 2006 and I had been in my current role since 2010. As a practitioner, I felt comfortable and confident in what I was doing; I was a good teacher. I saw my research as a way to build on this and further improve it. As a researcher, I was not at all confident in what I was doing. I looked to my supervisor as an all-knowing person, very much the 'teacher' in our supervisory relationship. Something I can reflect on now is the power relationship between myself and my supervisor. I hasten to add that my supervisor would not necessarily have seen himself as being the teacher or holding power, but I certainly viewed the relationship in this way, perhaps due to my own professional background.

One element of my professional role was to teach lessons which aimed to prepare students for application to, and study at, elite universities. For my doctoral research, I decided to examine how these lessons met their aims. As part of my doctoral research, I used reflexivity as an insider researcher. This process of reflexivity was essential to understanding the phenomena I was investigating, but it also led to an uncomfortable tension for me as a practitioner-researcher. My research enabled me to realize that I was using my social and cultural capital to train my students to perform in admissions interviews for elite universities; this was uncomfortable for me as a practitioner, and a part of me would still try to misrecognize that I was doing this and argue that in fact I was simply developing my students into better scholars. The conversations that I had with my supervisor helped me to negotiate this tension and to come to terms with the role I was playing in reproducing social inequality. I had come into the EdD feeling confident in my practitioner role, but the more I engaged with research and the intellectual leadership of my supervisor the more challenged and threatened I felt as a practitioner. It was one thing starting the EdD and feeling unsure of myself in a research setting, as I was new to being a researcher, but the EdD thinking and supervisory meetings caused me to feel unsure of myself in my professional setting and to question the professionalism I had developed over years. As I started to become an 'expert', and I still use the word very reluctantly, in my research area, and thus an intellectual leader, I was very aware of the risks associated with this in my practitioner role. There was a danger that my research would undermine what I was doing through my teaching practice. There was a complex interplay between how I negotiated my practitioner role and my researcher role. I left my teaching role in 2018, a year after completing my doctorate, to take up a position in a university so that I could engage more with research activity.

Vignette 2 (Jo): Shifting student identity

I was a full-time primary school teacher and subject leader when I started my part-time EdD. I had always wanted to be a teacher and aspired to move up the leadership ladder through senior leadership and into headship. However, my Masters in Education had sparked my interest in closely analysing my practice and challenging my thinking. I decided to embark on an EdD to further my career as well as to continue engaging in learning. The head teacher of my school was supportive of my decision and, as well as writing a reference, arranged for my non-contact time to be on Fridays to ensure I could attend the six taught weekends in each of the first two years.

When I arrived at the first EdD weekend, I found myself surrounded by educational professionals in leadership roles: head teachers, Ofsted inspectors, local-authority advisors as examples. As a middle leader in my school, I was daunted and somewhat intimidated by my colleagues. I wondered if I did not have enough leadership experience to engage, let alone succeed, at this level. I found the sessions challenging as they led me to question my everyday practice, my values and my assumptions about education. I was actively encouraged to trouble who I was and what I was on a regular basis. Returning to school after the EdD weekends, it was difficult to fall back into the same teaching and subject leadership when I so often questioned my very foundations.

Fellow teachers in school also seemed to struggle with my EdD work. Some questioned why I would spend my weekend doing extra work, others voiced their opinions about the limited value of 'academic work' and one even asked why I wanted to be a doctor when I didn't deal with blood well! As a result, I kept my identity as a teacher and as an EdD student quite separate in the beginning: in the week, I would be a teacher, at the weekends, I would read, write and think like a student. This became more challenging as time moved on. The more interwoven my research became with my practice, the harder it was to keep them separate. Sometimes the language of my research crept into conversations as a practitioner in school and these were not always in alignment with the senior leadership team. In addition, the multiplicity of roles adopted meant that my identity was conflicted and continually negotiated. I was a teacher, a leader, an 'expert' in school but also a learner, a student, a novice researcher, a writer, amongst others.

Two years into my EdD, a position as a professional tutor at a university was advertised in English, my specialist subject. I applied and was successful in securing the post. When I told my head teacher about the job offer, she said that she was very surprised and that I was a 'dark horse'. This perhaps highlights how hard I had worked to make sure that my EdD work was not interrupting my teaching practice or disrupting the status quo. My decision to move into higher education meant that I felt I could discuss my research more openly with both members of the school staff and within my new role. It also meant that I could locate myself solely as a research student when returning to the school to collect data.

Vignette 3 (Chris): Learning intellectual leadership through the EdD

I started the EdD in 2011, following a thirty-year career in education in England. I had been a teacher in secondary schools and had held posts at middle- and senior-leadership level. I had also worked for a local authority as a School Improvement Partner and had been a member of national educational bodies. When I began my EdD studies, I had no aspirations to work in higher education: the EdD was a personal challenge for me as I approached – so I thought – the end of a career in education. I studied part time while an independent consultant to schools, colleges, governing bodies, local authorities and academy trusts. Although I would not have used the phrase at that time, I must have been drawing on my professional experience to provide some sort of intellectual leadership – mostly on a performative, school improvement agenda – to the professionals who engaged my services. For example, I advised school governing bodies on the performance management of head teachers, observed lessons and provided feedback on teaching, analysed pupil performance data and schools' plans to raise attainment and improve progress.

From the start of the EdD, it quickly became clear that some of the taken-for-granted concepts that underpinned my professional work – *school effectiveness, impact, progress data, attainment gaps, performance and standards, quality assurance* – were problematic and not to be taken for granted at all. The immediate immersion into critical scholarship showed me the intellectual limitations attached to the functional quest for what works (or not) in schools. I began to question my assumptions about leadership and my understanding of equity and social justice. Within weeks of starting the EdD, I had begun to think and act differently in my work with schools. I relished the difference and felt that it strengthened my relationship with the teachers with whom I worked. On the other hand, colleagues in similar roles – I was doing commissioned school-improvement work as part of a local-authority team – appeared sceptical about the value of doctoral study. Nevertheless, I was proud to be continually learning and convinced that it was of both professional and personal benefit.

The EdD gave me the opportunity to develop a critical study of systemic reform: to problematize the system in which I had thrived as a professional and that had provided me with a living. Blair's 'Education, Education, Education' speech (Blair, 2001) had led to the launch of several high-cost policy initiatives in England, including Excellence in Cities, Education Action Zones, the Leading-Edge Partnership programme, Specialist Schools, City Challenge and the Academies Programme. I had held leading roles with all of them; now I had the opportunity to study and critique their intellectual foundation.

I welcomed that opportunity and wasn't too surprised that the EdD changed me as a person; after all, the EdD tutors warned us to expect that. What took me completely by surprise was my late-career move to employment in higher education in a 'teaching and scholarship' capacity, in which I continue to be involved in research projects, but also have teaching and management responsibilities. The combination of professional and academic experience fostered by the EdD enables me, I believe, to provide intellectual leadership to students at undergraduate and postgraduate level – also, to colleagues at an earlier stage in their academic careers.

Vignette 4 (Alex): Identity and action

As a professional educator, senior leader and teacher educator, I pretty much knew the what and how of my day job, but I often had an unclear – or no – understanding of the why. Although I'd worked in higher education for many years, I'd never for a second thought that I would ever be 'Dr Alex'. I didn't want to be; at that time it seemed to me that a doctorate would be irrelevant; all the people I knew who were academic doctors had PhDs; they were experts in obscure and opaque areas, and much cleverer than me, well-read, with quicksilver minds. In 2011 I hadn't heard of a 'professional doctorate', but as I was looking for ways to develop my career further, I came across the notion of a 'profdoc', a qualification that was at doctoral level but with a focus on a particular professional context and set of personal professional interests. For me, that was an EdD, a Doctorate in Education. At the time I was working for myself as an educational consultant and as an associate lecturer at a number of universities; in my spare time I was examining and contributing to textbooks. It was a varied portfolio, and I was increasingly aware that I needed to develop my educational leadership in a coherent way that was rooted in theory. So the EdD sounded perfect and I signed up.

I'd always been focused on social justice as a guiding principle for my work; that was born out of my upbringing in a liberal household where my parents had brought me up to 'do any job, as long as it's socially useful'. That's really why I was a teacher. I wanted to do more thinking about social justice and education. I was thrilled that in the first year of the EdD I met Mike Apple, John Bascom Professor of Curriculum and Instruction and Educational Policy Studies at the University of Wisconsin, Madison. I listened to him talking about social justice and about some of the key challenges facing education, including social and economic inequality, political instability, and other existential threats like climate change (and now, of course, the impact of a global pandemic). And I heard Mike say this: 'A position on the balcony may provide a comfortable seat to watch the fray, but answers can best be found by joining in the creative and determined efforts of building a counter-public. There is educational work to be done' (2013, p. 166).

Mike changed my professional thinking and so my professional life; I was able to connect the how and what of my professional beings and doings to the why, and to engage in thinking about critical pedagogy for the first time. Since then, I have tried not to sit on the balcony, but to develop my intellectual leadership in ways that mean I engage with the 'why' as well as the 'how' and the 'what'. The thinking I have engaged with as a result of my EdD has been the catalyst for a big change in my professional life; I am now a reader in education at a large UK university, and I hope I encourage other educators to join me in the important educational work that needs doing.

Discussion

In these vignettes, we have illustrated the complexity, challenges, location and practices of professional intellectual leadership, illuminated by the learning from our studies and our interactions with supervisors and peers during the EdD programme. While each of our stories provides individual insights into the perspectives and precarity that we continue to experience, there are some commonalities between our experiences that we examine by employing the principles of a theory-driven, deductive thematic analysis (Boyatzis, 1998; Hayes, 1997). We view those experiences through the three lenses identified earlier: the development of professional-doctoral student identities, the impact of professional doctorates on organizational change, and the imperative of critical reflexivity as a leader negotiating the roles of practitioner and researcher. This approach provides 'a detailed analysis of some aspect of the data' (Braun & Clarke, 2006, p. 84) and enables us to hone in on particular themes (Braun & Clarke, 2012) that are pertinent to professional intellectual leadership. We will consider each of the themes in turn and discuss how the data in the vignettes illuminate and speak to the theoretical ideas presented earlier.

The development of professional doctorate identities

All four of us have undergone a shift towards being an intellectual leader in our research area, realized through a mixture of research and teaching activities. This brings with it a risk of 'challenging accepted practices', a theme that is common to all of us. Sam and Jo became uncomfortable in their professional roles, sensing a danger that their research might undermine their day-to-day professional responsibilities or their relationships with work colleagues. Alex expresses this rather differently, metaphorically moving from a comfortable position 'on the balcony' to a closer, yet critical, relationship with practice and practitioners. Similarly, Chris found that the process of doctoral study, far from distancing him from the realities of practice, provided the intellectual tools to question certain concepts that had been taken for granted in his previous professional work. We all valued the support of our peers, not only for coping with the demands of assignment deadlines and workload, but also as we managed the challenges of questioning the status quo and understanding our intellectual transformation. Peer support provided empathy that exceeded anything that our work colleagues, family or friends could offer.

Impact on organizational change

Our impact on change in our own organizations included questioning matters of privilege and organizational culture (Sam); requiring professional colleagues to rethink their assumptions about the value of 'academic work' (Jo); raising doubts about national policy rationales and discourses (Chris); developing a stronger theoretical grounding for social-justice activism (Alex); and being a role model of the practitioner-as-student (all of us). We have argued in this chapter that such impacts constitute intellectual leadership, where the academic qualification of a doctorate is considerably enhanced by our credibility as professionals whose experience and expertise bring us close to the site of our empirical work. Being able to establish a trusting relationship, both with the leaders of our organizations and with our research participants, enabled us to generate richer data than might have been possible for researchers on a more conventional doctoral programme. We have been able to use the data generated in our four projects to create new knowledge embedded in practice, and to pose critical questions about the ambivalences and contradictions in an educational world that is troubled by ideological, political and operational tensions.

Critical reflexivity as a leader

Here, we ask ourselves how we 'have come to think and write and practise in a particular way, at that time and in that space' (Gunter, 2002, p. 7). It may be a coincidence that, for all of us, 'that space' is higher education in England, where we are all now employed in universities, whereas at the start of the EdD, three of us worked in or with the school sector. Working with experienced professionals and scholars, treating and addressing each other as colleagues, reflecting on practice and emerging theories, has demonstrated to us that our projects would not have developed as they did, nor had the impact that they had, were they not planned and realized within the ethos and framework of a professional doctorate. We remain professional practitioners with particular responsibility for the leadership of teaching and learning; at the same time, we are researching professionals who seek to understand and problematize the educational worlds in which we work.

The production of the vignettes for this paper shows in itself that we are critical thinkers, aware of our own positionality and of our own development as leaders throughout the process of achieving doctorates. Mackay & Tymon (2013) describe critical reflexivity as the 'conscious review of an individual's subjective position in their research' (p. 644). It is clear that this reviewing process is something that all four of us undertook, both formally through the process of engaging with the formative assessments and work of the professional doctorate, but also more informally in our private thinking. Our practice of engaging in critical reflexivity allowed for valuable reflection on areas where we had past experiences that led to having well-entrenched and 'taken for granted' assumptions, and to begin to question hegemonic thinking and practices. Nonetheless, critically examining our practices and thinking was precarious and uncomfortable; and it required effort and perseverance. For example, Sam talks about the tension she experienced as a practitioner-researcher, as she negotiated the process of 'train[ing] my students to perform in admissions interviews for elite universities'. The use of this language by Sam as she discusses her discomfort is not accidental; it reflects the hegemonic discourses of performativity that are embedded in aspects of our education system (Ball, 2003). Jo too talks about how she found the taught EdD sessions 'troubling' in terms of her thinking about education and emphasizes the dissonance between her developing thinking about leadership and the lived realities of enactment of her leadership back in school 'when she often questioned her very foundations'. Alex explains how the doctorate has enabled her to engage with thinking critically about the 'why' as well as the 'how' and the 'what'.

It is interesting that the critical reflexivity in which all of us engaged appears to be significant in leading us to move into roles as academics and intellectual leaders in the university system in England and away from roles in schools and colleges. Chris in particular explicitly refers to the importance of the EdD in facilitating him being able to provide intellectual leadership to his students, who are also often education practitioners in schools, as well as to early career academics. Interestingly, each of us found a professional space in higher education, moving away from schools and from advisory work as we completed our doctorates. Perhaps that reflected a move from being a 'researching professional' to that of being, at least in part a 'professional researcher'. The precarious leadership roles and work that we were engaging in in our previous careers were something we were perhaps ready to leave behind for the more secure spaces of HE where we could engage in critical debate and intellectual leadership without encountering the hostility and scepticism we had done previously. The imperative of critical reflexivity in negotiating the roles of practitioner and researcher, and the spaces which the lived realities of those roles occupy, in what are precarious times both for individuals and for the education system, are fundamental to the development of intellectual leadership, but this is a risky and uncomfortable process.

Conclusion

In this chapter, we have explored the contribution of the professional doctorate, and more specifically the EdD, to professional intellectual leadership. Through our examination of recent empirical research, our vignettes and our discussions, we have highlighted the complexity, precarity and opportunities of operating in the spaces between professional practitioner and researcher. The vignettes have provided a real insight into the ways in which professional intellectual leadership is questioned, challenged and developed. These are precarious times, both for individuals and for the education system, in which critical reflexivity is imperative for negotiating the interconnected roles of practitioner and researcher. However, the concept of precarity is a complex one. The term is often used in a functional sense that is negative: people are in a precarious position in education because of the risk of losing their job as a consequence of management decisions made to satisfy the market, for example, by short-term contracts or reactions to performance data. However, the EdD deliberately causes *intellectual and emotional* precarity, and this is a positive thing, because it leads to the sort of critical scholarship that we have evidenced in our doctoral projects and our vignettes in this chapter. The value of the EdD in providing a supportive, reflective and collegial environment in which to explore such precarities is, we argue, significant to the development of professional intellectual leaders and is important if we are to affect change more widely in education.

References

Akiva, T., Crowley, K., Russell, J. L., & Hecht, M. (2018). Leadership in out-of-school learning: The Educational Doctorate program at the University of Pittsburgh. *IJREE–International Journal for Research on Extended Education*, 5(2), 19–20. http://dx.doi.org/10.3224/ijree.v5i2.09

Apple, M. (2013). *Can education change society?* Routledge.

Ball, S. J. (2003). The teacher's soul and the terrors of performativity. *Journal of Education Policy*, 18(2), 215–28. https://doi.org/10.1080/0268093022000043065

Blair, T. (23 May 2001). Full text of Tony Blair's speech on education. *The Guardian*. https://www.theguardian.com/politics/2001/may/23/labour.tonyblair

Boud, D., Fillery-Travis, A., Pizzolato, N., & Sutton, B. (2018). The influence of professional doctorates on practice and the workplace. *Studies in Higher Education*, 43(5), 914–26. https://doi.org/10.1080/03075079.2018.1438121

Boyatzis, R. (1998). *Transforming qualitative information: Thematic analysis and code development*. Sage.

Boyce, B. A. (2012). Redefining the EdD: Seeking a separate identity. *Quest*, 64(1), 24–33. https://doi.org/10.1080/00336297.2012.653260

Braun, V., & Clarke, V. (2006). Using thematic analysis in psychology. *Qualitative Research in Psychology*, 3(2), 77–101. https://psycnet.apa.org/doi/10.1191/1478088706qp063oa

Braun, V., & Clarke, V. (2012). Thematic analysis. In H. Cooper, P. M. Camic, D. L. Long, A. T. Panter, D. Rindskopf, & K. J. Sher (Eds), *APA handbook of research methods in psychology, Vol. 2. Research designs: Quantitative, qualitative, neuropsychological, and biological* (pp. 57–71). American Psychological Association.

Burnard, P., Dragovic, T., Ottewell, K., & Lim, W. M. (2018). Voicing the professional doctorate and the researching professional's identity: Theorizing the EdD's uniqueness. *London Review of Education*, 16(1), 40–55. https://doi.org/10.18546/LRE.16.1.05

Colbeck, C. L. (2008). Professional Identity Development Theory and doctoral education. *New Directions for Teaching and Learning*, 2008(113), 9–16. http://dx.doi.org/10.1002/tl.304

Costley, C., & Armsby, P. (2007). Research influences on a professional doctorate. *Research in Post-Compulsory Education*, 12(3), 343–55. https://doi.org/10.1080/13596740701559803

Cunningham, B. (2018). Pensive professionalism: The role of 'required reflection' on a professional doctorate. *London Review of Education*, 16(1), 63–74. https://doi.org/10.18546/LRE.16.1.07

Dollarhide, C. T., Gibson, D. M., & Moss, J. M. (2013). Professional identity development of counselor education doctoral students. *Counselor Education and Supervision*, 52(2), 137–50. https://doi.org/10.1002/j.1556-6978.2013.00034

Eddy, P. L., & Rao, M. (2009). Leadership development in higher education programs. *Community College Enterprise*, 15(2), 7.

Ellis, C., & Bochner, A. P. (2000). Autoethnography, personal narrative, reflexivity: Researcher as subject. In N. K. Denzin & Y. S. Lincoln (Eds), *Handbook of qualitative research* (2nd ed., pp. 733–68). Sage.

Finlay, L. (2002). Negotiating the swamp: The opportunity and challenge of reflexivity in research practice. *Qualitative Research*, 2(2), 209–30. https://doi.org/10.1177/146879410200200205

Foot, R., Crowe, A. R., Tollafield, K. A., & Allan, C. E. (2014). Exploring doctoral student identity development using a self-study approach. *Teaching and Learning Inquiry*, 2(1), 103–18. https://doi.org/10.20343/teachlearninqu.2.1.103

Fox, A., & Allan, J. (2014). Doing reflexivity: Moments of unbecoming and becoming. *International Journal of Research & Method in Education*, 31(1), 101–12. https://doi.org/10.1080/1743727X.2013.787407

Fox, A., & Slade, B. (2014). What impact can organisations expect from professional doctorates? *Professional Development in Education*, 40(4), 546–60. https://doi.org/10.1080/19415257.2013.843579

Gunter, H. M. (2002). Purposes and positions in the field of education management: Putting Bourdieu to work. *Educational Management and Administration*, 30(1), 7–26. https://doi.org/10.1177/0263211X020301005

Hawkes, D., & Yerrabati, S. (2018). A systematic review of research on professional doctorates. *London Review of Education*, 16(1), 10–27. https://doi.org/10.18546/LRE.16.1.03

Hayes, P. (1997). Contexts in context. Context in knowledge representation and natural language. *AAAI Fall Symposium, November 1997, Cambridge, Massachusetts*. Massachusetts Institute of Technology.

Lawrence-Lightfoot, S. (2005). Reflections on portraiture: A dialogue between art and science. *Qualitative Inquiry*, 11, 3–15. https://doi.org/10.1177/1077800404270955

Lundgren-Resenterra, M., & Kahn, P. E. (2019). The organisational impact of undertaking a professional doctorate: Forming critical leaders. *British Educational Research Journal*, 45(2), 407–24. https://doi.org/10.1002/BERJ.3503

Lunt, I. (2018). Introduction to 'The EdD at 20: Lessons learned from professional doctorates'. *London Review of Education*, 16(1), 4–9. https://doi.org/10.18546/LRE.16.1.02

Mackay, M., & Tymon, A. (2013). Working with uncertainty to support the teaching of critical reflection. *Teaching in Higher Education*, 18(6), 643–55. https://doi.org/10.1080/13562517.2013.774355

Malfroy, J. (2004). Conceptualisation of a professional doctorate program: Focusing on practice and change. *The Australian Educational Researcher*, 31(2), 119–29. http://dx.doi.org/10.1007/BF03249520

Oleksiyenko, A., & Ruan, N. (2019). Intellectual leadership and academic communities: Issues for discussion and research. *Higher Education Quarterly*, 73, 406–18. https://doi.org/10.1111/HEQU.12199

Paterson, R. (2021). Academic identity interrupted: Reconciling issues of culture, discipline and profession. In M. Savva & L. P. Nygaard (Eds), *Becoming a scholar: Cross-cultural reflections on identity and agency in an education doctorate* (pp. 106–20). UCL Press. http://www.jstor.org/stable/j.ctv17ppc4v

Pratt, N., Tedder, M., Boyask, R., & Kelly, P. (2015). Pedagogic relations and professional change: A sociocultural analysis of students' learning in a professional doctorate. *Studies in Higher Education*, 40(1), 43–59. http://dx.doi.org/10.1080/03075079.2013.818640

Quality Assurance Agency (QAA) (2020). *Characteristics statement: Doctoral degree*.

Rayner, S., Lord, J., Parr, E., & Sharkey, R. (2015). 'Why has my world become more confusing than it used to be?' Professional doctoral students reflect on the development of their identity. *Management in Education*, 29(4), 158–63. https://doi.org/10.1177/0892020614567247

Robinson, C. (2018). The landscape of professional doctorate provision in English higher education institutions: Inconsistencies, tensions and unsustainability. *London Review of Education*, 16(1), 90–103. https://doi.org/10.18546/LRE.16.1.09

Scott, D., Brown, A., Lunt, I., & Thorne, L. (2004). *Professional doctorates: Integrating academic and professional knowledge.* Open University Press.

Smyth, J., & McInerney, P. (2013). Whose side are you on? Advocacy ethnography: Some methodological aspects of narrative portraits of disadvantaged young people, in socially critical research. *International Journal of Qualitative Studies in Education,* 26(1), 1–20. https://doi.org/10.1080/09518398.2011.604649

Taysum, A. (2006). The distinctiveness of the EdD within the university tradition. *Journal of Educational Administration and History,* 38(3), 323–34. https://doi.org/10.1080/00220620600984255

UK Council for Graduate Education (UKCGE) (2002). *Professional doctorates.*

Wellington, J., & Sikes, P. (2006). 'A doctorate in a tight compartment': Why do students choose a professional doctorate and what impact does it have on their personal and professional lives? *Studies in Higher Education,* 31(6), 723–34. https://doi.org/10.1080/03075070601004358

Wenger, E. (2010). Communities of practice and social learning systems: The career of a concept. In C. Blackmore (Ed.), *Social learning systems and communities of practice* (pp. 179–98). The Open University.

Crises and the Emergence of 'Estates' within Australian Universities

James Waghorne

Introduction

In their 1970 study of higher education in the UK Eric Ashby and Mary Anderson identified what they called a 'student estate' operating in UK universities (Ashby & Anderson, 1970). This they conceived of as a new kind of a coherent student voice, able to represent the special interests of students and influence university policy. The idea of describing this student movement as an 'estate' powerfully evoked the sense in which students adopted a more forthright, articulate and organized approach towards their studies and how they conceived of universities, moving beyond paternalist relationships that had typified previous generations. Indeed, as Ashby and Anderson reflect, students are members of the university, not its clients or its servants.

This way of portraying universities captured the contemporary surprise expressed at the energy of the student movement, which achieved an uncompromising spirit that brought discomfort to universities and academics, and challenged what universities represented and what their public role ought to be. The emphasis of Ashby and Anderson's work was on students, and this is typically where it is read (Forsyth, 2014), yet this way of reading universities presupposes other estates alongside the students and reveals the different interests that combine to make up universities. Highlighting the different groups offers insight into their different connection with universities' work, with the production of knowledge, the quality of teaching, the resourcing of research and the means and level of funding and allocation of resources. Ashby and Anderson's insight is that these groups each have different interests and expectations, and their combination has shaped universities.

This chapter traces the emergence of estates in Australian universities, arguing for the importance of moments of upheaval in prompting their formation. It shows how group vulnerability motivated the finding of common cause, instrumental in creating diverse forms of leadership within universities, helping to shape responses to crises and then policy beyond. Yet these origins had lasting effects for the way in which these estates represented their members, including gaps in their representation, and for the governing structures established to accommodate them and the form of discourse they created.

Crises and the emergence of estates within universities

The 'estates' reveal misgivings about leadership structures dominated by small central groups, and a desire among university members to influence and shape the policy of universities by defining collective interests and claiming their legitimacy because of their special autonomy within universities and their university-wide applicability. This differs from administrative structures that might otherwise suggest representation, such as Student Representative Councils, whose primary focus was on the student body and who, at least initially, advocated on smaller issues such as disciplinary measures imposed on individuals, and claimed no right to reshape the university.

The emergence of more organized interests in Australian universities was spurred in part by gradual underlying changes in the size and complexity of organizations, but also, crucially, as this chapter argues, by moments of abrupt change. The estates that formed sought to preserve the interests of groups within universities as institutions formed during moments of crisis. Once formed, these structures endured, evolving from their original form while also bringing continued influence in the subsequent decades. These 'estates' also emerged in response to one another, the power they directed to groups within universities, as an attempt to challenge that authority and assert the interests of other groups. What has emerged over the twentieth century is a transformation within universities' governance as three distinct estates won status and legitimacy that has since been formalized within university governance structures.

The shift was considerable. The nineteenth-century universities were institutions of individual personalities, known by the reputations of their professors and the august men who populated their senior administrative roles. They were the single such institution within their own state so they related directly to their state government supporters, often through private channels.

They were public institutions, funded in large measure out of the public purse, with corresponding public expectations. Their primary mission was teaching of the next generation of students in the skills needed to enter the professions and to impart on their students the fine learning to bring civilization; however, they were also subject to public appeals for assistance in their areas of expertise (Horne & Sherington, 2012; Selleck, 2003).

Universities were governed according to their Acts of Incorporation by self-elected lay committees, comprising public leaders from the judiciary, business and the professions. These committees formed policy that was then ratified by a body of graduates. Throughout, university chancellors and other leaders remained honorary, conducting their business in the evenings around their primary work. Academic policy was largely delegated to professorial committees of academics, but formally enacted by the other process. Students, meanwhile, had ostensible representation through their Student Representative Councils, and their Unions or Guilds. The accounts were kept by the Registrar and their assistants, who had no policy function beyond financial oversight. These arrangements recognized the different expertise of constituents and gave them positions of authority, yet the coherence across the members of these groups was limited, meaning that they could not be characterized as 'estates'.

The influence of these estates has been to redefine the meaning of universities, their work and how they were supported to do it by government, who could come and what responsibility universities had to their students and staff, and how they achieved it. Such relationships are never more critical than during moments of precarity, where circumstances create anxiety and uncertainty invites fresh approaches. These estates protected the interests of their members, while also claiming forms of institutional leadership drawn from the needs and experience of their members.

The executive estate

The first of the interests to organize was the executive estate, the formation of which was triggered by the 1930s Great Depression following the crash of the US stock market. University budgets were abruptly slashed, forcing decisions about how reduced resources would be allocated (Croucher & Waghorne, 2020, pp. 38–40). A full-time chief executive in this context offered a single decision maker able to both manage internal discussions and represent the university in public settings and, through the appointment of a professional manager, an executive arm of the university was established. These chief executives adopted the title 'vice-chancellor' in recognition of their leadership role within universities as well as their managerial function, and their status as an estate was buttressed by external links with government and counterparts across Australia.

That crisis that was instrumental in creating the executive estate proved influential in making the office a more intrusive force in the university than it might otherwise have been. The underlying value of increased managerial oversight had long been identified at Australian universities. The increasing size of universities, both in student numbers and in academic staff and degrees, increased their complexity. At the turn of the twentieth century Australian universities were characterized by tiny student numbers – the largest having only a few hundred – and academic cohorts counted at most in the dozens. However, during the twentieth century these numbers grew inexorably, demanding the appointment of increasing numbers of academic staff, including associate professors and other teaching staff to support the professoriate. These appointments supported widening specialization and the number of academic departments proliferated.

The growing size and scale of this work justified the formalization of administrative governance. From 1914, when the University of Sydney appointed Henry Barff Warden and Registrar, universities in Australia appointed salaried administrative officers who would undertake the ongoing management of the institution (Turney, Bygott & Chippendale, 1991). This structure borrowed deliberately from business practices, with the vice-chancellor serving as the 'chief executive officer' to reflect the responsibilities of the position and its business-like approach. Unlike presidents in US universities, the vice-chancellor would report to a governing board chaired by the chancellor. The vice-chancellor in turn chaired the professorial board, thus bridging the academic and administrative arms of the university, while preserving the checks and balances (Croucher & Waghorne, 2020).

The full-time administration of Australian universities was given impetus by the worldwide economic depression of the 1930s. The collapsing public purse led governments to slash university budgets, forcing them to respond with emergency measures including blanket salary reductions. The careful management of public resources during a period of scarcity gave authority to these individuals, who claimed the ability to determine the most efficient allocation of resources. This was most apparent at the University of Melbourne, which had sought unsuccessfully to secure funding to support this position for over fifty years until the Victorian state government finally gave way during the economic crisis (Selleck, 2003, pp. 202–5, 336–44, 591–2, 599–602, 659–61; 'Royal Commission on the University of Melbourne', 1904).

The creation of the position of full-time vice-chancellor dramatically extended the authority of university administration. Administrations set the agenda for their institutions, took initiatives, and their control of the budget allowed them to bring change. They also provided a figure-head able to represent universities in the community and with government. The Melbourne Vice-Chancellor, the geologist Raymond Priestley, undertook this role with particular vigour, launching an ongoing fundraising campaign of public addresses across the country, in so doing making new arguments about the purpose of the university and how its public ought to support it (Brown, 1990; Priestley, 1937a, 1937b; Ridley, 2002).

Through these actions, the salaried vice-chancellor and the administrative structures that surrounded them came to represent an 'executive estate' within universities. This individual, and their staff, claimed authority to speak on behalf of the institution, to represent its interests and to have the right to shape its activities. Emerging as it did from a need for financial prudence, the position also combined internal fiscal conservatism with outward boosterism, championing a vision of universities larger than their great professors, and asserting their place as servants of their institutions, rather than the reverse. Inherent in this estate was the elevation of bureaucratic processes in university operations and the standardization of university work (Fitzgerald, 2014).

An important expression of the growth of the administrative estate was the creation of the Australian Vice-Chancellors' Committee (AVCC) in 1934. This body comprised the vice-chancellors of Australian universities and offered a way of convening and fostering common positions on issues and comparing situations in their respective institutions. The AVCC emerged out of annual conferences of universities over the preceding decade, mostly led by senior professors. These conferences raised a range of issues about universities, including academic and administrative questions, but inconsistent participants broke discussion and limited the ongoing applicability of findings. After 1934 vice-chancellors wrested control and excluded the other staff, and the forum became the instrument of leadership. The change reflected the confidence of vice-chancellors that they could represent their institutions on this national stage, and also a desire to ensure that meetings were focused and purposeful, drawing on the authority and expertise of senior administrative leaders. The vice-chancellors joined the AVCC in their personal capacity – they were not ex-officio representatives of their universities – confirming these individuals' newfound confidence in their own standing (Hambly, 1979). The AVCC had no authority to commit any of its members to policy, but nevertheless provided a national forum for university leaders to meet, mostly in camera, to discuss policies of common interest (Croucher & Waghorne, 2020). Emerging from financial crisis and seizing on the need for administrative oversight, institutions such as the AVCC served to strengthen the dominion of the universities' CEOs into an executive estate.

The rise of executives has been strengthened by subsequent crises. During the Second World War, for example, it was these executives who were able to liaise with government, protecting the interests of universities, as they saw them, while supporting war initiatives, cooperating with government in the setting of wartime quotas in degrees. This form of leadership largely involved the allocation of resources, financial prudence as well as an overarching concern for the university's public reputation.

These moments gave the executive estate imprimatur to speak on behalf of the institution externally, while their command of information, learned from in camera committees and correspondence with government officials, bolstered their internal authority. In this way authority gained during short-term periods of institutional precarity produced lasting leadership structures, and cemented forms of external and internal engagement.

The academic and professional staff estate

The foundation of the academic and professional staff estate in part responded to the authority of the vice-chancellors. The agent of change was the national staff association, which formed during another major economic crisis for universities, on this occasion spurred by the end of special post-Second World War reconstruction funding. This funding and its associated instruments had almost doubled the number of university students and supported the appointments of large numbers of new staff. However, the funding was finite, and a new government had committed to reducing Commonwealth funding to state universities. The impending crunch was characterized by the AVCC as a 'crisis' (Australian Vice-Chancellors' Committee, 1952), leading to the appointment in 1957 of the Murray Committee, the chief outcome of which was the restoration of higher rates of Commonwealth funding alongside state government funding, but which also involved an endorsement of universities (Murray, Clunies Ross, Morris, Reid & Richards, 1957).

The organizers of the new staff association had two main objectives. First, and predominantly, staff sought to introduce an authoritative staff voice into university policy discussions, which they believed they had lost. One of the main organizers, Ken Buckley, recalled that many of his colleagues were returned soldiers who reacted against what they saw as a quiescent university staff. Instead, they wanted to assert their place in the university (Buckley, 1993). This involved a process through which university staff altered their position of objectivity and independence to one in which they took a more activist stance (Stortz & Panayotidis, 2006).

The radical vision of the university presented by FCCUSA was 'collegiality': that universities were 'collegial' institutions with policy made in combination by the universities' members, including academic staff and administrative staff (O'Brien, 2015). This idea had earlier historical resonances, particularly in the operation of academic committees (Barnes, 2020). While professors had long held sway on academic matters, the new Association included staff at all levels, arguing that their separate interests should align with those of the professors.

The University of Tasmania emerged as the centre of FCCUSA activity, spurred by the scandal provoked by the dismissal of Sydney Sparks Orr as professor of philosophy. Orr was dismissed on moral grounds, but he was also a strident critic of the management of the University, including a signed letter that contributed to the 1955 Royal Commission into that university (Davis, 2002; Pybus, 1993). The energy and fellow-feeling created by this issue gave relevance to the early federal staff body, which conceived of the debate as one of academic freedom and due process, particularly concerning the process of the University Council in hearing evidence without sharing it with Orr (Bessant, 1993).

Alongside academic freedom, the staff association formed to protect and increase salaries and pensions, academic tenure and other working conditions. John O'Brien, in his history of the National Tertiary Education Union, argues that the staff associations' 'foremost concern was the material issue of its members' economic interests, not the future of the sector' (O'Brien, 1993, p. 205). To achieve these ends it lobbied government agencies and senior politicians directly, including the prime minister, Robert Menzies. FAUSA's 1984 policy statement, for example, set out positions on all manner of industrial concerns including pay and conditions, academic freedom and equal opportunity, and the internal government of universities (Hearn, 1984). This practice broke down any deference to the executive estate and introduced a new representative interest into discussions.

Yet while industrial concerns pervaded, the staff association also claimed a wider remit through its journal, which showed a much wider set of concerns. A key contribution of the staff association to the discussion of universities was the establishment of its *Bulletin* to discuss issues in higher education, a continuing publication which later changed its name to *Vestes* and then *Australian University Review*. This magazine gave voice to staff concerns, allowing the federal council to comment on changes in government policy, as well as other issues of concern to staff. It also offered staff a platform for raising issues concerned with university leadership. In pursuing salary claims, the association conducted investigations into university systems internationally, to determine their common features and how they differed (e.g. Holmes, 1960; Murray, 1959; Sheffield, 1960). They also explored a wide range of broader subjects no less relevant to staff interests, such as the granting of full university status to the Newcastle University College (The Staff Association, 1958), how best to rearrange university libraries (Osborn, 1960), and university architecture (Winston, 1960), to take just three examples.

Recognizing the valence of this, the AVCC published its own journal, the *Australian University*, providing opportunity for discussion of themes of interest to university administrations. The AVCC presented the new journal as 'complementary' to *Vestes*, while eschewing the staff association matters (Prescott, 1963). Nevertheless, the decision to launch a counterpart journal reflected the friction between the two estates and a desire to control the narrative. While both provided opportunity for critical comment on university policy, the *Australian University* highlighted issues of governance structures, measures to assist students from less-affluent backgrounds and the growth of disciplines – matters of greater concern to administrators (Baxter, 1968; Budig, 1971; Butterfield & Kane, 1969).

The academic and professional staff estate thus emerged to challenge the executive estate and called for greater participation of staff in university policy. While the administrative estate persisted in the posture that they represented the whole of the university, the rise of the general staff made this position untenable.

The rise of the staff estate thus ushered in a new set of priorities, but also an alternative vision of universities' priorities and missions. This diversified the leadership of universities, ensuring executive accountability, while also pushing staff to consider their own local issues and grievances from a whole-of-university perspective. The friction between these leadership structures has persisted, becoming a feature of universities, undermining claims of the executive estate to speak for all universities, while also preventing a simple unitary entry point to universities.

The student estate

The emergence of a 'student estate' is usually attributed to the 1960s when the student movement adopted methods of public protest and took uncompromising stands against racism and the Vietnam War. The picture of students invading university spaces and 'sitting in', or storming council chambers to demand policy change, such as the provision of childcare services, all derive from this time when the student body claimed special insight into universities and the responsibility to change universities and make them accountable to their students (Webster, 2015). The 'student estate' as has been characterized by this chapter emerged much earlier, prompted by the economic trials of the 1930s for students. In other countries, National Unions of Students formed at different times (Day, 2012; McKay, 2015), but in Australia the National Union of Australian University Students formed in 1937 at the Australian Universities Conference held in Adelaide to advance student causes generally and contribute a student voice to national discussions about universities. The Adelaide conference reflects the mutual dependence of these estates. Vice-chancellors, who sponsored the travel of delegates to the Adelaide conference, encouraged them to organize (Ridley, 2002). Causes advanced by students in particular benefitted from the support and guidance of academic staff, especially junior staff.

In creating a national union, students were faced with interpreting what this would mean. Among the purposes of the NUAUS as expressed by its Constitution (NUAUS, 1937) was to 'study national and international questions relating to higher education and to the intellectual and material life of students', and take action on them (Constitution of the National Union of Australian University Students, 1937, s. 3(c); Hastings, 2003, pp. 138–39).

One of the areas that emerged was student health, which reflected the challenges faced by students during the period of disruption caused by economic depression and the Second World War, and also the tenor of the age when centralized organization, harnessing and organizing collective resources, was commonplace. Student cohorts working with academic staff pressed universities to establish student health centres. These centres offered screening for infectious diseases such as tuberculosis and would later extend into psychological and counselling services to university students (Clegg, 1956; Dickinson, 1976; McGee, 1933). Health concerns also led to moves to improve the quality of food served in student cafeterias (Janus, 1945).

Another concern was student housing, which issue became particularly acute during the Second World War when rationing limited construction of new housing (Darian-Smith, 2009; Macintyre, 2015). Student surveys at the University of Melbourne found that students were suffering under 'high rents, crowded conditions, unheated rooms, shortage of food, which was often bad, lack of proper study facilities, unhygienic surroundings, too much noise, bad sanitation, poor washing facilities, unnecessary restrictions and uncooperative landladies'. Unscrupulous locals were renting out 'sheds, garages, barns, stables, so-called sleep-outs and other flimsy structures at exorbitant rates'. Lodgings provided by churches eased the pressure but brought other problems as large dormitories offered no 'privacy or quietness'. One in ten students were found to be living in conditions the student meeting considered 'unsatisfactory' (Orams & Shavitsky, 1945). This information was then channelled into political discussion beyond the university, including to political members and trade unions.

These initiatives differed from previous student initiatives in that they were not altruistic, aimed at overcoming a social injustice or advancing a social cause; they were concerned to redefine universities' responsibilities to their students and the range of activities they supported (Brewis, 2014). These differed from the industrial concerns of staff, and the national union often limped along with meagre assets and individual universities periodically withdrawing their support.

Students at Melbourne University took up their cause by founding a Student Hostel in 1945, to be run by students as a non-profit cooperative. The hostel was established in a former hotel in the neighbouring suburb of Fitzroy with space for fourteen student residents. This initiative had been undertaken without the support of the University, which raised legal as well as moral objections, although three professors agreed to sign as trustees (Pascoe, 2011).

The Hostel was renewed by each year's SRC during the 1940s and 1950s as a pilot scheme that it hoped would lead to other initiatives on a larger scale. The SRC envisaged the Brunswick Street Hostel would be followed by a facility providing 500 beds, with special arrangements for both single and married students. It lobbied unsuccessfully for the Commonwealth Department of Post-war Reconstruction to provide housing for returned soldiers, and it lobbied the Victorian government to amend the University Act to require it to support student housing. This campaign bore some fruit in 1947, when the government funded the establishment of a student hostel on Drummond Street, Carlton, later named for the Vice-Chancellor, John Medley, as Medley Hall.

In raising and championing these issues, students challenged the paternalism that typified their place in universities. At Melbourne, students led by returned soldier Geoffrey Serle created an 'Orientation Week' in 1945 to provide students an extended welcome to the university and raise awareness of the services that were available to them. Students then pressed for this weeklong welcome to continue in the subsequent years with university support. Serle's message to students went beyond the customary welcome, urging them to participate in university leadership. Among the 'main functions' of the NUAUS, he told students, was 'to make student opinion heard on all matters affecting their welfare, subsidies, quotas, teaching methods, student housing, student health, etc.'. As with other student activities, this depended on participation from a sometimes apathetic or distracted student group: 'Its strength depends on your individual support and ideas … this is your Union, and through it our ideas and hopes reach fulfilment' (Serle, 1945, p. 4).

In asserting their interests, students opposed forms of paternalism that had characterized their treatment by the university in previous eras. Seizing student control of university institutions became a central organizing project of postwar students. Between 1946 and 1953 students at the University of Melbourne succeeded in converting the University Union, for students, staff and graduates, into a student-run affair tailored to the interests of its student members, the graduates and staff forming separate associations, although technically remaining eligible for membership to the union. Measures such as voting support for a student telephone line and funding for a typist for the NUAUS were opposed by the university for their cost, but were nevertheless confirmed by student-dominated organizing committees (Waghorne, 2022).

With or against

The emergence of estates revealed questions about whether these consisted of efforts to work within structures or to counter existing ones. The staff association combined these elements' contributing ideas and innovations to inform university governance, while also maintaining an unyielding opposition to centralized executive authority. The student movement was less obviously in this position, emerging during the long 1960s to adopt a more militant activism. The earlier manoeuvres served to prepare the way for these protest movements, and the ideas expressed in this period would shape that later period, particularly in its combination of cultural and political elements. Newly assertive students claimed a greater range of causes as falling within their remit, not only in the wider world, but those which affected the university itself, ranging from opposition to the White Australia Policy (the government policy of excluding immigrants from Asian countries), buoyed by support for international students and moves to support Indigenous peoples to access university (Clark, 2001, 2008; Curthoys, 2002; Darian-Smith & Waghorne, 2016; Tavan, 2008; Viviani, 1992). Among the largest issues was the Vietnam War, condemned by student opponents as an unjust war, calling into question universities' public role and place within the state committing war crimes (van Moorst, 2015). This was a transnational movement, applied to Australian conditions, combining cultural and political elements (Barcan, 2011; Hoefferle, 2012; Murphy, 2019; Piccini, 2016; Yeats, 2009; Young, 1977).

The student estate proved to be uncompromising, cutting across forms of decorum through its adoption of forms of protest. Its counter-cultural elements introduced a desire to explore alternative forms of representation. Actions such as the 'sit in' occupation of buildings and the painting of slogans, placards and posters around the campus, made the student estate difficult to contain. At its most militant, it rejected forms of assessment such as examination, arguing that university teaching should follow the interests and development of individual students, rather than having students adhere to fixed ideas of qualification (Wood, 1974). Within the militant student movement tension emerged over the benefit of maintaining independence and external critique of university policies or being co-opted into academic and government structures (Briedis, 2019).

The maintenance of an activist standing created a new form of precarity as the actions of student leaders exposed them to university and legal sanction. This form of leadership fostered a different approach to the student estate, characterized by risk-taking, an approach which proved effective in moving university executives to expand their offerings. Areas of advance included in childcare, which was not initially seen by some university leaders as an essential university service, and was achieved only after sustained student and staff pressure (Poynter & Rasmussen, 1996, pp. 408–12). Perhaps in an effort to contain the ardour of student leaders, but more obviously to capture their spirit and to recognize their ability to contribute to university policy, student leaders were co-opted into university academic and executive committees, cementing the place of the student estate within the university. The radical component remains, however, and will not be stifled.

The endurance of 'estates'

The emergence of estates has reshaped universities' character and the way they have determined policy. Universities recognized the emergence of the student estate in the 1960s by inviting student representatives to join governing bodies, and student representatives participate in faculty and school committees. The interests of the student estate are thus considered, and students participate in the government of universities, although with conditions (Cornelius-Bell, 2021; Rodgers, Freeman, Williams & Kane, 2011). Student organizations have also come to be seen as worthy conduits, contributing to 'connecting universities and their students' (Day, 2012). Staff also play a greater role in the operation of universities, gaining representation on governing councils. The academic committees have been 'democratized' by the inclusion of representatives from non-professorial bodies. Staff, students and executive members participated in regular, ad hoc conferences where issues could be raised and different perspectives shared (Wheelright, 1960).

These structural changes reflect the tendency for groups within these estates to win co-option into governing structures. Such moves are natural responses from universities concerned to listen to a wider range of perspectives, and for them to ensure that their activities meet the needs of their constituent groups. Yet these changes also risk dividing the common cause created during moments of precarity, with implications for future crises. 'Estates' are more flexible and amorphous than these governing structures can hope to be, and more able to challenge alternative forms of authority.

One reason for this is the difficulty of representation, as universities have grown inexorably, and with widening demographics of students especially, but also of staff. The task of representing all students could no longer rely on older forms of social groupings that applied in smaller cohorts. By the 1960s, universities such as those in Sydney and Melbourne had more than 15,000 students, while the newer institutions rapidly expanded. Enlarged student membership also broadened universities' social and ethnic composition. This reduced the prospect of common cause (Anderson, 1968). A student body of this size on the one hand offers validity to methods for writing in forms of representation, yet such formal structures cannot claim to represent their constituents.

This was also true for estates, but their undefined qualities offered greater scope for reform, even if this was not always achieved. While the national staff association represented university staff it did little to challenge the overwhelmingly masculine working culture at universities. As Thérèse Radic (1982) recalled, this was an environment by men for men, which women often found it difficult to break into. The first woman was not elected to its executive committee until 1971, reflecting the situation in which the association had formed and the forces which had brought it together after the war (Gaha, 1993). These organizations thus claimed to represent their constituencies more than they necessarily did. Similarly the student estate primarily represented its politically active members, at times alienating the wider body of students (Little, 1970). However, such shortcomings were more easily overcome by flexible structures and ones not reliant on one or two student representatives.

In place of stability representative structures, the concept of university estates promotes flexibility. One example of alternative approaches was the Free University established in Sydney in the late 1960s. Released from the shackles of university administration and the expectations of large university bureaucracies, this initiative supported new approaches potentially more suited to their students. This initiative enabled what Hannah Forsyth has described as 'blurr[ing]' the 'distinctions' between staff and students in the process of producing knowledge (Forsyth, 2015). In this way the FU was a manifestation of the staff and student estates, which empowered their members to pioneer new forms of knowledge production outside the hierarchies established by the governing structures created by establishing legislation.

The difference between the idea of 'estates' and representative structures was revealed in the dispute following the University of Melbourne's 1970 decision to exclude student activist Albert Langer from enrolling on character grounds. Student groups responded by occupying the administration building and voted to withdraw their representatives from University and faculty committees (Poynter & Rasmussen, 1996, p. 399). The postgraduate representative on the University Council, Chris Ryan, resigned over the event, explaining that his presence on the committee 'adds legitimacy' to Council decisions giving the erroneous impression that 'due consideration has been given to student views' (Chris Ryan, cited in Francis & Lenaghan, 1989, p. 17).

Students voted for an enquiry into the forms of governance at the university, a proposal accepted by the University Council in an extraordinary concession symptomatic of the pressure caused by the action of different estates. The Council's motion acknowledged the place of the different estates, inviting proposals from 'representative groups within the university community' (University of Melbourne Council Minutes, 7 June 1971). However, in discussions about how to organize this inquiry, the participants moved in favour of establishing a standing committee to conduct an ongoing inquiry to issues as they arose, a proposal which became the University Assembly, formed in 1974. The Assembly, comprising representatives of academic and other staff, students and graduates, aimed to serve as a 'permanent consultative body'. Concerns from all participants could be raised and discussed; sub-committees conducted research projects into larger issues to inform debate. The Assembly's intention was to create a structure by which the interests of staff and students could be advanced, although the Assembly that emerged was limited to making recommendations to the University Council, rather than committing the University to make change. Even for this, the Assembly's submissions carried the weight of having emerged from the community and could not be summarily dismissed (Roskam, 1989). The Assembly lasted until 1989, when it was disbanded (Stavropoulos, 1989).

The demise of the University Assembly reflected the rise of new forms of management within universities which acted to concentrate authority in the hands of administrators and imposed external forms of accountability that contained staff independence. Students, meanwhile, found themselves pressed to acquire skills with limited opportunity for exploration (Walter & Holbrook, 2018), while increased competition and expectations on staff have squeezed opportunities for collective action (Lipton, 2019). By 1993, the staff association became the National Tertiary Education Union, concerned with protecting the work and conditions of its members (O'Brien, 2015). Staff have expressed concern about the shifts and called for greater staff autonomy (Connell, 2019). Perhaps this latest crisis will lead to a renewal of the interests of student estates.

Conclusion

The closure of university campuses across Australia during the Covid-19 pandemic, and the gradual return of staff and students, has revealed how fragmented universities can seem and the importance of informal connections in forming collective identity. The disconnection of many staff from one another, of staff from students and all from the body of the university itself shows the importance of geographic proximity in establishing university hierarchies.

Moments such as these reshape the collective experience of groups within universities, exposing underlying issues that might otherwise be overlooked. Past crises have prompted the group identification of the administration, staff and students, and the formation of 'estates', offering means for groups to articulate and represent their own distinctive interests. Their emergence, prompted by circumstance but reflecting underlying and often long-standing interests, has shown the role of diverse forms of intellectual leadership during times of precarity in ensuring responses respond to the needs of a range of interests.

Crises such as these have been instrumental in reshaping the Australian university, and these uncommon times have shaped their emergence and contributed to their ill-fitting qualities. The endurance of these 'estates' after the crisis passes has been less clear. During calmer times, common causes can diminish, and issues such as their partial representation loom larger. University governance structures have also sought to capture these estates, incorporating them into committees' ostensibly representative of their groups. While such initiatives are worthy of support in some regard, the danger that diverse interests are co-opted into larger, immovable systems, shows the continuing value of the less structured affiliations provided by 'estates'. These offer more flexible and dynamic means of representing the diverse interests that make up universities in both more placid moments and times of crisis.

References

Anderson, D. S. (1968). The prospect of student power in Australia. *The Australian University*, 6(3), 207–21.

Ashby, E., & Anderson, M. (1970). *The rise of the student estate in Britain*. Harvard University Press.

Australian Vice-Chancellors' Committee (1952). *A crisis in the finances and development of the Australian universities.*

Barcan, A. (2011). *From New Left to Factional Left: Fifty years of student activism at Sydney University*. Australian Scholarly Publishing.

Barnes, J. (2020). Collegial governance in postwar Australian universities. *History of Education Review*, 49(2), 149–64. https://doi.org/10.1108/HER-12-2019-0050

Baxter, J. P. (1968). The role of the vice-chancellor in the University of New South Wales. *The Australian University*, 6(1), 4–13.

Bessant, B. (1993). FAUSA and academic freedom. In P. Chapman (Ed.), *40 years of FAUSA: Four decades of representing university staff* (pp. 8–10). National Tertiary Education Union.

Brewis, G. (2014). *A social history of student volunteering: Britain and beyond, 1880–1980*. Palgrave MacMillan.

Briedis, T. (2019). 'I'm never coming back from that trip': The 1994 ANU occupation and student protest beyond the 1960s. *Journal of Australian Studies*, 43(2), 188–202. https://doi.org/10.1080/14443058.2019.1611620

Brown, N. (1990). Aspirations and constraints in Australian universities in the 1950s. In F. B. Smith & P. Crichton (Eds), *Ideas for histories of universities in Australia* (pp. 72–93). Division of Historical Studies, Research School of Social Sciences, Australian National University.

Buckley, K. (1993). Early years: The origins of FCUSAA. In Chapman, P. (Ed.), *40 years of FAUSA, 1952–1992: Four decades of representing university staff* (pp. 3–5). National Tertiary Education Union.

Budig, G. A. (1971). Recent changes in the American college presidency. *The Australian University*, 9(1), 49–57.

Butterfield, M., & Kane, L. (1969). A new look at the part-time student: Academic performance. *The Australian University*, 7(3), 226–49.

Clark, J. (2001). Abschol: More than a scholarship scheme. *National Library of Australia News*, 12(1), 11–13. https://doi.org/10.3316/aeipt.112016

Clark, J. (2008). *Aborigines and activism: Race, Aborigines and the coming of the Sixties to Australia*. Pearson.

Clegg, H. A. (1956). Student health services. *The British Medical Journal*, 2(4991), 520–2.

Connell, R. (2019). *The good university: What universities actually do and why it's time for radical change*. Monash University Press.

Constitution of the National Union of Australian University Students (1937). John Foster Papers, 1981.0150. University of Melbourne Archives.

Cornelius-Bell, A. (2021). University governance, radicalism and the market economy: Where student power gave way to economics and educative possibility to the corporate university. *International Journal of Social Sciences & Educational Studies*, 8(2), 76–87. http://dx.doi.org/10.23918/ijsses.v8i2p76

Croucher, G., & Waghorne, J. (2020). *Australian universities: A history of common cause*. UNSW Press.

Curthoys, A. (2002). *Freedom ride: A freedom rider remembers*. Allen & Unwin.

Darian-Smith, K. (2009). *On the homefront: Melbourne in wartime, 1939–45* (2nd ed.) Melbourne University Publishing.

Darian-Smith, K., & Waghorne, J. (2016). Australian-Asian sociability, student activism, and the university challenge to White Australia in the 1950s. *Australian Journal of Politics and History*, 62(2), 203–18. https://doi.org/10.1111/ajph.12245

Davis, R. (2002). The battle for collegiality in Tasmania: The 1955 Royal Commission and the Orr aftermath. In J. Biggs & R. Davis (Eds), *The subversion of Australian universities* (pp. 41–51). Fund for Intellectual Dissent.

Day, M. (2012). Dubious causes of no interest to students? The development of National Union of Students in the United Kingdom. *European Journal of Higher Education*, 2(1), 32–46. https://doi.org/10.1080/21568235.2012.683699

Dickinson, K. G. (1976). Student health services. *The British Medical Journal*, 2(6045), 1177–8.

Fitzgerald, T. (2014). Scholarly traditions and the role of the professoriate in uncertain times. *Journal of Educational Administration and History*, 46(2), 207–19. http://dx.doi.org/10.1080/00220620.2014.889092

Forsyth, H. (2014). *A history of the modern Australian university*. NewSouth Publishing.

Forsyth, H. (2015). Expanding higher education: Institutional responses in Australia from the post-war era to the 1970s. *Paedagogica Historica*, 51(3), 365–80. https://doi.org/10.1080/00309230.2014.929592

Francis, C., & Lenaghan, N. (1989). Bricks, mortar and all that: Assembly antecedents. In P. Stavropoulos (Ed.), *Short circuit!: The Melbourne University Assembly, 1974–1989* (pp. 9–40). The Assembly.

Gaha, J. (1993). Women and the development of an industrial agenda in FAUSA. In P. Chapman (Ed.), *40 years in FAUSA, 1952–1992: Four decades of representing university staff* (pp. 20–3). National Tertiary Education Union.

Hambly, F. S. (1979). Australian Vice-Chancellors' Committee. *Journal of Tertiary Education Administration*, 1(1), 64–71.

Hastings, G. (2003). *It can't happen here: A political history of student activism*. The Students' Association of Flinders University.

Hearn, J. M. (1984). Industrial activity and political influence: Strengthening the nexus in academic unions. *Vestes*, 27(2), 2–7.

Hoefferle, C. (2012). *British student activism in the long sixties*. Routledge.

Holmes, F. W. (1960). Current problems of the New Zealand universities. *Vestes*, 3(1), 37–44.

Horne, J., & Sherington, G. (2012). *Sydney: The making of a public university*. Melbourne University Publishing.

Janus. (1945). Mens Sana .... *Farrago*, 21(20), 1.

Lipton, B. (2019). Closed doors: Academic collegiality, isolation, competition and resistance in the contemporary Australian university. In M. Breeze, Y. Taylor, & C. Costa (Eds), *Time and space in the neoliberal university: Futures and fractures in higher education* (pp. 15–42). Palgrave Macmillan.

Little, G. (1970). *The university experience: An Australian study*. Melbourne University Press.

Macintyre, S. (2015). *Australia's boldest experiment: War and reconstruction in the 1940s*. NewSouth.

McGee, N. W. (1933). Student health service. *The Journal of Higher Education*, 4(9), 475–9.

McKay, C. E. A. (2015). *A history of the National Union of South African Students (NUSAS), 1956–1970* [Unpublished PhD thesis]. University of South Africa.

Murphy, K. (2019). The countercultural New Left 'Down Under': Student activism at the University of New England, Australia. *The Sixties*, 12(2), 178–204. https://doi.org/10.1080/17541328.2019.1674486

Murray, K. A. H. (1959). The work of the University Grants Committee in Great Britain. *Vestes*, 2(1), 2–7.

Murray, K. A. H., Clunies Ross, I., Morris, C. R., Reid, A. J., & Richards, J. C. (1957). *Report of the Murray Committee on Australian Universities, September 1957*. A. J. Arthur, Commonwealth Government Printer.

NUAUS. (1937). *Constitution*. John Foster Papers, 1981.0150. University of Melbourne Archives.

O'Brien, J. M. (1993). The collective organization of Australian academic staff 1949–1983. *Journal of Industrial Relations*, 35(2), 195–220. https://doi.org/10.1177/002218569303500201

O'Brien, J. M. (2015). *National Tertiary Education Union: A most unlikely union*. UNSW Press.

Orams, H., & Shavitsky, A. (1945). Big news in housing: Sub-committee reports. *Farrago*, 21(20), 3.

Osborn, A. D. (1960). The turning point for university libraries. *Vestes*, 3(1), 21–5.

Pascoe, S. J. (2011). *The social and spatial construction of student housing: The University of Melbourne in an age of expansion* [Unpublished Masters dissertation]. The University of Melbourne.

Piccini, J. (2016). *Transnational protest, Australia and the 1960s*. Palgrave Macmillan.

Poynter, J. R., & Rasmussen, C. (1996). *A place apart: The University of Melbourne: Decades of challenge*. Melbourne University Press.

Prescott, S. L. (1963). The Australian University: An introduction. *The Australian University*, 1(1), 1–3.

Priestley, R. E. (1937a). *Problems of the English-speaking university world*. The Hassell Press.

Priestley, R. E. (1937b). *The university and national life: Three addresses to Victorian political organisations*. Melbourne University Press.

Pybus, C. (1993). *Gross moral turpitude: The Orr case revisited*. William Heinemann.

Radic, T. (1982). Still life with mirrors. In P. Grimshaw & L. Strahan (Eds), *The half-open door: Sixteen modern Australian women look at professional life and achievement* (pp. 30–53). Hale & Iremonger.

Ridley, R. (Ed.) (2002). *The diary of a Vice-Chancellor, Raymond Priestley: University of Melbourne, 1935–1938*. Melbourne University Press.

Rodgers, T., Freeman, R., Williams, J., & Kane, D. (2011). Students and the governance of higher education: A UK perspective. *Tertiary Education and Management*, 17(3), 247–60. https://doi.org/10.1080/13583883.2011.586046

Roskam, J. (1989). The drafting of the Statute. In P. Stavropoulos (Ed.), *Short circuit!: The Melbourne University Assembly, 1974–1989* (pp. 41–55). The Assembly.

Royal Commission on the University of Melbourne (1904). *Final report on government administration, teaching work and finances of the University of Melbourne: With appendices*. R. S. Brain, Govt. Printer.

Selleck, R. J. W. (2003). *The shop: The University of Melbourne, 1850–1939*. Melbourne University Press.

Serle, G. (1945). We're unionists you know! *Farrago*, 21(1), 4.

Sheffield, E. F. (1960). Canadian government aid to universities. *Vestes*, 3(2), 20–6.

Stavropoulos, P. (Ed.) (1989). *Short circuit!: The Melbourne University Assembly, 1974–1989*. The Assembly.

Stortz, P., & Panayotidis, E. L. (2006). 'Have you ever looked into a Professor's soul?': Historical constructions of the professoriate in Canada. In P. Stortz & E. L. Panayotidis (Eds), *Historical identities: The professoriate in Canada* (pp. 351–80). University of Toronto Press.

Tavan, G. (2008). Immigration: Control or colour bar? The immigration reform movement, 1959–1966. *Australian Historical Studies*, 32(117), 181–200. http://dx.doi.org/10.1080/10314610108596160

The Staff Association (1958). A policy for the development of Newcastle University College. *The Federal Council Bulletin*, 1(4), 3–4.

Turney, C., Bygott, U., & Chippendale, P. (1991). *Australia's first: A history of the University of Sydney, Volume 1, 1850–1939*. Hale & Iremonger.

van Moorst, H. (2015). The Vietnam moratorium: Protest and resistance. In S. Blackburn (Ed.), *Breaking out: Memories of Melbourne in the 1970s*. Hale & Iremonger.

Viviani, N. (Ed.) (1992). *The abolition of the White Australia Policy: The immigration reform movement revisited*. Centre for the Study of Australia–Asia Relations.

Waghorne, J. (2022). *By students, for students: A history of the Melbourne University Union*. Australian Scholarly.

Walter, J., & Holbrook, C. (2018). Policy narratives in historical transition: A case study in contemporary history. *Australian Historical Studies*, 49(2), 221–36. https://doi.org/10.1080/1031461X.2018.1441886

Webster, S. L. (2015). *Protest activity in the British Student Movement, 1945–2011* [Unpublished PhD dissertation]. University of Manchester.

Wheelright, T. (1960). Proposal for Australian Universities Conference. *Vestes*, 3(1), 62–3.

Winston, D. (1960). Building our universities. *Vestes*, 3(4), 25–8.

Wood, D. G. (1974). Formal examinations: Do they serve any useful purpose? *Cranks and nuts*, 1974, 62–4. http://hdl.handle.net/11343/274967

Yeats, K. (2009). *Australian New Left politics, 1956–1972* [Unpublished PhD dissertation]. University of Melbourne.

Young, N. (1977). *An infantile disorder?: The crisis and decline of the New Left*. Routledge.

10

The Need for Critical Intellectual Leadership in US Community Colleges during Precarious Times

David L. Levinson and Katherine R. Rowell

Introduction

The development of community colleges in the United States was inexorably tied to differentiating lower strata of students within the academic enterprise. As private higher education grew in the United States during the post-civil war, there was a desire to maintain the exclusivity of the enterprise by creating a 'junior-college' segment. The pejorative nature of this term reflected this development as the president of the University of Chicago was instrumental in creating Joliet Junior College in 1901. In the 1890s, William Raney Harper, then president of the University of Chicago – an extremely prestigious private institution in the United States – segmented the University of Chicago to reflect a senior and junior division (Durry, 2003). This junior division, synonymous with US community colleges that offer a two-year associate degree, was viewed as inferior from its inception, and its faculty and administrators were often intentionally excluded from disciplinary association membership.

Historically, disciplinary associations in the United States often disregarded faculty working at community colleges. Mary Huber (2021) notes that some of the reasons for this non-inclusion include requirements of doctoral degrees and emphasis on scholarship rather than teaching. She writes, 'Indeed, many societies have historically paid short shrift to the most immediate professional concern of many community college faculty – teaching itself' (2021, p. 11). Although many disciplinary associations are increasingly working to be more inclusive of community college faculty and their students, this historical disciplinary dismissal of the work happening at community colleges further exacerbated the status issues of community college faculty and their students in the higher education system in the United States.

Community colleges remain on the lowest rung in the US higher education status hierarchy. As open-admission institutions, ideologically, they represent the inclusive opportunity available to all in the United States to pursue the 'American Dream'. However, they are often viewed as promulgating an inferior product because they eschew selectivity. As evidence, many point to their relatively low graduation/completion rates, that 70–80 per cent of their students enrol in remedial education, and how community colleges 'cool out' student ambition as illustrative of poor quality as they reproduce existing social inequality.

The rapid development of community colleges in the United States during the twentieth century brought an ideological universalism of postsecondary education to all. As higher education institutions openly admit students and bypass the competitive processes that govern entry into most baccalaureate and above colleges and universities, community colleges are potential sites for inclusion and equity. While they constitute 43 per cent of US higher education enrolment, they account for 53 per cent of all Native American student enrolments, 50 per cent of Hispanic students and 40 per cent of Black students (AACC, 2022). As open access, relatively low-cost institutions, community colleges have often been characterized as 'democracies colleges' (Boggs, 2012). We argue, however, that their potential is limited due to their colonized position within US higher education. The relentless tension between career/vocational/workforce training versus liberal arts education, their contradictory location within the nexus of US federalism and growth in consumerist models of higher education whereby institutions aggressively market themselves as guarantors of occupational success all marginalize community college students. Given their relatively low position in the US social class structure, these students are besieged with a variety of social needs, resulting in only one-third being able to enrol full-time.

To move the potential of community colleges forward, we argue that community college leadership and disciplinary associations need to reframe their structures and approaches to become 'democracies colleges'. They must develop institutional configurations conducive to models of learning that enable students to overcome the structural barriers they face. Their relatively low-cost and open admission policies provide potential upwardly mobile pathways to those historically excluded from the 'American Dream'. However, given they are 'bottom-feeders' in the United States' higher education pecking order, community colleges are often placed in a reactive mode. They are structurally in a weak position to resist what comes down from those wielding economic and political power. College administrators are often left to manage institutions subject to underfunded mandates. Full-time faculty struggle with large teaching loads as their numbers dwindle, with an increasing number of contingent faculty hired to balance budgets. Disciplinary associations in the United States have published statements and studies on the issues of working conditions for 'contingent' faculty. Still, these studies and reports are often ignored by community college administrators. Unfortunately, due to their 'status', community college faculty are not as connected to best disciplinary practices in teaching and learning. Disciplinary integration is often forfeited in favour of educational reforms that promise a relatively quick fix to the problem of incompletion, which collectively come under the umbrella of student success strategies. However, these strategies are directed towards full-time students, who constitute only one-third of the community college student body, and their long-term effectiveness is often dubious (Isserles, 2021).

From its beginning, the 'Community College' was founded as a lower stratum higher education system with less funding and resources to educate the masses and the marginalized. The system, one could argue, was designed to maintain inequality, and, thus, there has always been a tension about higher education at the community college. This unequal system has left community colleges to serve students more at the whim of state and local governments and capitalistic economic systems. Thus, rather than offer marginalized and first-generation students opportunities to achieve the dream of higher education, community college administrators have unwittingly become 'managers', and their faculty have become 'employees' with little to no voice or institutional power.

Our standpoint

As community college practitioners, we approach this issue from very different positions. Kathy, a professor of sociology for over thirty years, was the first community college president of the North Central Sociological Association and one of only two community college sociologists to receive the American Sociological Association Distinguished Contributions to Teaching Award. David served as a community college president and administrator for thirty years, periodically teaching sociology to community college students, and higher education leadership to graduate students.

Being positionally situated from very different vantage points, we have a plethora of experiential and institutional knowledge textured by occupying very different organizational positions. Kathy and David served as co-chairs of the American Sociological Association Community College Task Force from 2012 to 2017 and have worked to engage in conversations about community college issues within the discipline of sociology. Although this chapter focuses on leadership at the community college, we also note that the lack of connection between disciplinary associations and community college faculty and administrators has left community faculty with little disciplinary support for their work. Thus, they have less institutional power around curriculum and pedagogical practice issues.

We have witnessed how community colleges can be transformative in students' lives. We can point to the scores of students who have thrived and radically altered their lives. However, we have experienced both the challenges and limitations, some attributed to the uneven preparation of our students and learning deficits that reflect 'the hidden injuries of class' (Sennett & Cobb, 1972), and others to the institutional structure of community colleges, where the hallowed academic tradition of shared governance is glossed as administrators often take a 'command and control' perspective on leadership. This perspective trickles down throughout the levels of leadership at community colleges, with departmental chairs being viewed as 'supervisors' rather than colleagues. Unfortunately, community colleges view 'leadership' as a management function. For example, there is a growing trend where community college presidents use the term 'Chief Executive Officer' (a term often used for corporations). This leadership trend lends itself to seeing faculty and students as needing to be managed, and thus the focus is on 'training' and increased rules and policies to reduce organizational problems. The curriculum is increasingly 'standardized', resulting in faculty having less academic freedom. We argue this approach results in a lack of understanding of the barriers students encounter, making it difficult for faculty to teach and students to learn at community colleges. It also divides administration and faculty, whose solidarity is needed for community colleges to address current inequities.

We suggest that community college leaders benefit from reframing leadership strategies to consider the sociological imagination and 'pedagogy of the oppressed' approaches, including understanding the structural barriers that community college students face, such as poverty and racism. As will be argued in our conclusion, it's a perspective that we urge administrators, faculty and staff to take to realize the transformative potential of community colleges. We recommend a critical leadership approach, not just a critical pedagogy.

Colonialism, federalism and neoliberalism

Three significant factors have created a situation where the leadership of community colleges is disconnected from the faculty and students: the colonized history of community colleges, the advent of 'New Federalism',[1] which promulgates market-based solutions to systemic social problems, and the dominance of private market-based solutions in higher education. These factors have continued to create a structure where community college faculty and students remain at the bottom of the higher education ladder in the United States. In contrast, academic managers have become an enlarged professional–managerial class (Ehrenreich & Ehrenreich, 1978) in higher education. With faculty and administration often working with ideologically different values, students are deprived of the tools to transcend existing inequality and white supremacy structures, with little to no support from the disciplinary associations.

Colonialism

In order to understand community colleges in the United States, it is essential to view them under the guise of colonialism. As Itzigsohn and Brown argue, modernity can only be understood in relation to colonialism. They state (2020, p. 15): 'The defining characteristics of modernity for Du Bois were colonialism and the creation of race, the invention of whiteness, and the global denial of humanity and multiple forms of exclusion, oppression, exploitation and dispossession constructed along racial lines.'

The creation of land-grant institutions in the United States, which marked the beginning of a higher education system in the United States, was clearly a colonial act for it literally took land from indigenous populations. As Davarian L. Baldwin (2021, p. 28) notes:

> The Morrill Act [of 1862] first distributed public-domain lands to states that could then be used or sold to build the financial endowments of universities. However, the 10.7 million acres for this project were indigenous lands, confiscated through seize or suspect land treaties.

The seizure was accomplished by over 160 'violence-based treaties and land seizures' impacting on 'approximately 250 tribes, bands and communities' (Lee & Ahtone, 2020).[2] We argue that the low stature of community colleges parallels and embodies structures of racial oppression and white privilege. In many ways, they reflect the underside of what W. E. B. DuBois characterizes as the 'color line'.

Community colleges have historically been under-funded, viewed with disdain by notable educational historians and sociologists (e.g. Clark, 1960; Jencks & Riesman, 1968) despite their importance for educating a disproportionate number of non-white, low-income students compared to other sectors of US higher education. It was not until passage of the Morrill Act of 1890 that there was an explicit requirement that land grant institutions provide higher education for non-whites. This was accomplished, however, by segregating non-white students into Historically Black Colleges and Universities (HBCUs).[3]

Federalism: 'Old' and 'new'

The idea of 'separate but equal' is a theme that resonates throughout US history and illustrates the convergence of colonialism and federalism.

Open access has been hampered ironically through measures designed to promote universal admission. As stated by Bilmes and Brooks (2022, A11), 'the GI Bill (The Servicemen's Readjustment Act of 1944, commonly known as the G.I. Bill, was a law that provided a range of benefits for some of the returning World War II veterans) was one of the worst social injustices of the 20th century'. They discuss how the distribution of funds from this historic legislation was left to the states, resulting in the absence of homeownership (Rothstein, 2017) and educational opportunities for Black Americans. Black students were relegated to underfunded HBCUs at the time, staffed by faculty with a lack of credentials and devoid of any entry into skilled trades. This resulted in HBCUs not only as segregated institutions but as constituting a segmented stratum. However, it has been to the credit of HBCUs to provide unmatched opportunities for Black students despite funding inequities (UNCF, 2022).

Community colleges stand at the crossroads of what has been termed the 'New Federalism' in the United States. The tenth amendment of the US Constitution asserts the importance of localized state rights and asserts that unless prescribed to the federal government's powers, the states garner legislative authority. 'States' rights' have become the calling card of the New Right in the United States. Typically evoked in the content of the alleged oppressive nature of the federal government, when it comes to education policy, this has become manifest with respect to the 'school choice' movement and the increasing presence of 'charter schools' which are viewed as an escape clause from the perceived monopolization and state control of public schooling.

Situating community colleges within the problematic New Federalism, it is important to note that although localized at the state level, which accounts for substantial variation in their governance structures among the fifty states, they are impacted significantly by federal policies. Pell grants, which are an essential source of funding for 'low-income' students, emanate from federal appropriations, and the recent allocation of Covid-19 Higher Education Emergency Relief Funds (HEERF) has staved off the fiscal insolvency of many community colleges, given precipitous declines in enrolment and increasing operating costs. Furthermore, as the tension between localized and national politics increases – a tension often expressed as regressive 'state's rights' within US political discourse – a nationalized, coordinated role for community colleges is potentially undermined. This was recently illustrated by the failure of the Biden administration's attempt at 'free community college' nationwide, which is especially ironic given that First Lady Jill Biden is a professor at Northern Virginia Community College.

Neoliberalism

The dominance of market force in higher education is increasingly prevalent in the United States. 'Outsourced' entities providing everything from Management Information Systems (MIS) to dominating searches for higher education leaders often bypass higher education's shared governance traditions.

The impact of austerity politics on higher education (Nixon, 2017) has been a dominant theme during the beginning decades of the twenty-first century. For the United States, it has meant a reduction in fiscal support for higher education and a concomitant rise in tuition for public and primarily private higher education. Concurrently, there has been a rise in for-profit higher education (e.g. Capella University, University of Phoenix) that has experienced substantial growth. However, concerns have recently been hindered by distorting student success. Such players have partially used Pell grant appropriations for low-income students to finance these operations. In addition, these institutions packaged high-interest student loans to applicants in a bait-and-switch operation that resulted in insurmountable student debt, preying on the career ambitions of working-class students.

However, other players, such as the University of Southern New Hampshire (SNU), a non-profit, have exponentially increased their online student component and serve over 100,000 students in their online division. Many analysts have heralded SNU's 'disruptive' (Christenson & Eyring, 2011) higher education strategies. The virtual environment found at SNU became more common place due to the Covid-19 pandemic. 'Blended' courses, consisting of in-person and online learning, have become more commonplace (Marcus, 2022), though the net effect on student completion has yet to be determined.

Besides being replete with discussions about needing to 'disrupt' the current model of education (Christensen & Eyring, 2011), many assert that higher education needs to learn from market reforms that have occurred in other industries. A recent example is Arthur Levine and Scott Van Pelt's *The Great Upheaval: Higher Education's Past, Present and Uncertain Future* (2021), which offers the following prognosis on what will change:

> 1) institutional control of higher education will decrease, and the power of higher education consumers will increase; 2) With near-universal access to digital devices and the Internet, students will seek from higher education the same things they are getting from music, movie, and newspaper industries; 3) new content producers and distributors will enter the higher education marketplace, driving up institutional competition and consumer choice and driving down prices; 4) the industrial era model of higher education, focusing on time, process and teaching, will be eclipsed by a knowledge economy successor rooted in outcomes and learning; and 5) the dominance of degrees and just in case education will diminish; non degree certificates and just-in-time education will increase in status and value.

Such deterministic projections gloss over the larger neoliberal, market-based forces at work. The commodification of higher education creates a precarious situation for public institutions, whose state appropriations as a percentage of operating costs have steadily declined while predatory private, and often for-profits, steer students to these institutions by promising degree completion and gainful employment which seldom occur.

US higher education should be viewed in the context of creeping neoliberalism (Tucker, 2020). The dominance of the marketplace is evident in many areas: increasing use of contingent faculty; the contracting-out of many services such as information technology; and the dominant use of search firms (head-hunters) to fill administrative positions, which has resulted in insecure employment conditions for many workers. The 'gig' economy, represented by the 'Uberization' of work, has resulted in employment without the traditional benefits. The rise of contingent faculty in higher education, especially within community colleges, is symptomatic of this more considerable socio-political formation development.

Another area where external forces have been especially active in community college reform has been a plethora of foundations and non-profit organizations.

Community college reform has been their 'bread and butter'. Organizations such as Achieve the Dream (ATD), Complete College America (CCA), Aspen Institute and EAB have produced policy recommendations that have dominated the community college student success debate. Related to this area, several foundations, such as Lumina and Gates, have funded types of research that have structured policy. The Community College Research Center (CCRC) at Teachers College, Columbia University, constitutes the most extensive amount of research. The publication of its 2015 Redesigning America's Community Colleges has been highly influential (Bailey, Smith Jaggars & Jenkins, 2015).

Community colleges are the dominant site for non-white student enrolment in US higher education, and a large percentage – 43 per cent – of students enrolled in higher education attend community colleges. They are a welcome antidote to the alleged meritocracy (Sandel, 2020) that dominates the higher education admissions game in the United States, which some have termed tyrannical or 'testocratic merit' (Guinier, 2015), which underpins the status rankings of 'competitive' universities and colleges. Community colleges also attract the lowest social class of students in tandem with inequities regarding race and ethnicity. Guinier talks about the 'tyranny of merit' as currently defined, something that higher education in the United States reproduces.

The 'status-seeking' nature of higher education and wedding to the belief of an ingrained meritocracy is problematic, as Michael Young underscored in this satirical *The Rise of the Meritocracy, 1870–2033* (1958) where merit is correlated with the rise of class privilege. Similarly, Lani Guinier, in *The Tyranny of the Meritocracy: Democratizing Higher Education in America* (2015), talks about the perversion of higher education, focusing totally on admission and not mission, perpetuating a testocracy in the process. For colleges, this has been operationalized through SATs. A plethora of research shows that such measures of technical competence are related to social class/socio-economic status, resulting in the privileged reproducing themselves.

It is noteworthy that two-thirds of community college students enrol part-time, reflecting student engagement in work and family responsibilities. And as Mayra Olivares-Ureta (2022) argues, there is especially a disregard for single mothers, who make up a substantial number of community college students who depend on holistic services. Although they constitute the majority of community college attendees, they are, for the most part, forgotten when it comes to pundits who scribe about community colleges. The community college 'student success movement', which is critiqued so skilfully by Robin Isserles (2021), targets those who already are full-time and strategizes to make those who are part-time into full-time students.

How the US Department of Education conceptualizes graduation rates also furthers and reproduces inequality. The number of full-time students who attain an associate degree in three years or baccalaureate in six years excludes close to two-thirds of students who attend community colleges part-time. By definition, the majority of students in community colleges are failures!

The Voluntary Framework of Accountability (VFA) development offers an essential corrective to the current US Department of Education classification system based on graduation rates, a measure, as previously discussed, not applicable to two-thirds of community college students. The VFA can be summarized as follows:

> In general, the VFA cohort was defined to be very widely inclusive and to examine the progress and outcomes of all students who enroll at the community college. The VFA uses a retrospective cohort tracking method for measuring the progress (after two years) and outcomes (after six years) of a student population that includes all students who enter in the fall who are first-timers at that college and attend part-time or full time. Additionally, the VFA looks at the progress and outcomes of a sub cohort of students defined as those students who earned 12 credit hours by the end of the initial 2 years of the 6-year tracking period. The measures address developmental education progress, student milestones and progress, and relevant 6-year outcomes such as credential (degree or certificate) attainment, transfer, and persistence.
>
> (American Association of Community Colleges, 2012, p. 8)

One of the primary insights of the sociology of education has to do with how educational institutions reproduce social inequality (Coleman, 1990). Bowles & Gintis (1976), in their classic study *Schooling in Capitalist America*, argued that none of IQ, heredity, nor cognitive differences explained intergenerational education inequality; it was due to the persistence and reproduction of social class. Regarding higher education, Parsons & Platt (1973) argue that the differentiation found within higher education institutions reflects the social construct of the larger society. This can be seen through the obsession with status rankings of higher education institutions, whereby colleges and universities manipulate various metrics to achieve high placement in published guides that have little to do with indices of student learning. The differentiation of two-year colleges from the larger higher education enterprise should be viewed in the context of a larger industrializing society of the 1890s, which brought about an expansion of postsecondary education in the United States with a relative need for differentiation and division of labour. According to Parsons & Platt (1973), the mushrooming of the 'cognitive complex' was a key differentiating factor of the modern world, and with respect to higher education, community colleges embodied a residual underside of the 'cognitive complex' from their start. Wilson (2021) argues that the subjugation of community colleges was by design. Community College fiscal appropriations are only about 50 per cent of what is afforded to public universities and four-year colleges. Although there has been considerable interest in rendering community colleges 'tuition-free', as enacted by Tennessee (ironically a 'red state'), this was exorcized from President Biden's legislative agenda (Startz, 2021). So even though community colleges serve the most vulnerable students in the United States, they receive fewer resources than other higher education institutions, thus reinforcing the cycle of poverty and inequity (The Century Foundation, 2019).

Despite demographic changes which underscore a strategic need for institutions to serve an 'adult' population, community colleges continue to use the traditional organizational progress and outcomes of a sub-cohort of students as defined in the VFA, as previously discussed. Such structures silo academic activity, student affairs and continuing/adult education. The organizational structure of these institutions isomorphically rests on control by a managerial class (Meng, Tian, Chiang, & Cai, 2020) that is often at odds with the faculty and staff. While full-time faculty have been progressively retrenched as more contingent faculty are hired, the number of administrators has grown over time. Ultimately this is harmful to students as a wider gulf exists between these stakeholder groups.

> Whereas most community college faculty relationally and holistically conceived of their work, administrators generally favored instrumental and bureaucratic techniques, leading us to argue that the generosity of these educators is highly managed. Similar to earlier writing on managed professionals, we found that administrators expected faculty to entrust their efforts to care for students to bureaucratic devices. However, faculty often considered such systems ineffective. Ultimately, we assert that the instrumental framing of community college faculty work expectations adversely affects not just faculty but students, and we offer recommendations for community college leaders and faculty development offices.
>
> (Aguilar-Smith & Gonzales, 2021)

Towards a critical intellectual leadership

Our experience has been that community college administrators are primarily engaged in management, not intellectual leadership. Inadequate appropriations and political pressures to keep tuition low result in recurrent fiscal hardships. Precarious conditions of faculty employment, where the majority are contingent labourers and work with little or no employment protection, have become a strategy for maintaining solvency. Their employment is often conditional upon a sufficient number of students enrolling in a course, which is often unknown until the beginning of a semester. The majority of these faculty have weak ties to disciplinary associations and are typically provided with syllabi that they need to follow, making academic freedom a precarious dimension of employment.

Community college administrators are often solely managers, and although they may emanate from the faculty, they no longer have faculty status as administrators. The gulf between instruction and management is vast, whereby many organizational reforms are literally from the top – administrators – to faculty, staff and students. A feature of their colonized status, the absence of robust and shared governance in community colleges often thwarts faculty and staff engagement, resulting in a 'legitimation crisis' (Habermas, 1975) in implemented reforms and policies.

Disciplinary associations have a precarious presence in community colleges. Very few community college faculty appear on the editorial/advisory boards of disciplinary journals, whilst high teaching loads often preclude engaging in research, and there is a lack of professional development funds and time to attend annual disciplinary meetings.

To change this precarious state of being, there needs to be a reconceptualization of intellectual leadership that transforms a simple managerial approach into that of a community organizer. Such a transformation will also depend on an organizational structure that adapts to what students need to cultivate their talents. The need for a 'full-service' community college is paramount.

The concept of a 'full-service' school applies to community colleges with respect to recent findings concerning what makes for a 'successful' student. The typical silos of academic vs student affairs do not serve current student needs or interests, which the Covid-19 pandemic has magnified.

The pandemic illuminated the precarious enrolment of students in community colleges. Enrolments in US community colleges have declined 14.8 per cent since 2019 (National Student Clearinghouse Research Center, 2022), the largest percentage drop in any higher education sector. Given the rise in unemployment during the pandemic, it would have been reasonable to expect enrolments to increase, as they often do during times of economic crisis. However, this dip may reflect the hardships when instruction went online. Not all have broadband access, and other familial responsibilities may have interceded, such as caring for children when public schools were closed. Given the predominance of growing food insecurity, childcare challenges and the overall exacerbation of pre-existing inequities, the pandemic brought to bear these and other challenges, such as mental and physical health, that disproportionately affected constituents attending community colleges.

Forced to pivot to online instruction in March 2020 due to Covid-19, community colleges have experienced subsequent enrolment declines, accompanied by increased health and food security needs by students who remained. As a result, community colleges were further strained due to the pandemic, engaging in unprecedented crisis management. Community colleges have received three rounds of Higher Education Emergency Relief Funds (HEERF) under the American Rescue Fund from the federal government, with half of these funds going to direct student support and the remainder for institutional needs. Although these appropriations have staved off immediate financial disaster, they were episodic and will not necessarily sustain the financial viability of colleges. However, the allocation of HEERF funds suggests a pathway whereby the federal government can provide additional funding to community colleges.

This is an opportune moment for community colleges to redefine their institutional role. For example, while the availability of low-wage service sector employment has captured students' interest, they may not understand the full implications of the limited mobility in such occupations. However, this would be a perfect time to enlighten students by introducing research to enable them to understand their life chances fully. For example, those in retail jobs might benefit from a close reading of *Walking Mannequins: How Race and Gender Inequalities Shape Retail Clothing Work* (Misra & Walters., 2022) which provides an ethnographic study of the trials and tribulations of women retail workers.

This underscores what we believe is another dimension of precarious intellectual leadership in community colleges: the weak presence of disciplines. Another initiative that can enhance the role of community colleges in US academic leadership would be for disciplinary societies to examine how community college faculty and their students are marginalized. Recently we co-chaired an American Sociological Association (ASA) task force on sociology faculty in the community college (ASA Taskforce, 2017). It was refreshing to learn that most faculty are 'pulled' to community colleges by their commitment to social justice. However, they are often conflicted by a competing institutional versus professional identification. They are confronted with the innovation du jour that administrators are promulgating as the next best thing for student success. These initiatives command substantial institutional resources. Faculty yearn for professional development within sociology. However, the latter is usurped by other administrative priorities.

In the summer of 2021, a special issue of *New Directions in Community Colleges* included articles from eleven disciplines about the growing recognition of the importance of including community college faculty and their students in disciplinary association agendas and work (Maier, Rowell & Macdonald, 2021a, 2021b). Over 100 community college faculty and administrators attended a virtual conference funded by the National Science Foundation (NSF) in January 2022 to discuss these issues. Increasingly, disciplinary associations recognize the importance of including community college faculty and students in their missions as an important diversity, equity and inclusion issue (Rowell, Maier, & MacDonald, 2022). Also, through their respective graduate programmes, academic disciplines can better reach out to prospective faculty. Unfortunately, doctoral-trained faculty often shun community college employment. Mentors and advisors typically advise graduate students that a career teaching in a community college means sacrificing research given the typical teaching load of fifteen credit hours per semester, which guarantees estrangement from their discipline.

Given that community colleges disproportionately enrol non-white students compared to other US higher education sectors, and community college faculty are drawn to these institutions due to their commitment to social justice, it is incumbent that changes occur to realize their agency to bring about social change. Community college leadership in the United States still tends to be white and male. However, some current initiatives, such as the Lakin Institute, part of the National Council on Black American Affairs (NCBAA), engender a pipeline for Black leadership in community colleges.

A challenge facing community colleges is that two-thirds of all students attend part-time, whose average age is twenty-seven. Given their preponderance in other spheres of social life – such as work and family – this cries out for a new model of higher education to serve these students. However, most community colleges remain wedded to an organizational model that replicates undergraduate, residential colleges designed for eighteen- to twenty-two-year-olds. As recently underscored by Robin Isserles (2021), the current 'student success movement' in the United States neglects these students and runs the risk of marginalizing most community college students who are in desperate need of a new paideia. Tragically, the students in most need of the mission of community colleges in the United States are often those less helped.

We have practised and seen the impact of adopting a 'pedagogy of the oppressed' (Freire, 1970) and the fruits of a 'sociological imagination' (Mills, 1959). Although our students typically have a rich/nuanced repertoire of life experiences, they often don't see how elements of social structure impact their lives. A sociological imagination, which C. Wright Mills defines as the intersection of biography (personal experiences) and history (social structure/social forces), is a very empowering tool. They are a prime audience for what has been termed 'public sociology' (Burawoy, 2005). Community College leadership would benefit from understanding and addressing the unequal social structures that make it difficult for the students they serve to succeed.

Paulo Freire's *Pedagogy of the Oppressed* (1970), where he articulates critical pedagogy as teaching learners to examine power structures and patterns of inequality, is at the heart of what drives much of the community college sociology professoriate. For Freire, the narrative is the fundamental vehicle for teaching, a dialogic, interactive approach to instruction, and a collaborative approach between student and instructor. It is imperative that community college leadership understand power structures and patterns of inequality to move the student success agenda in the United States.

bell hooks' work *Teaching to Transgress* (1994) focuses on intersectionality as critical dimensions of oppression and inequity are similarly crucial for developing a transformative analytical perspective on the part of community college sociologists; however, it is not a perspective or 'standpoint' shared by many community college administrators. The community engagement role of community colleges represents a critical transformative moment. The late bell hooks' last academic appointment was at Berea College, an institution known for its egalitarian governance structure and equitable sharing of organizational responsibilities. Such an organizational model would be ideal for community colleges and allow them to enjoy priority in US higher education.

Conclusion

US higher education needs to be decolonized for community colleges to undertake an intellectual leadership role. As Go (2016) advocates, we first need to understand the colonized history, which is something we've attempted to do in this chapter. Community college leaders can be genuinely transformational by adopting the principles of engaged critical pedagogy that resonate with the biographical experiences of First-Generation College Students (FGCS), who are often non-white, low-income and first-generation students. A critical leadership model is needed for community colleges to become transformative entities for those who have been typically marginalized from higher education. Not until community college leadership begins to understand and solve some of the social problems and structural barriers facing the students they serve can they become 'democracies colleges'.

Notes

1. The 'New Federalism' can be viewed as part of the rise of neoliberalism associated with the presidency of Ronald Reagan, which involves reducing the role of the federal government in regulating social policies, letting markets act in an unfettered fashion and providing local states with a high degree of autonomy, viewed as endemic of the US constitution. Ironically, even though Reagan's firing of over 11,000 air traffic controllers in 1981 was an autocratic federal action, this 'union-busting' of the Professional Air-Traffic Controllers Association (PATCO) was viewed as the defining gauntlet of a new federalist era.
2. It is interesting to note that within the fifty-two universities initially created, less than 0.5 per cent of their enrolment in 2019–20 comprised Alaskan/Native American students (https://www.landgrabu.org/).
3. HBCUs have proven to be highly effective in providing upward mobility for non-white students. For a current list of HBCUs and a discussion about their effectiveness see https://sites.ed.gov/whhbcu/one-hundred-and-five-historically-black-colleges-and-universities/

References

Aguilar-Smith, S., & Gonzales, L. (2021). A study of community college faculty work expectations: Generous educators and their managed generosity. *Community College Journal of Research and Practice*, 45(3), 184–204. https://doi.org/10.1080/10668926.2019.1666062

American Association of Community Colleges (AACC) (2012). *The voluntary framework of accountability: Developing measures of community college effectiveness and outcomes.* https://vfa.aacc.nche.edu/Documents/VFAOutcomesReportWebFINAL.pdf

American Association of Community Colleges (AACC) (2022). *Fast facts.* https://www.aacc.nche.edu/wp-content/uploads/2022/04/AACC_2022_Fact_Sheet-Rev-4_11_22.pdf

ASA Taskforce (2017). *Final report of the ASA Taskforce on community college faculty.* https://www.asanet.org/sites/default/files/asa_cc_taskforce_report.pdf

Bailey, T., Smith Jaggars, S., & Jenkins, D. (2015). *Redesigning America's community colleges: A clearer path to student success.* Harvard University Press.

Baldwin D. L. (2021). *In the shadow of the ivory tower: How universities are plundering our cities.* Bold Type Books.

Bilmes, L., & Brooks, C. (23 February 2022). The GI Bill was one of the worst racial injustices of the 20th century. Congress can fix it. *Boston Globe*, A11.

Boggs, G. (2012). The evolution of the community college in America: Democracy's colleges. *Community College Journal*, 82(4), 36–9.

Bowles, S., & Gintis, H. (1976). *Schooling in capitalist America.* Basic Books.

Burawoy, M. (2005). For public sociology. *American Sociological Review*, 70(1), 4–28. https://doi.org/10.1177/000312240507000102

Christensen, C., & Eyring, H. (2011). *The innovative university.* Jossey-Bass.

Clark, B. (1960). The cooling-out function in higher education. *American Journal of Sociology*, 65(6), 569–76. https://doi.org/10.1086/222787

Coleman, J. (1990). *Equality and achievement in education.* Westview Press.

Durry, R. (2003). Community colleges in America: A historical perspective. *Inquiry*, 8(1).

Ehrenreich, B., & Ehrenreich, J. (1978). The professional-managerial class. In P. Walker (Ed.), *Between labor and capital.* Black Rose Books.

Freire, P. (1970). *Pedagogy of the oppressed.* Continuum.

Go, J. (2016). *Postcolonial thought and social theory.* Oxford University Press.

Guinier, L. (2015). *The tyranny of the meritocracy: Democratizing higher education in America.* Beacon Press.

Habermas, J. (1975). *Legitimation crisis.* Beacon Press.

hooks, b. (1994). *Teaching to transgress.* Routledge.

Huber, M. T. (2021). Foreword: Community college faculty as disciplinary colleagues. *New Directions for Community Colleges*, 2021(194), 11–13. https://doi.org/10.1002/cc.20448

Isserles, R. G. (2021). *The cost of completion: Student success in community college.* Johns Hopkins University Press.

Itzigsohn, J., & Brown, K. (2020). *The sociology of W. E. B. DuBois.* NYU Press.

Jencks, C., & Riesman, D. (1968). *The academic revolution.* Doubleday and Company.

Lee, R., & Ahtone, T. (30 March 2020). Land-grab universities. Expropriated Indigenous Land is the foundation of the land-grant university system. *High Country News.* https://www.hcn.org/issues/52.4/indigenous-affairs-education-land-grab-universities

Levine, A., & Van Pelt, S. (2021). *The great upheaval: Higher education's past, present and uncertain future.* Johns Hopkins University Press.

Maier, M., Rowell, K. R., & Macdonald, R. H. (2021a). Disciplinary societies and community colleges: Partners in progress. *New Directions for Community Colleges*, 2021(194), 159–71.

Maier, M., Rowell, K. R., & Macdonald, R. H. (2021b). Editors' notes. *New Directions for Community Colleges*, 2021(194), 7–9.

Marcus, J. (6 March 2022). What researchers learned about online higher education during the pandemic. *Hechinger Report*. https://hechingerreport.org/what-researchers-learned-about-online-higher-education-during-the-pandemic/

Meng, F. H., Tian, X.-M., Chiang, T.-H., & Cai, Y. (2020). The State role in excellent universities policies in the era of globalization: The case of China. In S. Rider, M. A. Peters, M. Hyvönen, & T. Besley (Eds), *World class universities. Evaluating education: Normative systems and institutional practices* (pp. 197–217). Springer. https://doi.org/10.1007/978-981-15-7598-3_12

Mills, C. W. (1959). *The sociological imagination*. Oxford University Press.

Misra, J., & Walters., K. (2022). *Walking mannequins: How race and gender inequalities shape retail clothing work*. University of California Press.

National Student Clearinghouse Research Center (26 May 2022). https://nscresearchcenter.org/current-term-enrollment-estimates/

Nixon, J. (Ed.) (2017). *Higher education in austerity Europe*. Bloomsbury Academic.

Olivares-Ureta, M. (2022). From at risk to at promise: Fighting fiercely for the community college students we have to safeguard the futures they deserve. *Teachers College Record*. ID number: 24015. https://www.tcrecord.org

Parsons, T., & Platt, G. (1973). *The American university*. Harvard University Press.

Rothstein, R. (2017). *The color of law*. Liverlight.

Rowell, K., Maier, M., & Macdonald, R. H. (7 March 2022). Disciplinary society engagement with community college faculty: A key element for increasing diversity, equity, and inclusion. *Teachers College Record*. ID number: 23997. https://www.tcrecord.org

Sandel, M. (2020). *The tyranny of merit*. Farrar, Straus and Giroux.

Sennett, R., & Cobb, J. (1972). *The hidden injuries of class*. W. W. Norton and Company.

Startz, D. (15 September 2021). Free community college: Progress is being made, but pitfalls remain. *Brookings*. https://www.brookings.edu/blog/brown-center-chalkboard/2021/09/15/free-community-college-progress-is-being-made-but-pitfalls-remain/

The Century Foundation (2019). Recommendations for providing community colleges with the resources they need. *The Century Foundation*. https://tcf.org/content/report/recommendations-providing-community-colleges-resources-need/?agreed=1&agreed=1&agreed=1

Tucker, A. (2020). *Democracy against liberalism*. Polity Press.

UNCF (2022). *Why choose an HBCU?* https://uncf.org/pages/why-choose-an-hbcu

Wilson, A. (2021). Exclusion and extraction: Situation spirit murdering in community college. *Journal of Educational Foundations*, 34(1), 47–67.

Young, M. (1958). *Rise of the meritocracy*. Routledge.

Thinking Critically about Intellectual Leadership in Precarious Times

Tanya Fitzgerald, Helen M Gunter and Jon Nixon, Editors

Introduction

The primary purpose of the research and analysis reported in this book is to provoke readers to think critically about intellectual leadership in precarious times. It was not our intention to offer technical solutions, but rather to frame critical questions about the unevenness, ambivalences and disruptions that now mark everyday life and interactions. At the first stages of this project, our social reality was intertwined with a global pandemic, and within the UK and European context BREXIT. What has occurred since then has been the invasion of Ukraine by Russia, economic recession and inflation, government instability in countries such as Australia, England, France and Italy, increased surveillance and violent suppression of the activities and freedoms of women and girls in countries such as Afghanistan, Iran and the United States, and the continued rise of populism together with the integration of far right and authoritarian political parties into the mainstream of erstwhile social democratic states. Existential crises mean that there seems to be little space for thoughtful and critical debate based on research and expertise.

Across national regions, historical circumstances have impacted differentially on the economic and social conditions underlying the development of higher education. For example, within the national regions of the UK, a thirteen-year reign of the Conservative party in control of the UK government – the first government from 2010 was hefted into power through coalition with the Liberal Democratic Party – pushed through economic policies that have proved detrimental to the continuing sustainability of the public sector including national health and state education. Those economic policies were referred to as 'austerity', i.e. an ideologically driven set of policies aimed at the shrinkage of public sector funding (the small state) and the escalation of accumulated profit (deregulation) for which the public was told 'there is no alternative'. (It even had a catchy acronym – TINA.)

There was, of course, an alternative, but one which relied upon reform, public investment and political will. Such an approach requires forms of institutional leadership at governmental and institutional levels that will provide stability, continuity and cohesion across educational sectors that are a product of and contribute to democratizing forms of intellectual leadership. This is a huge agenda, and one we would like to stimulate rather than determine, and so in these concluding reflections we would like to engage with the contributions made by our co-authors, and then consider the shift from intellectual compliance towards intellectual leadership.

Intellectual leadership in precarious times

The projects reported in this book have provided evidence and analysis that examine what it means to undertake intellectual leadership in precarious times. Importantly precarity is a form of perilous uncertainty, and while world-leading research and teaching may demand letting go of accepted ways of thinking, or 'thinking without a banister' (Arendt, 2018), what is distinctive about our evidence and analysis is the clear evidence that research is now deliberately located in uncertain times that threaten our abilities and capacities to produce new ways of thinking and doing, because we have to hold onto performative banisters through producing spreadsheets that describe value. We recognize that there are damaging trends to public investment in knowledge production, with a shift from collective to privatized security, where struggles for limited resources combined with a strange interplay of metrics and lying have generated a populist claimocracy about what is known, what is worth knowing and who knows best (Gunter, 2023). Intellectual leadership within higher education has been seriously wounded, and while important research continues to debate intellectual leadership (see other books in the series, https://www.bloomsbury.com/uk/series/perspectives-on-leadership-in-higher-education), along with the current challenges for public intellectuals (see McCulloch & Peterson, 2022) and for universities (see Thrift, 2022), our approach has been to raise questions about the actuality of and possibility for intellectual leadership at a time of precarity.

The fact of the production of this book (along with other research outputs that our co-authors and ourselves have referenced) demonstrates that such intellectual leadership is possible at a time of precarity. Within the nine chapters our co-authors present evidence and arguments that are not comprehensive of the experiences of those who work in higher education – that would be impossible – but do speak to the wider issues of constructive and destructive forms of precarity that we raised in Chapter 1. Notably we presented a way of thinking about intellectual leadership within contextual precarization that is personal, organizational, existential and geopolitical, and while all of the research projects reported in the chapters engage with the interplay of such contextual dynamics, we intend providing a summary by using illustrations from particular chapters.

1. *Personal:* Precarity has a detrimental impact on the agency of the higher education workforce, in ways that ruin not only working lives but also health and family. Our co-authors have demonstrated the personal nature of what it means to be corporatized in regard to projects, outputs and teaching in order to manage risk and to trust (and be trusted) in global markets. What this means in terms of strategic as well as day-to-day difficulties is directly engaged with by Parr et al. (Chapter 8) and Waghorne (Chapter 9), whereby they locate the complexities within the realities of lives over time. Both engage with the negativity of precarity that threatens intellectual work, but both also identify the productive potential of taking a risk, whereby Waghorne focuses on student activism and participation in learning, and Parr et al. on those active students who navigate the performative demands of the work place, showing the potential for shifting from their role from researching professionals into professional researchers.

2. *Organizational:* Precarity has a negative impact on the design and conduct of formal roles through to practices that interplay structure with personal agency in ways that corporatize intellectual leadership. Our co-authors have demonstrated how and why the methodologies of knowledge production have been manufactured through digitization, and value-factured through brand marketing, in order to secure status in league tables and so generate and meet global consumer demands. The calculative meaning of what can be thought, said and done is evident in the chapters by Oleksiyenko (Chapter 1) and Jones (Chapter 2), whereby they examine how the personal is reworked and often disposed of through how markets impact on the cost of knowledge production. Jones

examines the corporatization of the university and how the introduction of metrics (e.g. research quality audits, student surveys) is a form of 'corporatizing disruption' to the purposes, conduct and impact of research, and Oleksiyenko is also concerned with deficit approaches to intellectual leadership where the illegal Russian invasion of Ukraine in 2022 has been supported by those who work in universities.

3. *Existential:* Precarity threatens the security and existence of both the personal and organizational in higher education. Our co-authors have demonstrated the neoliberal and populist visceral attacks on the people and the institutions that conduct research and demonstrate expertise – the global researcher is meant to have a demonstrated impact but at the same time is often silenced as irrelevant, and so is outflanked by responsive and modern international consultancy companies, think tanks and private laboratories. How the personal and organizational interplay is evident in the chapters by Hall (Chapter 5), O'Connor (Chapter 6) and Rider (Chapter 7), whereby they examine how the need to make changes to intellectual leadership based on social justice goals can be highly problematic. Hall characterizes professors as 'university labourers' who are driven to forms of corporate intellectual leadership through the 'academic *peloton*' that invest in corporate processes that measure and declare worth, and O'Connor examines how the composition of the workforce is a contributory factor in such lethal cultures, but shows that while more women have taken up the role of university president in Ireland they tend to be born and/or educated outside of Ireland and from a STEM background, so the capacity of a system to be more inclusive remains limited. These are matters that concern Rider through examining the notion and reality of academic freedom, whereby the introduction of line management and group identification challenges the vitality and legitimacy of epistemic communities based on self-governance. Consequently, confronting Hall's academic labourer and O'Connor's troubling of social justice transformations both require an approach to the fact of plurality that Rider identifies as being based on a system of rights and obligations for, towards and within knowledge production.

4. *Geopolitical:* Precarity as an existential threat to the person and organization is global and local, historic and contemporary. Our co-authors have engaged with the meaning and lived realities of neoliberal managerialism through, for example, how this is reworked in national and regional systems and how the purposes and practices of intellectual

leadership are being reworked through a shift in the purposes of higher education to primarily a site for training (Collini, 2011). The dimensions of the geopolitical are evident in the chapters by Tran et al. (Chapter 4) and Levinson and Rowell (Chapter 10), where they examine how the autonomy necessary for debate has been constrained to meet global markets.

At an international level Tran et al. focus on inclusive transnational research collaborations and student mobility in ways that demonstrate the productive contribution of 'academic diplomacy' for knowledge production, but at the same time they show how this is vulnerable to geopolitical turbulence, and at a local level Levinson and Rowell establish how there is potential in community colleges in the United States for making such inclusivity work in practice through how educational access and experience can be decolonized in a way that enables student engagement in intellectual leadership.

Our co-authors have provided important new evidence and analysis which demonstrates that intellectual leadership is wounded, but not yet dead. Hence your reading of this book as an intellectual activist is vitally important, and how you engage with the ideas, evidence and ideas matters and is integral to the revival and survival of democratic inclusion and security. However, we wonder, given the identified trends, if this type of book could be produced in ten years' time – who will do the research, how will it be funded and who will publish it? We therefore turn to not just saving intellectual leadership but how we might consider developing it.

Developing intellectual leadership

We argue that researchers and teachers as intellectual leaders practise leading and leadership through providing theoretical searchlights and the evidence base necessary for challenging and providing the basis for new and radical agendas. Consequently, as noted, we set out to examine the terrain on which intellectual leadership is located as a way of supporting agenda processes that can support activism (Collins, 2013). That is, the plurality within, for and about intellectual leadership has the capacity to nurture public democratic discourses, to engage with a range of communities, and to reinvigorate the environmental conditions that give rise to and shape public intellectualism (Desch, 2016). At least two conditions are helpful here: first, the issue of access, or how 'we make expertise of all kinds systematically findable' in ways that support citizenship (Noveck, 2016, p. 8); and second, a focus on normalized intellectual work with a right to do research: 'All human beings are, in this sense, researchers, since all human beings make decisions that require them to make systematic forays beyond their current knowledge horizons' (Appadurai, 2006, p. 167). Thus, we see intellectual leadership as intertwined with intellectual participation, and with the production of new knowledge and new insights that give rise to social and institutional reforms (Smyth & Hattam, 2000) – reforms that do not necessarily align with hierarchical compliance, performativity or productivity (Macfarlane, 2012).

We deliberately link the public intellectual with leadership as this connects academic values, scholarship and service to the idea of leadership. Our overt signal here is that the *idea* of leadership is critical and we ought to therefore move away from linking leadership with a portfolio of activities or an institutional role. Intellectual leadership might well be exercised by an individual, and marked by a scholarly commitment to debate, advocacy and collegiality in a wide variety of educational and managerial contexts. Stevenson (2012, p. 349) identifies 'the roles of constructer, organiser, permanent persuader' as integral to intellectual leadership. Thus, an intellectual leader is, in essence, a scholarly architect, who may or may not have a formal organizational role but who creates the necessary relational conditions, or intellectual culture, that fosters the communal emergence of new ideas, or even new answers, to complex problems with/in public or professional space and time.

The metaphor of architecture is crucial here because it relates the notion of overall design to that of planning, construction and usability. All the contributors to (and readers of) this book are – in their own ways and their own very different contexts – architects of a civic society (emergent, imagined, half realized) in which education in general and higher education in particular has a vital role to play in the development of individual flourishing, social well-being and economic sustainability.

What emerges from the accounts and analyses provided in the previous chapters is the notion of the intellectual leader as a constructive disruptor: generating new forms of knowledge, transgressing established or taken-for-granted boundaries, committed to a critical community of scholars and fostering shared values of academic citizenship. Intellectual leadership therefore does not occur in a vacuum, but rather is a complex and complicated set of activities that draw on scholarly or professional expertise and critical inquiry in the public realm. As Oleksiyenko and Ruan (2019) contend, intellectual leadership is the 'cardinal leverage' for transformation (p. 406) that enables the 'breaking of norms and boundaries for the purposes of advancing new knowledge' (p. 407). This therefore suggests that intellectual leadership is not primarily concerned with the status quo but rather invokes a level of public responsibility to tackle ideas and knowledge, no matter how precarious the social, political or intellectual climate. Intellectual leadership is, we suggest, about creating open and discursive spaces for debate, inquiry and critique, which is inextricably bound up with the freedom to research, to teach and to speak (Uslu & Welch, 2018).

Evident across the book's contributions is the critical significance of intellectual leadership in precarious times. In each of the chapters the authors have engaged with the concept and construct of intellectual leadership and through their own reflections have highlighted the vitality and importance of intellectual work. In doing so, the authors have illuminated the issues in their problematization of intellectual leadership for yourselves as readers and their understanding of how precarity manifests itself across institutional, social, cultural, economic and political contexts. Furthermore, arising from these debates is the recognition of the critical role of public intellectuals to interrogate and protect 'fearless speech' (Peters, 2022, p. 9). As editors we are particularly struck by John Berger's (2008) comment (as a novelist, essayist and art critic):

> When I think now about what we were doing twenty years ago, I'm struck by the precariousness of our situation then, a precariousness which we, engaged in our struggle, mostly ignored or didn't see. And this is strangely reassuring in face of what we are up against today, for it suggests precariousness is our strength.
>
> (p. 192)

The challenge now is not to mask precarity within higher education structures, policies, processes and institutional cultures, but to identify through your own research the possibilities for change that can be provoked as we as intellectual leaders respond to scholarly uncertainties, and incorporate new ideas, values, understandings, knowledge, purpose and action into our everyday work and everyday interactions.

The previous chapters draw on the work of scholars and researchers working in a wide variety of interdisciplinary fields and disciplines. Many of the chapters include an historical perspective in, for example, the contextualizing of their authors' arguments, the historical grounding of the ideas being developed, and the calling to account of absences and silences in the accounts and records of the past. Calling truth to power is crucial in this context and central to what we understand by intellectual leadership. The pathbreaking work of Peter Fryer in the mid-1980s (building on the earlier work of Folarin Shyllon and others) and the later work of David Olusoga, in calling to account the racist selectivity in the UK historical record, are – to identify but one example – central to this radical tradition of 'calling truth to power' (Clark, 2022; Fryer, 2018; Kidman, O'Malley, Macdonald, Roa & Wallis, 2022; Malik, 2023; Olusoga, 2021; Shyllon, 1977).

In her essay on *Truth and Politics*, in which in the wake of the controversy following the publication in 1963 of her *Eichmann in Jerusalem*, Hannah Arendt argued that '[f]acts and events are infinitely more fragile things than axioms, discoveries, theories – even the most wildly speculative ones – produced by the human mind' (Arendt, 1977, p. 231). Arendt was a great interpreter of history but insisted on the primacy of the factual. Once a factual truth is lost, she argued, no rational effort will ever bring it back: 'Perhaps the chances that Euclidian mathematics or Einstein's theory of relativity – let alone Plato's philosophy – would have been reproduced in time if their authors had been prevented from handing them down to posterity are not very good.' But, she insisted, 'they are infinitely better than the chances that a fact of importance, forgotten or, more likely, lied away, will one day be rediscovered' (pp. 231–2).

Arendt's commitment to the importance of grounding truth in facts has particular resonance at a time when politicians and pundits are well aware of the malleability of facts and the power of disinformation. This has led to what Peter Osborne – commenting specifically on the UK and US administrations during the tenures of Johnson and Trump – calls 'a new moral barbarism' in which 'lying, cupidity and lack of integrity' have become 'essential qualities' for those seeking power (Osborne, 2021, p. 6). This raises the question of how, in our existential present, we have responsibility for handing on to future generations a truthful record of what it means to be living in the first quarter of the twenty-first century.

We live in an increasingly precarious world. Ten years ago a global financial crisis shook the neoliberal consensus to its foundations, leaving much of the world precariously balanced between a discredited though still dominant neoliberal economic order and a populist and anti-liberal order that, although as yet only emergent, is gaining not only influence but also political power. 'We are entering', as the historian Tony Judt (2010, p. 207) then suggested in his final work, 'upon a time of troubles'. In the decade following Judt's valedictory utterance, his somewhat gloomy prognosis has been fully vindicated.

There are, as the chapters in this collection highlight, compelling reasons for optimism. In spite of often destructive precarity the research reported within and outside of this book continues to be produced, and even in dark times, we can expect and do see illumination from ideas and analysis through forms of constructive precarity (Arendt, 1993). Our awareness of precariousness reinforces the critical importance of dialogic and communal forms of leadership that are deeply and inextricably connected to intellectual work. 'Speaking the truth to power is', as Edward Said put it, 'no Panglossian idealism: it is carefully weighing the alternatives, picking the right one, and then intelligently representing it where it can do the most good and cause the right change' (Said, 1994, p. 75). Speaking truth to power requires judgement, which in turn requires the evidence on which judgements are formed and critiqued, and the guts to speak considered judgements when necessary.

References

Appadurai, A. (2006). The right to research. *Globalisation, Societies and Education*, 4(2), 167–77. https://doi.org/10.1080/14767720600750696

Arendt, H. (1977). *Between past and future: Eight exercises in political thought*. Penguin Books (First published by Faber and Faber, 1961, and with additional material by Viking Press, 1968).

Arendt, H. (1993). *Men in dark times*. A Harvest Book, Harcourt Brace & Company.

Arendt, H. (2018). *Thinking without a banister: Essays in understanding 1953–1975, Edited with an introduction by Jerome Kohn*. Schocken Books.

Berger, J. (2008). *From A to X: A story in letters*. Verso Books.

Clark, A. (2022). *Making Australian history*. Vintage Books.

Collini, S. (25 August 2011). From Robbins to McKinsey. *London Review of Books*, 33(16), 9–14.

Collins, P. H. (2013). *On intellectual activism*. Temple University Press.

Desch, M. (Ed.) (2016). *Public intellectuals in the global arena: Professors or pundits*. University of Notre Dame Press.

Fryer, P. (2018). *Staying power: The history of black people in Britain*. Pluto (First published in 1984).

Gunter, H. M. (2023). *A political sociology of education policy*. Policy Press.

Judt, T. (2010). *Ill fares the land*. Penguin.

Kidman, J., O'Malley, V., Macdonald, L., Roa, T., & Wallis, K. (2022). *Fragments from a contested past: Remembrance denial and New Zealand history*. Bridget Williams Books.

Macfarlane, B. (2012). *Intellectual leadership in higher education*. Routledge.

Malik, K. (2023). *Not so black and white, a history of race from white supremacy to identity politics*. Hurst & Company.

McCulloch, G., & Peterson, A. (2022). Public intellectuals and education in a changing society. *British Journal of Educational Studies*, 70(5), 533–7. https://doi.org/10.1080/00071005.2022.2154422

Noveck, B. S. (28 November 2016). Enough of experts: Data, democracy and the future of expertise. *Academy of Social Sciences Professional Briefings*, 10, 1–8. https://www.socialsciencespace.com/2016/11/enough-experts-data-democracy-future-expertise/

Oleksiyenko, A., & Ruan, N. (2019). Intellectual leadership and academic communities: Issues for discussion and research. *Higher Education Quarterly*, 73(4), 406–18. https://doi.org/10.1111/hequ.12199

Olusoga, D. (2021). *Black and British: A forgotten history* (Revised ed.). Picador.

Osborne, P. (2021). *The assault on truth: Boris Johnson, Donald Trump and the emergence of a new moral barbarism*. Simon and Schuster.

Peters, M. (2022). Public intellectuals, viral modernity and the problem of truth. *British Journal of Educational Studies*, 70(5), 557–73. https://doi.org/10.1080/00071005.2022.2141859

Said, E. W. (1994). *Representations of the Intellectual: The 1993 Reith lectures*. Vintage.

Shyllon, F. (1977). *Black people in Britain: 1555–833*. Oxford University Press for the Institute of Race Relations.

Smyth, J., & Hattam, R. (2000). Intellectual as hustler: Researching against the grain of the market. *British Educational Research Journals*, 26(2), 157–75. https://doi.org/10.1080/01411920050000926

Stevenson, H. (2012). Teacher leadership as intellectual leadership: Creating spaces for alternative voices in the English school system. *Professional Development in Education*, 38(2), 345–60. https://doi.org/10.1080/19415257.2012.657880

Thrift, N. (2022). *The pursuit of possibility*. Policy Press.

Uslu, B., & Welch, A. (2018). The influence of universities' organisational features on professorial intellectual leadership. *Studies in Higher Education*, 43(3), 571–15. https://doi.org/10/1080/03075079.2016.1185774

Index

abolition 83
    academic peloton 87–9, 93–4, 200
    competition 83–7
    knowledge production 89–92
    of professor-as-entrepreneurial-knowledge-producer 83–5 (*see also* professor(s))
academic and professional staff estate 164–7
academic capitalism 11
academic disciplines 139, 192
academic expertise 49–51
academic freedom 33, 36, 51–2, 67, 71–2, 121–2, 125, 135, 165, 182, 190, 200
    intellectual collaboration 67
    origins of 125–7
academic labour 8, 43, 83, 90, 92
academic liberalism 132–4
academic proletariat 24. *See also* precariat
academics quitting 81
accountability 3, 13, 25, 42, 44, 55, 91, 93–4, 106, 166, 173
Ahmed, S. 92
alienation 43, 91
Alvesson, M. 103
American Dream 180
American Sociological Association (ASA) 191
Anderson, M. 159
Andreotti, V. 86
anti-intellectualism 1, 48–9
anxiety 69, 82, 88, 161
Arendt, H. 204
Artificial Intelligence (AI) 6–7
Ashby, E. 159
Asia-Pacific 63
Australia-China relationships 64–5
Australian National University (ANU) 66–7
Australian universities 61–4, 66–7, 70–1, 160, 162–3, 167
    academic/professional staff estate 164–6
    administrative officers 162–3

aid package to Ukraine 66–7
    and China relationship 64–5
    estates, emergence of 160–1
    executive estate 161–4
    New Colombo Plan 64
    political interference 69–71
    Russian institutions and 67–8
    student estate 167–9
Australian University Review 166
Australian Vice-Chancellors' Committee (AVCC) 163–4, 166
Authentica Habita 125
authoritarian 1, 25, 43, 48, 66, 71, 121
authoritarianism 11, 26, 61, 67–8
autonomy 22, 51–2, 55, 65, 69, 93, 121–2, 128, 129, 135, 160, 173, 194 n.1, 201

Baldwin, D. L. 183
Barbarossa, F. (Emperor) 125–6
Berger, J. 203
Berlant, L. 3, 4
Bernstein, R. J. 10
Bhopal, K. 8
Bilmes, L. 184
Birstein, V. J. 27
Blackmore, J. 102
Boberg, J. 131–2
Boud, D. 143
Bourdieu, P. 4, 92–3
Brooks, C. 184
Brown, K. 183
bullying 24, 88
Butler, J. 3, 4

centralization of power 24–6, 43–5, 71–2, 101–5, 203–5
change(s) 2–3, 43–4, 62, 102–3, 140–5, 147, 152–3, 171, 189
collegiality 52–4, 122–3, 165, 202
Collini, S. 3
Colombo Plan, Australia 62–3

colonial 62, 81, 93, 183
colonialism 183–4
commercialization 2, 62–3, 70–1, 85, 88, 93
Committee of University Chairs (CUC) 46–7
commodification 85, 94, 103, 186
community colleges, The United States 179–81
   colonialism 183–4
   contingent faculty 181
   critical intellectual leadership 190–3
   curriculum 182
   disciplinary associations 179–82, 191–2
   during Covid-19 pandemic 190–1
   federalism 184–5
   foundations and non-profit organizations 186–7
   full-service 190
   leadership 180–2
   neoliberalism 185–9
   non-white student enrolment 187, 192
   pedagogy of the oppressed 182, 193
   students' transformation 182
   student success movement 187–8
   subjugation of 189
competition 3, 34, 48, 53, 68, 83–6, 90, 94–5, 128, 144, 173, 186
Connell, R. W. 2, 14
contextual precarization 7, 199
contingent faculty 181, 186, 189
contract of indefinite duration (CID) 105
corporate universities 26–7
Covid-19 pandemic 6, 9, 61, 64–5, 70, 73, 84, 101, 104–7, 109–10, 113, 173, 185, 190–1
   academic impact 61
   enrolments in US community colleges 190–1
   financial crash 84
   Higher Education Emergency Relief Funds 185, 191
   Irish HE system, impact of 104–7
   Sino-Australia relationship 64–5
   universities in England 9
   women's leadership positions 102, 104, 109–10
critical leadership 102–3, 182, 194

critical reflexivity 140–2, 145–7, 152–5
critical thinking 23, 25, 27, 35, 131, 197–8
   developing intellectual leadership 201–5
   in precarious times 198–201
culture(s) 1, 21, 31, 34–5, 48, 53–5, 71–2, 81–7, 89–92, 103, 106–7, 112, 114, 125, 153, 172, 200, 202–3
   gender 112–14
   Global North institutions 84–7
   peloton/HE sector 87–8
   Russian 31
   of silencing and secrecy 81, 83
   Ukrainian 34–5
   wars 54–5, 71, 82

Davis, A. J. 86
Dearing Committee 44
democracies colleges 180. *See also* community colleges, The United States
democracy 1, 10–12, 66, 71, 121–3, 130–1, 133, 135–6
disciplinary 2, 49–50, 53, 69, 83, 88, 89, 90–3, 109–10, 125, 131, 160, 179–83, 190–2
disciplinary associations 179–83, 190–2
discourse(s) 10, 22–4, 27, 34, 36, 41–3, 45–8, 51, 53–4, 103, 145, 153–4, 185, 201

educational hubs 63–4
educational leadership 11, 139, 141–2, 144, 146, 151
Education, doctorate (EdD) 139–43, 146–54. *See also* professional doctorates
   learning intellectual leadership 149–50
   opportunities 141
entrepreneurial 30, 45, 83, 85, 90
entrepreneurialism 91
entrepreneurship 82, 86, 88, 93
epistemic 36, 121–3, 132–3, 200
epistemic oligarchy 123
estate 159–61. *See also* student estate
   academic and professional staff 164–7
   endurance of 171–3

executive 161–4
  protest movements 169–70
  and representative structures 172
  within universities 160–1
European Union 63, 108, 123–4
executive estate 161–6
existential 7, 8, 10, 14, 151, 197, 199, 200, 204
existential precarization 9–10, 200
expertise. *See* academic expertise

Federal Council of University Staff Associations of Australia (FCUSAA)/ Federal Association of Australian Staff Associations (FAUSA) 165
federalism 180, 183–5, 194 n.1
feminist 102, 110. *See also* women's leadership positions
feudal society 3
Foreign Influence Transparency Scheme 69
Forsyth, H. 172
Fulbright programme, The United States 62
Fuller, S. 123, 132–4, 136 n.3
funding 5, 8–9, 19, 36, 53, 63, 65–8, 70, 83, 88, 101, 105–8, 110, 121, 123, 125–6, 130, 133, 159, 162, 164, 169, 181, 184–5, 191
Furstenberg, S. 121

Gadamer, H.-G. 10
Geiselberger, H. 1
gender 8, 14, 44–5, 56, 68, 71, 101–4, 107–11, 113–14, 122, 191
  equality 101–2, 107–9
  profile 109–13
geopolitics 61–2, 68–70, 72
  of international education 62–4
  Russia-Ukraine war and intellectual collaboration 66–8
  Sino-Australia relationship 64–6
  tensions 61–2, 71
  transnational research collaborations 68–72
geopoltical precarity 9–10, 200–1
Gessen, M. 27
The GI Bill (The Servicemen's Readjustment Act of 1944) 184
glass cliff 101–4, 109, 113

global discourse 22
Global North institutions 81–2, 84, 89, 91, 123
  governance of 123
  knowledge production in 89–91
global rankings 9, 104
governance 3, 6, 14, 22, 36, 41–57, 72, 83, 104, 110, 121–3, 131, 134, 136, 160, 162, 166, 169, 172, 174, 182, 185, 190, 193, 200. *See also* university governance
  democratized 131–2
  group's code of 46–7
  precarity in 43
Great Depression 161
gross inequalities 5
Guinier, L. 187
Gunn, A. 9
Gustavsson, S. 133–4

Hawkes, D. 143
Heathershaw, J. 121
hierarchical compliance 26, 202
hierarchical obedience 26
hierarchy 2, 27, 88, 108, 180
higher education (HE) 1–2. *See also* international education
  Australia 61–4, 66–7, 70–1, 160, 162–3, 167 (*see also* Australian universities)
  economy and 6, 9
  England 9, 12, 41, 52, 83–4, 149–50, 153–4, 197
  equitable system of 3
  governance (*see* governance; university governance)
  intellectual leadership in 2, 7, 21–2 (*see also* intellectual leadership)
  internationalization of 61–2
  Ireland 104–8, 110, 113, 200 (*see also* Ireland, higher education)
  knowledge production and 6
  neo-Soviets and neoliberals administration in 25–6
  on-line teaching and learning 6
  precarity in 6–7
  risk reasons 6
  Russia 22–3, 66–8, 200

The United States 8, 12, 107–8, 179–80, 183–5, 187, 189 (*see also* The United States)
Westernization of 66
women and positional leadership in 107–9
working lives in 5–7
Higher Education and Research Act 2017 44
Higher Education Emergency Relief Funds (HEERF) 185, 191
higher education institutions (HEIs) 9, 12, 41, 180, 188–9
   leadership 102–3
   managerialism 102
   women's leadership positions 107–9
Higher Education Statistics Agency 44–5
Historically Black Colleges and Universities (HBCUs) 184, 194 n.3
Holland, D. 14
housekeeping 108, 112, 132
Huber, M. 179
Hull, G. T. 92

identity(ies) 2, 4, 31, 34–5, 48, 81–3, 85, 92, 139–43, 145–50, 152
   practitioner and researcher 145–6
   professional doctorate vignette 146, 148–51
independence 51–2
   academic freedom 51
   autonomy 51–2
informal interactions 112
innovative leadership 84–5. *See also* intellectual leadership
Institutes of Technology (IoTs) 105
integrity 21, 23, 36, 130, 133, 204
intellectual collaboration 61–2, 66–8, 70, 73. *See also* transnational intellectual collaboration
intellectual existence 27
intellectual freedom/independence 21, 51–2, 70, 113
intellectual influencers 24
intellectual leadership 2, 7, 10–14, 21, 23, 42, 48, 54–6, 61–3, 68–72, 82–4, 86–7, 89–92, 102, 124, 139–54, 174, 190–1, 197–203
   capability development 91, 201–5

constructive disruptor 202–3
educational professionals 139–40
higher education and 2, 21–2
and international research collaboration 68–72
learning through EdD vignette 149–50
in precarious university 23–6
professor's role in 11–12, 21
truthfulness and 10–11
value-frames 85–6
virtues of truth/accuracy 11
intellectual position 24
intellectual work 13–14, 68, 70, 83, 88–95, 199, 202–3, 205
international collaborations 62, 67–71, 73
international education 62–5, 68, 70. *See also* geopolitics
   national political agendas 63–4
   programmes 62–4
   public diplomacy goals 63
   weaponization of 64–5
intersectional 83, 86, 90, 193
Ireland, higher education 104–8, 110, 113, 200
   Covid-19 pandemic impact 104–7
   funding 105–7
   gender profile, transformation of 109–13
   leadership 102–3
   neoliberal managerialism 103–4
   online lectures 106
   Protection of Employees (Fixed-Term Work) Act 2003 105
   student enrolment 105–6
   women's leadership positions 107–9
Isserles, R. 187–8, 192
Itzigsohn, J. 183
Ivancheva, M. 7

Jarratt Report 44
Jessop, B. 11
Jones, S. 8–9, 14, 199
Joyce, J. 27, 36

Kakabadse, A. 45, 47
knowledge economy 12, 56, 186
knowledge production 5–6, 12–14, 22, 62, 82–3, 87, 89–94, 144, 172, 198–201

intellectual work as 89–92
transnational research collaborations 61–2
Kukharskyy, B. 33
Kuraev, A. 23, 27

Lave, J. 14
leadership 2, 11–12, 21–3, 25–6, 29, 35, 42, 53, 56, 66–8, 81, 84, 88–9, 91–3, 101–4, 107, 122, 134–5, 141–6, 148–50, 153–4, 160–4, 166, 169–70, 180–3, 192–3, 201–2, 205. *See also* intellectual leadership; positional leadership; women's leadership positions
  cultures and practices 91
  gender equality 101–2
  positions 81, 101–4, 107–9, 146
learning intellectual leadership vignette 149–50
legal protection 125, 128
liberalism 63, 133–4. *See also* academic liberalism
Lindberg, D. 126–7
local governance 41–2
low-paid workers 5–6
Lukács, G. 90
luxury leadership 11
Lynch, K. 103

Macfarlane, B. 11, 23, 42, 56
managerialism 2–3, 21–2, 41, 84, 102–4, 106, 113, 122, 200
managerial revolution 126
Marcuse, H. 85–6, 89
Marginson, S. 69
marketization 2, 42, 49, 55, 103
McCaig, C. 42
methodological practices 82–3, 89–90, 92–3, 199
micro-aggressions 113
micropolitics 113
military-industrial complex 25
Millar, K. M. 4
Mill, J. S. 134, 136
Mills, C. W. 193
Mintrom, M. 9
Moratti, S. 112
Morrill Act 183–4

Morrish, L. 52
Murray Committee (report of the) Australia 164

nationalism 1, 26
national research assessments 85
National Student Survey (NSS) 50
National Tertiary Education Union 165, 173
National Union of Australian University Students (NUAUS) 167
neoliberalism 23–5, 34, 102–4, 108, 113, 185–9, 194 n.1, 200, 204
neo-Soviets and neoliberals administration 25–6
New Colombo Plan 64

O'Brien, J. 165
Office for Students (OfS) 44, 48
Oleksiyenko, A. 199, 200, 202
Olivares-Ureta, M. 187
online lectures 106
organizational change 140, 141, 143–5, 152–3
organizational precarity 8, 199–200

Parsons, T. 188–9
pathological developments/cultures 22, 82, 88, 92
pedagogy 46, 151, 182, 193–4
peer-reviewed inquiry 25
peloton 83, 87–9, 93–4, 200
performance dashboard 50
personal precarity 7–8, 199
Piketty, T. 5
Platt, G. 188–9
political liberalism 133
positional leadership 107–10, 113
post-feudal capitalism 3
post-school education 2–3
post-soviet higher education 22–3
post-truth 22, 27, 33, 49
power 2, 9–11, 23–4, 26–8, 30, 34–6, 42–5, 52, 54, 57, 61–3, 69, 71–2, 81–2, 85, 88, 92–3, 101–5, 107–8, 112–13, 124–5, 130–1, 134, 144, 147, 160, 181–2, 184, 186, 193, 197, 203–5
  executive 62–3, 71–2
  positional 102–13

and privilege 24, 26, 144
truth to 203–5
practitioner and researcher vignette 147–8
precariat 5, 24. *See also* academic proletariat
precarious intellectuals 24, 191
precarious university 21, 26
   intellectual leadership 23–6
   modern discourse of 27
   performance management 82
   professors 82–3
   studies of Russian intellectuals 28–33
   true reflection 27–8
precarity 2–10, 13–14, 21–4, 26–7, 34–6, 41–3, 48–9, 52, 54, 56, 62, 81–2, 94, 140–2, 152, 161, 164, 170–1, 174, 198–200, 203–5
   artificial intelligence 6–7
   contextual 7
   critical thinking 197–8
   dimensions of 6–10
   educational professionals 140
   on equity 7
   existential 9–10, 200
   forms of 4
   geopolitical 9–10, 200–1
   in governance 42–3
   independence 51–2
   of knowledge 13
   low-paid workers 5–6
   obligation and dependency 3
   organizational/institutions 8, 81–2, 199–200
   personal 7–8, 199
   sector 49–50
   slow death 3–4
precarization 6–7, 11, 199
   contextual precarization 7, 199
   existential precarization 9–10, 200
   expertise precarization 49–51
   geopolitical precarization 9–10, 200–1
   organizational precarization 81–2, 199–200
   personal precarization 7–8, 199
   sector precarization 49–50
Prelec, T. 121
president. *See* rector; vice chancellor
Priestley, R. 163
Primary education exchange and learning-abroad programmes 63

Privilegium Scholasticum 125
professional doctorates 139–41, 143–6, 152
   collaboration 145
   developmental identities 152
   educational leadership and 141–2
   experiences of 146–7
   identity and action 150–1
   leadership/teaching commitments 145–6
   learning intellectual leadership 149–50
   on organizational change 143, 153
   practitioner/researcher, roles of 145–8, 153–4
   self-awareness 144
   student identities 142–3, 148–9
   traditional PhD and 140–1
   trust 144
   vigilance 144
   vignettes 147–51
professional intellectual leadership 139, 141–2, 152
professor(s) 2, 11, 26, 28–9, 31–5, 82–3, 85–95, 108, 165, 181, 185
   academic peloton 87–9, 93–4, 200
   competition 84–7
   critical thinking 23, 25
   as entrepreneurial-knowledge-producer 83, 85
   idealization of 89–90
   identities and meanings 82–3
   in intellectual leadership 11–12, 21
   in organizational roles 11
   self-exploitation 83
proportionality principle 123–5
Protection of Employees (Fixed-Term Work) Act 2003 105
public colleges and universities 5
public intellectuals 34, 67, 71–2, 104, 143, 198, 201–3
public policymaking 8

Quality Assurance Agency (QAA) 140
quit lit. *See* academics quitting

Rachman, G. 9–10
racial-patriarchal cultures 86, 92
Radchenko, S. 33
Radic, T. 172
Ranson, S. 12–13
rector 29, 101, 104, 107, 109

republicanism 122
Research Excellence Framework (REF) 50, 85
resilience 21, 51, 88
Rhoades, G. 5
rigid ideology 25
Rowlands, J. 43
Ruan, N. 21, 202–3
Russia-Ukraine war 66–8

Said, E. W. 205
Sakharov, A. 35
Schofield, A. 55
Scott, P. 45, 49, 52
Second World War 164, 167–8
sector precarization 49–50
self-awareness 143–4
self-care 85–6
self-censorship 26
self-exploitation 83–7
self-governance corporations 122, 126–7, 131–2
settler-colonialism 92
sexual violence 81
Shattock, M. 41, 44, 54
Shepherd, S. 103, 109
Sikes, P. 141
Sino-Australian international education relationship 64–5
Slaughter, S. 5
Smith, B. 92
Snyder, T. 34
social inequality 147, 180, 188–9
social injustices 7, 168, 184
sociological imagination 182, 193
soldierism 26
staff association 164–6, 169, 171–3
Standing, G. 4
State Employment Control Framework 105
stereotype 104, 108
Stevenson, H. 202
student estate 159, 167–73
  crises and emergence of 160–1
student fees 106, 126–8
student identity, professional doctorate 140–3
  vignette 148–9
Student Representative Councils 160–1
subsidiarity principle 123–5
  collegial bodies in 134

surveillance models 26, 50
Sveningsson, S. 103

Technological Universities (TUs) 105, 110
THE Impact Ranking (THE) 108
Trakman, L. 55
transnational intellectual collaboration 62, 66, 70, 73. *See also* international education
transnational research partnership 61, 69, 73
truth/truthfulness 10–11, 27–8, 33, 35, 94, 203–5

United Kingdom Council for Graduate Education 140–1
The United States 8, 12, 61–2, 64–5, 68, 107–8, 122, 146, 179–81, 183–5, 187, 189, 192–3, 197, 201
  community colleges (*see* community colleges, The United States)
  disciplinary associations in 179–83, 190–2
  Fulbright programme 62
  junior division 179
  New Federalism 184, 194 n.1
  during pandemic 64–5
  tyranny of merit 187
  women's leadership positions 107–8
University Assembly 173
university governance 41–56, 72, 134, 160, 169, 174
  anti-intellectualism 48–9
  collegiality 52–4
  committees 161
  corporatized 55
  democratic governance in 131–2
  discourses of 45–8
  effectiveness 46, 55
  efficiency and competitiveness 56
  expertise precarization 49–51
  financial sustainability 48, 54–5
  funding 49
  governors power 45
  intellectual independence 51–2
  knowledge economy 56
  one-size-fits-all model of 55–6
  profit-making consultants 46
  sector precarization 49

senates 44
skills gaps 50
university management 43, 68–9, 71, 124, 130, 132
   competitive culture 86
   documental changes 41
   gender 101
   innovative leadership 84–5
   intellectual leadership 69
   local governance practices 41–2
   peloton 88–9
   rankings 69–70
   representative structures 172
university staff 46–7, 54, 165, 171

value(s) 1, 8, 12–13, 41–2, 48–9, 53–4, 57, 62, 81–7, 89, 91–4, 102–4, 113, 141, 144, 148, 150, 153, 155, 174, 183, 198–9, 202–3

vice chancellor 44, 47, 52, 87, 101, 104, 109, 111, 162–4, 167, 169. *See also* rector; president
vigilance 143–4
virtues of truth/accuracy 10–11
Voluntary Framework of Accountability (VFA) 188
vulnerability 21, 70, 73, 121, 160

Wellington, J. 141
Williams, B. 10–11
Wilson, A. 189
Wolin, S. S. 11
Women's leadership positions 102, 104, 106–13
Wood, R. 111–12

Yerrabati, S. 143

www.ingramcontent.com/pod-product-compliance
Lightning Source LLC
Chambersburg PA
CBHW052108300426
44116CB00010B/1580